Sophrosune in the Greek Novel

Also available from Bloomsbury

Epic, Novel and the Progress of Antiquity, Ahuvia Kahane
Greek Literature in the Roman Empire, Jason Konig
The Poetics of Phantasia, Anne Sheppard

Sophrosune in the Greek Novel

Reading Reactions to Desire

Rachel Bird

BLOOMSBURY ACADEMIC
LONDON • NEW YORK • OXFORD • NEW DELHI • SYDNEY

BLOOMSBURY ACADEMIC
Bloomsbury Publishing Plc
50 Bedford Square, London, WC1B 3DP, UK
1385 Broadway, New York, NY 10018, USA

BLOOMSBURY, BLOOMSBURY ACADEMIC and the Diana logo are trademarks
of Bloomsbury Publishing Plc

First published in Great Britain 2021

For legal purposes the Acknowledgements on p. vi constitute an extension
of this copyright page.

Cover design: Terry Woodley
Cover image: Ask Me No More (1906) by Sir Lawrence Alma-Tadema (1836-1912).
Photo by: Photo 12/Universal Images Group via Getty Images

A catalogue record for this book is available from the British Library.

Library of Congress Cataloging-in-Publication Data
Names: Bird, Rachel, author.
Title: Sophrosune in the Greek novel : reading reactions to desire / Rachel Bird.
Description: New York : Bloomsbury Academic, 2020. | Includes bibliographical references and index.
| Summary: "This book offers the first comprehensive evaluation of ethics in the ancient Greek novel,
demonstrating how their representation of the cardinal virtue sophrosune positions these texts in
their literary, philosophical and cultural contexts. Sophrosune encompasses the dispositions and
psychological states of temperance, self-control, chastity, sanity and moderation. The Greek novels
are the first examples of lengthy prose fiction in the Greek world, composed between the first
century BCE and the fourth century CE. Each novel is concerned with a pair of beautiful, aristocratic
lovers who undergo trials and tribulations, before a successful resolution is reached. Bird focuses on
the extant examples of the genre (Chariton's Callirhoe, Xenophon of Ephesus' Ephesiaca, Longus'
Daphnis and Chloe, Achilles Tatius' Leucippe and Clitophon and Heliodorus' Aethiopica), which all
have the virtue of sophrosune at their heart. As each pair of lovers strives to retain their chastity in
the face of adversity, and under extreme pressure from eros, it is essential to understand how this
virtue is represented in the characters within each novel. Invited modes of reading also involve
sophrosune, and the author provides an important exploration of how sophrosune in the reader is
both encouraged and undermined by these works of fiction"—Provided by publisher.
Identifiers: LCCN 2020024310 (print) | LCCN 2020024311 (ebook) |
ISBN 9781350108646 (hardback) | ISBN 9781350108653 (epub) | ISBN 9781350108660 (ebook)
Subjects: LCSH: Greek fiction—History and criticism. | Temperance (Virtue) in literature. |
Ethics in literature.
Classification: LCC PA3267 .B57 2020 (print) | LCC PA3267 (ebook) | DDC 883/.0109—dc23
LC record available at https://lccn.loc.gov/2020024310
LC ebook record available at https://lccn.loc.gov/2020024311

ISBN: HB: 978-1-3501-0864-6
        ePDF: 978-1-3501-0866-0
        eBook: 978-1-3501-0865-3

Typeset by RefineCatch Limited, Bungay, Suffolk

To find out more about our authors and books visit www.bloomsbury.com
and sign up for our newsletters

Contents

Acknowledgements

This book originated in my Classics PhD thesis composed at Swansea University, and submitted in 2016. Without the guidance and support of the staff in the Department of Classics, Ancient History and Egyptology at Swansea, this book would not have been possible. In particular, I would like to express my gratitude for the intelligent input of Ian Repath, who read and commented upon many early drafts of chapters included in this work when supervising the original thesis, and offered welcome and witty advice during the production of this book. John Morgan has provided invaluable tips and comments, and genuine support, both as the internal examiner of the thesis and in subsequent years. This work has also benefitted from discussions, both formal and informal, with Fritz-Gregor Herrmann, who also read and critiqued draft material. Tim Whitmarsh's feedback as external examiner of the thesis helped me to develop and, I hope, enhance my ideas as the editing process progressed. I am also indebted to insightful comments provided when I have presented papers related to this book at various conferences and colloquia by, not limited to but including, Stephen Trzaskoma, Koen De Temmerman, Aldo Tagliabue, Nicolò D'Alconzo, Claire Rachel Jackson, Olivier Demerre, Benedek Kruchio and those scholars already mentioned above. To all members of the KYKNOS Research Group, and those who attend the regular Reading Group at Swansea, with whom I have often had fruitful conversations, academic and otherwise, I say a heartfelt 'thank you'. I am also grateful to family and friends for being an ongoing and much appreciated source of strength. I offer thanks to the anonymous reviewers for Bloomsbury for their pertinent remarks and guidance, and to Alice Wright and Lily Mac Mahon at Bloomsbury Academic for their excellent support throughout the editing process. Any errors that remain are entirely my own.

Finally, I would like to thank my parents, whose unfailing love and support enabled me to complete this book, which I dedicate to them.

Introduction

The Greek novel, as a genre,[1] is defined by its erotic content, representing in each extant example a central relationship between a pair of lovers, who must overcome trials and tribulations on the path of true love. The novels have emerged as key markers of how Greek culture under the auspices of Rome encompasses an awareness of erotics contextualised by Classical and Hellenistic influence. However, these texts also look towards a new way of defining love and sexuality in literature. The role of *sōphrosunē* is discussed in varying amounts of detail by several commentators,[2] but no comprehensive and sustained analysis exists, an omission which is rectified by the present work. From the discussion below of key critiques involving gender and erotics, it is evident that desire within the texts and on a metaliterary level is much discussed. The key virtue of *sōphrosunē* deserves a similar level of attention: it is a factor which is abundantly present in characterizations and is, I will argue, intrinsic to the reading process.

Turning to the way in which the novels treat this cardinal virtue will allow us to appreciate its crucial role as a marker of Hellenic identity both inside and outside the texts. To briefly outline my approach: by working from the text outwards, my aim is to draw from these narratives a sense of how *sōphrosunē* informs any reading of the erotic dynamics which are expressed through these novels. Following on from the first chapter, which will be concerned with characterization within the texts, the focus will next be on how the reader is encouraged to respond to voyeurism and to the ebb and flow of *erōs* and *sōphrosunē* at key moments in the novels. A key factor in the novels is the *eugenia* or nobility of the heroes and heroines: this involves an intrinsic regard for virtue, and in particular, for *sōphrosunē*, which is either evident from the outset of the couples' adventures, or is clearly apparent as events progress. This possession of *sōphrosunē* in the well-bred, and well-educated protagonists of the genre also suggests that the authors of these texts expect their readership to attain to a similar regard for the virtue, and this is reflected in the nature of readerly *sōphrosunē*, which will be discussed in Chapters 2 and 3. This move from internal to external dynamics allows for a complete understanding of how the virtue influences, or is encouraged in, characters and readers alike. *approve*

In the following sections of this introduction, an overview of directly relevant and recent scholarship will be provided before attention turns to context in terms of the representation of *sōphrosunē* in Greek literature and philosophy which is pertinent to the Greek novels. Finally, detail about the aims and structure of the following chapters will be included.

*

It has been one of the major concerns of scholars, particularly since Foucault's seminal *The History of Sexuality vol. III: the Care of the Self*,[3] to focus on *erōs* in the novels, and to consider the genre's role and importance in the development of sexual ethics.[4] Konstan argues that the novels construct equality in the relationships of their protagonists, with constancy at the heart of these relationships.[5] These overarching claims can miss some of the nuances of the texts, particularly in the more subversive elements present in Achilles Tatius, for example. However, Konstan's work helps us to perceive how these texts have a clear thread of morality, in terms of sexual ethics, running through them, which is something which will be explored further in the present work.

Goldhill's response to Foucault's view of the novels encapsulates key features of contemporary discourse on sexuality, while recognising the centrality of *sōphrosunē*; as he puts it: 'The realignment of the care for the flesh that is characteristic of later antiquity brings with it a realignment of a new contestation of the senses of sophrosune, an ideological matrix in which the novel also plays a significant role.'[6] Thus, Goldhill builds on Foucault's recognition of a cultural shift in the Imperial era, with a new emphasis on the individual and their role as desiring subject, though constrained by ethical concerns. However, he questions whether cultural reality is reflected in the texts on which he focuses. Crucially, Goldhill discusses the playfulness and ingenuity of Longus, Achilles Tatius and Heliodorus in approaching the themes of desire and fidelity, something which goes beyond Foucault's focus. Goldhill raises questions regarding readerly *sōphrosunē* in Longus, when he discusses the proem and asks whether this 'prophylactic prayer' for self-control is programmatic for readers,[7] a question which is pertinent for the present study.

In terms of feminist criticism and gender theory, there are three studies on the Greek novels which invite discussion here: Haynes' *Fashioning the Feminine in the Greek Novel*,[8] Morales' *Vision and Narrative in Achilles Tatius' Leucippe and Clitophon*,[9] and Jones' *Playing the Man: Performing Masculinities in the*

Greek Novel.[10] Haynes' discussion focuses on the apparent primacy of the 'feminine' in the novels, exploring how the strong female roles in the texts are constructed in terms of cultural dynamics. Haynes ultimately suggests that the image of a Greek woman who resists violation is representative of Hellenic identity and superiority in the Roman world.[11] Morales' *Vision and Narrative in Achilles Tatius' Leucippe and Clitophon* is the only monograph on that novel, and the author includes some key analysis of sexuality, gender and the gaze, all of which is relevant for the present work. Morales' discussions of how vision operates in the representation of Leucippe is particularly interesting, as she navigates the tricky issue of Clitophon's narrative focalization and how this can be evaluated via the theory of the gaze.[12] Jones' *Playing the Man* provides crucial analysis of how masculinity is constructed and represented within the Greek novel. With discussions based around *paideia*, *andreia* and sexual ideology, Jones provides a cohesive view of how masculinity is performed in the novels, with close readings of key passages, using modern theories of the performance of gender roles. All of these texts address key aspects of how gender informs our readings of the Greek novels, and include feminist criticism, such as gaze theory (as previously identified in the work of Mulvey),[13] and ideas surrounding male and female subjectivity and agency. When looking at *sōphrosunē* in the novels, notions of gender and feminist theory are relevant to any modern reading, addressing pivotal questions around the socially informed nature of constructions of narrative, characterization and reader-response.

Morgan's *Longus: Daphnis and Chloe* argues for a serious reading of Longus, and he explores factors such as intertextuality, and narrative techniques, such as focalization.[14] He also focuses on the erotics of this text, demonstrating how the education of Daphnis and Chloe in the name and deeds of love is represented with humour, but also with serious intent. From the perspective of the present work, Morgan's book allows space to explore how Longus' text, with its nuanced and subtle features, invites disparate readings and interpretations.

Two further major studies on the Greek novel merit my attention here. Whitmarsh's *Narrative and Identity in the Ancient Greek Novel: Returning Romance* builds on the author's prolific output in the field of ancient fiction and provides analyses considering both cultural context and narrative dynamics. One of the key discussions therein which is crucial for the present work is that regarding the role of *erōs* or desire in the reading experience,[15] something which opens up room for discussing how *sōphrosunē* is also intrinsic to the reading process, as discussed in Chapter 3 of this book. De Temmerman's study on characterization in the Greek novel provides comprehensive treatment of this aspect in each of the texts.[16] The emphasis on how characterization is a crucial factor in these texts directly challenges the earlier predominant focus in scholarship which denies character development in the novels. De Temmerman demonstrates the extent to which much of the characterization in these texts is subtly nuanced and rich. His study emphasizes the rhetorical nature of characterization in these texts, and how this is related to narrative representation. His view of how *sōphrosunē* is involved in certain characterizations is a factor which is taken further in my own discussion in Chapter 1 of the present work.

*

Sōphrosunē is crucial to Greek ethics, philosophy and culture. As a concept, it is continually redefined throughout antiquity, from its origins in the archaic world, where it stood for sanity and mortal limitations and was representative of the opposite of the heroic nature, to its representation in the Christian era where it entailed a closeness to God in terms of abnegation and rejection of worldly pleasures. The concept has crucial political resonance in the Classical era, which is evident in the work of the tragedians and the sophists, and of course in the Platonic dialogues. Its psychological aspects become more prominent in the Classical era and continue in importance in philosophy in the Hellenistic era. *Sōphrosunē* is seen on a popular level to control the appetites and provide harmony to the soul, instilling moderation in those who possess it. This popular view of the concept is intrinsic to the philosophical view too: Plato cites the virtue as the one which is attainable to all, while also recognizing its loftier religious connotations; Stoicism views the virtue as one which suppresses the emotions, which is essential for a virtuous or happy life. In the Greek world of the Imperial era, in which the novels were produced, *sōphrosunē* retains its centrality in the philosophical schools and continues to be viewed as a popular virtue, which restrains appetites.

Rademaker defines the 'moral' and 'intellectual' senses of *sōphrōn* and its cognates as follows:

> For the intellectual sense, the translations commonly given include 'of sound mind', 'discreet', 'prudent' and (when used of non-animate entities) 'reasonable'; the moral sense prompts translations like 'having control of the sensual desires', 'temperate', self-controlled', 'chaste' and (when used of non-animate entities) 'moderate'.[17]

For our purposes in this book, it will be the 'moral' sense of the term and concept which is foregrounded, given the nature of the texts with which we are concerned.

Discussion will also be limited to those texts and schools of thought which directly inform the views of *sōphrosunē* as represented in the Greek novels, or to those authors or texts to which the novels allude, when concerned with *sōphrosunē*.

Tragedy: Euripides

Euripides uses to full advantage the variety of meanings which can be attached to the term *sōphrosunē*, and he alludes to the concept far more frequently than the other tragedians. It is in the work of Euripides that the student of the ancient Greek novel can perceive the roots of much of the usage in those later texts, as the poet often alludes to the moral sense of the concept as it relates to sexual self-restraint and chastity. The ambiguous moral senses of the concept are particularly crucial for the *Hippolytus* and the *Bacchae*, where opposing characters have separate (mis)conceptions of what *sōphrosunē* is. Euripides exploits the inherent difficulties of the differing implications associated with the concept in order to enhance the emotional and intellectual impact of his tragedies.

While North recognises the significance of the treatments of *sōphrosunē* in the *Hippolytus* and *Bacchae*, and discusses the implications in some depth,[18] it is Rademaker who classes the approaches to this concept seen in these plays, along with *Medea* and the farmer in *Electra*, as representative of 'different views' in contrast to the more traditional representations of *sōphrosunē* seen in other Euripidean tragedies.[19] The focus here will be on the *Hippolytus* and the *Medea*, as both works demonstrate how Euripides creates tension between conflicting views of *sōphrosunē* in characters afflicted with *erōs*, something which is highly relevant in the Greek novels.

The moral conflicts in the *Hippolytus* are represented in terms of *sōphrosunē*, with Hippolytus and Phaedra each having differing views of the concept. Hippolytus believes himself to be *sōphrōn* as he is devoted to Artemis and to the chastity which the goddess represents. However, his *hubris* in dismissing Aphrodite and his arrogance imply that he also lacks the virtue in moral terms, which is recognised by Phaedra, who says he must learn to be *sōphrōn* (731).[20] Also, North points to Hippolytus' 'fanatically cruel and intemperate' tirade against Phaedra and his denunciation of women as evidence of his *hubris*.[21] Conversely, Phaedra, who suffers because of her desire for Hippolytus, tries to conquer her love for him with *sōphrosunē*, but is not *sōphrōn* because she has adulterous desire. Rademaker suggests that the two characters complement each other, and that both are *sōphrōn* and not *sōphrōn*, and 'confound conventional and simplistic ideals of *sōphrosunē*.'[22] There are complex consequences stemming from Euripides' representation of this virtue in the *Hippolytus*: ritual purity in sexual terms is seen to be undermined by arrogance, so that the appearance of *sōphrosunē* does not imply its true essence; those suffering from the effects of *erōs* cannot be viewed as exemplars of *sōphrosunē*, but the way in which they respond to their erotic desire is potentially more demonstrative of their possession of the virtue. Thus, rather than defining *sōphrosunē* as 'chastity' in terms of the actual state of being chaste, it is clear that for Euripides, the concept encompasses the moral struggle to retain chastity or fidelity under erotic duress, and this is highly significant when we come to look at *sōphrosunē* in the Greek novels.

North illustrates how in both the *Hippolytus* and the *Medea* the idea of *sōphrōn erōs* (love in moderation, without the extreme passion which leads to jealousy and violence) is a recurrent theme, assigned to the Chorus in each of these two tragedies.[23] To turn to the *Medea*, Jason's view is that jealous women are not *sōphrōn*, but sexually-obsessed (*Medea*, 1365–1369), a view which echoes that found in the representation of Andromache and Hermione in the *Andromache*, as Rademaker notes.[24] Jason's dismissal of Medea as non-*sōphrōn* after she has killed their children, picks up on his earlier efforts to convince her to lay aside her jealous rage preceding the Chorus' ode at 627ff. The ode itself illustrates the danger of non-*sōphrōn erōs*. North suggests that the choral ode implies that if Medea is without *sōphrosunē*, Jason is without *erōs*.[25] However, this view of the implications of the ode is countered by Rademaker, who does not read the *strophe* and *antistrophe* as both pertaining to Medea's case, rather he suggests that the Chorus refer to Jason's excessive *erōs* for the daughter of Creon in the *strophe* and to their own hope to avoid the jealous state of mind of Medea in the *antistrophe*. Thus, he argues, it is not implied that the situation stems from the excessive *erōs* of Medea for Jason. Rademaker claims that Medea's excessive love is nowhere in the tragedy blamed for her anger, which instead is brought about by Jason's inability to keep his part of the deal, that is to respect their marriage.[26] To suggest that Medea's motivation is not coloured by sexual jealousy at all is a little misguided in my view. While her sense of dishonour and injustice is crucial to her thirst for vengeance, it is also the case that her emotional response to the situation is rooted in that original sexual desire for Jason. While this is not explicitly illustrated in the tragedy, it is implied by her emotive speeches and by the symptoms described in the initial speech of the Nurse (16–35), following on from the Nurse's assertion that 'νῦν δ' ἐχθρὰ πάντα, καὶ νοσεῖ τὰ φίλτατα.' 'But now hatred is everything, and dearest love becomes sick.' (My translation). Thus, Medea is non-*sōphrōn* in the sense that she is overcome with sexual jealousy, but I would add, in line with Rademaker, that Jason sees only her jealousy and not his own dishonour, so that Medea is not the archetypal non-*sōphrōn* woman,[27] and he, despite his claims of prudence in choosing his new wife, is also non-*sōphrōn* in his desire for the young princess.

Euripides demonstrates a flexibility in how *sōphrosunē* can be nuanced to serve the purposes or viewpoints of his characters, and it is clear from the brief appraisal above of the representation of the concept in the *Hippolytus* and the *Medea* that in the erotic sphere, the term and its cognates can refer to chastity, the motivation behind fidelity, fidelity itself, self-control (in terms of emotion) and prudence.

Xenophon

Xenophon's representation of *sōphrosunē* in the *Cyropaedia* is relevant to the representation of *sōphrosunē* in the extant examples of the Greek novel, so deserves detailed treatment here.[28] In the *Cyropaedia*, Xenophon focuses on how an education in virtue (with particular emphasis on *sōphrosunē*) is central to the development of an idealised ruler, and he also includes discussion regarding the all-encompassing power of beauty and *erōs* in the Panthea episodes. The latter aspect makes this text, rather than any of the rest of the Xenophontic corpus, pertinent for this study.[29]

Parallels between the *Cyropaedia* and Chariton's *Callirhoe* are recognised in recent scholarship, with the role of Panthea, her devotion to her husband, and the divergent responses of Cyrus and Araspas to her beauty being of particular importance.[30] Xenophon of Ephesus' allusions to the story of Abradatas and Panthea in the *Cyropaedia* are also discussed.[31]

In addition to the recognised allusions to the *Cyropaedia* by Chariton and Xenophon of Ephesus, there may well be a generic debt to this fictional biography.[32] When considering how the diversion in the *Cyropaedia* involving Panthea might prefigure the plot of a Greek novel, one must look at events from the perspectives of Abradatas and Panthea, rather than from the perspective of Cyrus. The couple's misfortune in being separated is in part the responsibility of Cyrus, whose subsequent gallantry would cast him in the role of a benevolent antagonist. Araspas, as the principle threat to Panthea's chastity, is successfully defeated in his amorous advances through the intelligence of Panthea in reporting him to Cyrus. When Panthea and Abradatas are reunited, readers of the novel would be happy for events to stop there, but Abradatas' death and Panthea's consequent suicide provide tragedy instead.

Cyrus' *sōphrosunē* is one of the qualities which his education has instilled in him, and it is, consequently, of prime importance to his characterization. The episodes involving Panthea demonstrate how it is not only in the military and governing spheres that he is shown to possess the virtue, but also in the sphere of *erōs*. The fact that Cyrus displays *sōphrosunē* regarding Panthea is made explicit when she tells Abradatas that Cyrus has exercised the virtue (6.1.47). The ruler's determination to avoid becoming susceptible to beauty and therefore *erōs* (*Cyr.* 5.1.7–12) is also a crucial character trait, which emphasizes his *sōphrosunē* in the erotic sphere.

To turn to the representation of Panthea: she is described with the term *sōphrosunē* by Cyrus, when he states he shall honour her following the death of Abradatas (7.3.12). It is perhaps significant that Cyrus recognises Panthea's *sōphrosunē*, just as she recognises his: the possession of this virtue seems to allow the possessor to see it in another. The emphasis throughout the episodes concerning her is on her fidelity and love towards her husband, which is evident when Cyrus refers to her with the term *sōphrosunē*. While Panthea's *aidōs* and *sōphrosunē* are implicit for the most part (the term *aidōs* is not used,[33] and *sōphrosunē* only on the one occasion referred to above, just as her story is about to end), her fidelity and love for her husband are explicit throughout, and it is clear that it is her devotion to him which earns her the compliments from Cyrus at 7.3.12.

The above discussion regarding Xenophon's use of the moral senses of *sōphrosunē* in the *Cyropaedia* demonstrates how in the sphere of philosophy and fictionalized biography in the fifth/fourth centuries there is a concern to engage with *sōphrosunē* as the virtue which results in self-restraint in erotically and morally challenging situations. Xenophon's approach to the concept, although in some respects paradigmatic for the approach in the Greek novel, is less complex than that which we see in Euripides and Plato: the latter of which is my next concern.

Plato

It is no small or simple task to evaluate the moral uses of *sōphrosunē* in the Platonic corpus, and I will necessarily limit my discussion to four dialogues which I perceive as directly relevant to the Greek novel as a genre: the *Charmides*, the *Symposium*, the *Republic* and the *Phaedrus*.[34] In North's diachronic study, she states that with Plato.

> ... the development of this concept reaches a climax. Not only did he reconsider most of the earlier interpretations of the virtue which had emerged from the Archaic and Classical worlds – now shattered forever by the crises of the late fifth century – and reintegrate them into a new unity, but he so extended its scope that all subsequent interpretations were the result, in some fashion, of his achievement.[35]

While North is correct in stating the evaluative and analytical radicalism which Plato brings to his discussions of *sōphrosunē*, I do not concur with her claim for a linear 'development' of the concept. I would rather infer from Plato's use of the concept that he teases out and explicates meanings and implications of the term and concept which are present to some degree in previous Greek thought.

Charmides

In this dialogue, Socrates and his interlocutors attempt to arrive at a definition of *sōphrosunē* in order to establish whether the young Charmides possesses the virtue, as his guardian, Critias, claims. The various definitions of *sōphrosunē* arrived at in the dialogue are unsatisfactory, at least for Socrates, and the dialogue ends in *aporia*. The discussion demonstrates how difficulties arise, as connections between virtue and knowledge are explored, with each solution to the problem of 'what sort of thing *sōphrosunē* is' ('ὁποῖόν τι ἡ σωφροσύνη':159a) becoming more complicated, and more challenging for Socrates' interlocutors. The dialogue markedly avoids any definition of *sōphrosunē* which involves control of appetites or passions as found in the *Republic* and the *Phaedrus*, but, as Rademaker suggests, this aspect of *sōphrosunē* is represented in the frame of the dialogue (as discussed below) and remains unchallenged.[36]

As far as the Greek novel is concerned, the genre does not engage with the intricacies of this discussion: it is the frame of the dialogue which is most pertinent in this context. Socrates' demonstration of his sexual *sōphrosunē* when he glimpses beneath the beautiful Charmides' cloak but manages to master himself (155d) is emblematic of how voyeurism challenges one's possession of the virtue, and we see examples of voyeuristic opportunism and various reactions, both *sōphrōn* and otherwise, in each of the novels. Not every instance of voyeurism or potential voyeurism recalls the Charmides directly (although I will argue for direct reference in Chariton's and Achilles Tatius' novels). However, I suggest that there is an implicit understanding on the part of the authors of the novels that Socrates, in the frame of the *Charmides* (and as represented by Alcibiades in the *Symposium*, as will be discussed below), is an archetypal example of someone who possesses *sōphrosunē* in a sexual context. Charmides' extreme beauty, which is acknowledged by all, can also be seen to prefigure the representation of the novels' protagonists, and Socrates' susceptibility to the youth's physical appearance can be aligned with reactions to the protagonists from characters within the texts, but can also be compared to readerly reactions to opportunities for voyeurism. Socrates' concern for the boy's soul rather than just for his physical beauty (154d) is not undermined by his reaction to Charmides' body, but is reflected in Socrates' self-mastery and his ongoing efforts to discover whether Charmides really knows what *sōphrosunē* is, which Socrates says is necessary before he can be said to possess it.

To varying degrees in the novels, the beautiful protagonists undergo ethical challenges to prove that they possess various virtues: the first among them is *sōphrosunē*. Thus, while sustained engagement with the discussion about *sōphrosunē* is not evident, the frame and Socrates' ethical aims in this dialogue are highly relevant in these texts, and there is clear engagement from the authors of the novels with Plato's authorial strategy as he represents Socrates as erotically susceptible to beauty but capable of retaining *sōphrosunē*.

Symposium

The speech of Alcibiades, which contains his account of Socrates' unassailable *sōphrosunē* (216b–219d), is of crucial importance in our discussion of the moral senses of Platonic *sōphrosunē*. Not only is Socrates' *sōphrosunē* in the sense of 'control of desires' present in Alcibiades' speech (Socrates is resistant to the seduction of Alcibiades), but his self-mastery in other areas, such as under physical hardship or in warfare, is clear too, thus demonstrating how Socrates is able to combine the virtues of *andreia* and *karteria* with *sōphrosunē*, often viewed as incompatible.[37] In the novels of Longus and Achilles Tatius, there are parodic versions of this chaste encounter.[38] Alcibiades' encomium to Socrates follows on from the encomia to Erōs, thus aligning the philosopher and the god, and highlighting the philosopher's status among his contemporaries. It is against this background, which is both humorous in how it is presented and serious in terms of its message about *sōphrosunē*, that Longus and Achilles Tatius work, with results which are ironic and, I think, question the attainability, and indeed the desirability, of such Socratic *sōphrosunē* for the novels' protagonists.

Republic

In the *Republic*, there are several important roles for *sōphrosunē*. In the discussion concerning the education of the prospective guardians of the city, *sōphrosunē* is highlighted as one of the four virtues which are necessary for the young guardians to acquire. Indeed, it is the one virtue every citizen, irrespective of specific classification, must possess. When introducing the need for *sōphrosunē* to be taught, Socrates asks this question:

> Σωφροσύνης δὲ ὡς πλήθει οὐ τὰ τοιαῦτα [δὲ] μέγιστα, ἀρχόντων μὲν ὑπηκόους εἶναι, αὐτοὺς δὲ ἄρχοντας τῶν περὶ πότους καὶ ἀφροδίσια καὶ περὶ ἐδωδὰς ἡδονῶν;
>
> And for the general population is not the main thing about self-control that while they are to be the subjects of those who govern them, they themselves are to be in control of the pleasures derived from drink, sex and food?

389d–e[39]

This proposed description, which is not contested by Socrates' interlocutor, is highly relevant in the novels, where *sōphrosunē* is most often represented in this 'popular' sense, particularly in conjunction with the challenge of erotic desire. The later discussion concerning *sōphrosunē* at 430e–432a involves consideration of its place in the city. Socrates conveys the difficulty in comprehending the idea of the self controlling the self (a problem raised at another level in the *Charmides*) and this problem is solved by the division of the soul into 'better' and 'worse' parts (430e–431a), which leads on to the similar division of the people in the city (431b–d). The virtue is subsequently defined as a kind of *harmonia* which spreads throughout the whole city (431e). The discussion then builds towards the theory of the tripartite soul, which develops from 435b. *Sōphrosunē* is crucial to the correct governance of this divided soul, allowing the harmonious cooperation between each part (442c–d).

There is engagement with this section of the *Republic*, which is concerned with the partition of the soul, in Chariton's *Callirhoe*, Achilles Tatius' *Leucippe and Clitophon*, and Heliodorus' *Aethiopica*, as Repath recognises.[40] The theme of education which is addressed in Books 2 and 3 of the *Republic* is also important in Longus' *Daphnis and Chloe*, as Herrmann suggests.[41] These interactions are significant for my purposes, given the importance of *sōphrosunē* to the tripartite soul and to the education of the guardians as outlined in the above discussion. I will aim to analyse fully how the novelists' use of terminology and ideas which are rooted in the *Republic* helps to elucidate the ways in which they represent *sōphrosunē*. It is principally these earlier parts of the dialogue which are relevant for the novels' representation of *sōphrosunē*, rather than the later discussions regarding the advanced education of those guardians who are capable of becoming philosopher–rulers, which encompasses contemplation of the Forms of the cardinal virtues, including that of *sōphrosunē*.[42] This suggests that, for the novel authors, the important aspects of *sōphrosunē* are its centrality in the psychological make-up of elite youth (acquired through education) and its ability to hold desire in check (or at least to regulate it), both of which concerns are addressed in Books 2 to 4 of the *Republic*.

Phaedrus

There are sixteen instances of *sōphrosunē* and its cognates in the *Phaedrus*,[43] and the concentration of these terms (10/16) in Socrates' second speech (243e9–257b9) demonstrates how central the concept is to this part of the dialogue. This speech is Socrates' second response to Lysias', intended to refute the latter's claim that the non-lover's sexual approaches should be accepted whereas the lover's should not, because the non-lover is sane, while the lover is not. At the beginning of Socrates' speech, he uses *sōphrosunē* in opposition to *mania*, and this 'sanity' is human, while the 'madness' is divine. In this early section of the speech, where he refers to three different kinds of divine madness, Socrates is preparing the ground for the fourth kind of divine madness, which is that coming from Erōs. At several points in the speech, particularly in the early sections, the implied meaning is that of sanity (244a5; 244b2; 245a8; 245b4; 256e5). Later, as Socrates narrates the Myth of the Soul, *sōphrosunē* takes on a 'higher' meaning as its true nature or Form is at issue (247d6; 250b2; 254b7),[44] or it is referred to as acting in the soul of the lover (253d6). Here a straightforward translation into English is not easy: Rowe opts for 'self-control' where the true nature of *sōphrosunē* is referred to, but this is not altogether ideal. 'Self-control' for us may well evoke aspects of disposition the Greeks would have referred to as *enkrateia*, so this translation potentially falls some way short of the ethical import which the virtue of *sōphrosunē* is surely intended to have at these junctures. A broader term such as 'decency' may fit better. Rowe's 'restraint' when referring to the *sōphrosunē* which is found in the 'good horse' of the soul is apt, given that the horse is naturally restrained as it is obedient to the control of the charioteer of the soul.[45] These disparate meanings imply a breadth in the scope of the term as it is represented by Plato in this text, which must be considered when discussing any potential allusions to these representations by the authors of the novels.

This dialogue is recognised as a major influence on second-century Greek literature.[46] In terms of the Greek novels, the setting of the dialogue and the content of Socrates' second speech are of importance for Achilles Tatius, and, perhaps to a lesser extent, Longus and Heliodorus. The allusions that are already recognised by scholars have consequences for any evaluation of the way in which *sōphrosunē* is represented in Achilles Tatius' and Heliodorus' texts in particular.[47] Commentators recognise that intertextuality with the *Phaedrus* demonstrates that this dialogue was central to rhetorical education in the second century.[48] This engagement with the text allows insight into how the authors of the novels viewed it as fundamental to erotic theory. Further, just as *erōs* and *sōphrosunē* are in tension in the novels, the erotic content of Socrates' second speech is underpinned by his reverence for *sōphrosunē*, and this point is not lost on authors such as Achilles Tatius and Heliodorus, who allude to the *Phaedrus* with Socrates' ethical concerns in mind.

I acknowledge that how *sōphrosunē* is represented is not always the principal concern of Achilles Tatius and Heliodorus when they allude to the *Phaedrus*: the roles of beauty, pleasure and, of course, desire are more important in places. What I suggest is that *sōphrosunē* is just as prevalent in certain allusions and, even where it is not recalled by direct verbal echoes, it is in the background as the virtue which is necessary for the philosophical reaction to erotic desire, which is at the heart of Socrates' message in his second speech.

Aristotle

It is in Aristotle's *Nichomachean Ethics* that we find the philosopher's clear conception of *sōphrosunē* in moral terms which relate to the individual. Aristotle states that the soul has three faculties (vegetative, appetitive, rational – *Nic. Eth.* 1102b13–25), and ethical virtue belongs to the second of these and is gained through habituation. *Sōphrosunē* is identified as a category of moral virtue (1103a6–7), 'which Aristotle defines as acting in the best way in relation to pleasures and pains (1104b27–28), and which he locates in a mean between excess and deficiency (1107a2–6).'[49] There is here a clear emphasis on practical rather than contemplative morality, which is mirrored in the middle and late Stoa, as we shall see below.

The doctrine of the Mean is key to Aristotle's concept of *sōphrosunē*, and North notes how the virtue is not merely defined in this doctrine, but is at its very foundation.[50] This is indeed the case, as Aristotle emphasizes how ethical virtues are the Mean between two extreme states, one of excess and one of deficiency (1106a26–b28), and attaining this balance must involve moderation, or *sōphrosunē*. Although the concept is crucial to the doctrine of the Mean, and thus to Aristotle's ethics, North observes how *sōphrosunē* is also narrowed in scope in the *Nicomachean Ethics*. It is the function of *sōphrosunē* to find the Mean in respect to *hēdonae* (1107b4–6, 1117b 23–26), and the virtue is limited to the restraint of bodily pleasures (eating, drinking, sex – 1118a 23–26).[51] North also notes the inherent 'humanism' in Aristotle's view of *sōphrosunē*: the possessor of the virtue does not abstain from pleasure, but enjoys it in moderation (1119a11–20, 1153a27–35).[52]

Book 7 of the *Nicomachean Ethics* makes what North calls 'the first rigorous distinction in Greek thought between *sōphrosunē* and *enkrateia*'.[53] This is significant for this study of the Greek novel, as both terms are used to depict forms of self-mastery relating to erotic desire in those texts. The important point arising from Aristotle's distinction is that the person who is *enkratēs* knows that the appetites are wrong and struggles against them, while the person who is *sōphrōn* does not experience those appetites (the implication surely being that s/he has habituated her/his resistance to them) and so does not need to struggle (1145b1–15; 1146a1–15).

There is one further element of Aristotle's approach to *sōphrosunē* to note before moving on. There is a distinction made between the *sōphrosunē* of the ruler and of men and the *sōphrosunē* of the ruled and of women. North summarizes this as follows:

> For the ruler – and for a man – *sōphrosunē* is conducive to command. For one who is ruled – and for a woman – it is conducive to obedience (1260a 20–24; 1277b 17ff).
>
>   This view of feminine *aretē* aligns Aristotle with most of the Greeks (except Socrates and Plato) and recalls especially the attitude of Sophocles' Ajax towards Tecmessa.[54]

Aristotle's rejection of the homogeneity of virtue (including *sōphrosunē*) for the sexes and for ruler and subject marks his distance from the doctrine of Plato (and hence Socrates). It will be important to see how gender informs the representation of *sōphrosunē* in the Greek novel, and to note whether the influence of Aristotle colours these representations to any extent.

The Stoics

Stoicism is the most crucial post-Aristotelian philosophy for the study of *sōphrosunē* in moral terms, given its reach both temporally and geographically, and given its clear emphasis on the complete control or suppression of passions and desires. The original sources for Stoicism are fragmentary, but we can find some elucidation for the middle and late Stoa in the writings of Cicero, Epictetus, Seneca, Marcus Aurelius and Musonius Rufus.[55] The way in which this philosophy is transmitted across the linguistic and cultural divide demonstrates its continuing and persistent influence up to the Imperial era. As Long notes, our evidence for Stoicism springs from when it had already become an authorized doctrine, rather than when it was a developing philosophical system.[56]

Diogenes Laertius states that for the Stoics, the primary virtues are wisdom (φρόνησις), courage (ἀνδρεία), justice (δικαιοσύνη) and *sōphrosunē* (D.L. VII.92). An important distinction between the Stoic view of *sōphrosunē* and that of the Peripatetics, is that for the Old Stoa, *sōphrosunē* is not moderation: the virtue implies the extirpation of the passions, rather than their moderation. Zeno, Cleanthes and Ariston of Chios (the latter as represented by Galen – *SVF* 1.374) held to the concept of unitary *aretē*, and *aretē* was called *sōphrosunē* when it was necessary to choose the Good and avoid Evil. Plutarch ascribes to Ariston another definition: as North puts it: 'when virtue regulates desire and defines the moderate and the seasonable in pleasures, it is called *sōphrosunē* (SVF 1. 375).' North states that these two definitions are not contradictory but complementary.[57] However, Ariston's second definition as stated by Plutarch does divert somewhat from the standard idea purported in the Stoa that πάθη should be suppressed completely rather than regulated. This is particularly important for the Greek novel where exemplary *sōphrosunē* is a response to desires, usually erotic, and does not denote the absence of such desires/passions.

North notes two definitions of *sōphrosunē* attributed to Chrysippus:

> One says that *sōphrosunē* is knowledge (*epistēmē*) of things to be chosen and avoided or neither; its antithesis, *akolasia*, is the ignorance of these matters (SVF 3. 262). In the other definition its chief function is to render the impulses steady and to achieve theoretical knowledge of them, while its secondary function is to contemplate and put into practice the objects of the other three virtues (SVF 3. 280).[58]

In these definitions, intellectual and moral senses are somewhat combined: one must have knowledge of what is good ('things to be chosen' – that is, the right choices) in order to practise *sōphrosunē*, and one must understand the impulses in order to control them. Another point emphasized by North, and which is relevant for this study, is that Chrysippus stated that 'aretē is identical for gods and mortals, for men and women (SVF 3.245, 246, 253, 254) – a return to the Socratic position which Aristotle had rejected.'[59]

For Panaetius, there are several crucial developments regarding Stoic ethics and hence *sōphrosunē*. These are summarized by North as follows: virtue is divided into the two categories of 'theoretical' and 'practical' (D.L. VII.92), and in Cicero's *De Officiis* (1.5.17), in which Panaetius' views are reflected, *sōphrosunē* belongs to the second category. According to Aulus Gellius (12.5) Panaetius rejects *apatheia*. This view is supported by Cicero (*De Officiis* 2.5.18 – there is a need to control the passions, not extirpate them). Panaetius also denied that virtue is enough for happiness; he recognised the need for health, affluence, and strength as well as virtue (D.L. VII.128). An important feature of Panaetius' ethics is the doctrine of the *prepon* (*decorum*, 'what is fitting'). According to North, this doctrine is inseparable from Panaetius' concept of *sōphrosunē*. At the root of the doctrine of the *prepon* is the idea that virtue stems from the appetites and impulses. This is a move away from Zeno's and Chrysippus' theories which have the *logos* or intellect as responsible for *aretē*.[60] I will not enter into a detailed analysis of the *prepon* here, but it is important to recognise that, as North suggests, and as is illustrated by Cicero, the doctrine allows for the practical and aesthetic application of Stoic virtue and *sōphrosunē* (which is at the heart of Cicero's *decorum speciale*, which creates harmony in the soul) in the life of the Roman elite.[61]

North asserts that the later Stoa (Musonius Rufus, Seneca, Epictetus, Marcus Aurelius) '. . . abandoned any pretence of an interest in the theoretical aspects of *aretē*. Without exception these philosophers were concerned with the practical applications of Stoic philosophy.' Therefore, they have a very similar doctrine in ethical terms to the Platonists and Cynics. 'One of the concepts they share is the definition of *sōphrosunē* as the restraint of the appetites.'[62] Two points which North makes about the distinctions made by Musonius Rufus are interesting when considering the Greek novels: while for Musonius Rufus, *sōphrosunē* is a private, individual element, and is not related to the state, he does refer to his belief that it is a ruler's duty to be an example of *sōphrosunē* for his subjects (in the fragment *That Kings Should be Philosophers* VIII). The other point to note is that Musonius Rufus analyses the *sōphrosunē* of women in his *Whether Women Should Study Philosophy*, and states that it is the duty of the *sōphrōn* woman to 'avoid unlawful loves and any kind of incontinence or appetite; to hate strife, extravagance, and ornamentation; to control anger and grief and every other passion (III, p10)'.[63] This idea about female *sōphrosunē* is important when considering the way in which the concept is gendered in the novels.

The brief summary above of the most important ideas and developments for Stoicism regarding *sōphrosunē* demonstrates how the virtue is nuanced according to its temporal and cultural context and according to its different proponents. The implications for this study of the virtue in the Greek novels will be seen in how the moral perspectives of the later Stoa continue to impact upon this genre.

Plutarch (Middle Platonists)

North's view that the Middle Platonists did not produce any truly original innovations regarding *sōphrosunē* holds true.[64] However, as one of the major spokesmen of the Middle Platonists, Plutarch produced work which elucidated the contemporary philosophical view of this virtue in his *Moralia*. This would not be particularly noteworthy for a general overview of the concept, but one dialogue is relevant for the study of the virtue in the Greek novel: the *Amatorius* (*Mor.* 748e–771e).[65] This dialogue focuses on the discussions which stem from a crisis which arises when Ismenodora, a wealthy young widow in Thespiae, falls for a younger man whom she then wants to marry, eventually 'kidnapping' him in order to secure the wedding. The text explores ideas about how heterosexual monogamous relationships can be viewed as worthy in philosophical terms.[66] The narrative structure of the work is significant: Flavian and Plutarch's son, Autobulus, are having a conversation, and Autobulus narrates how his father, shortly after his marriage, travelled to Thespiae to sacrifice to Erōs, and subsequently, along with various friends, became involved in the debates which ensued following the incident concerning Ismenodora and the handsome youth, Bacchon.[67]

The most important factor of this dialogue for this study is the question of exactly how Plutarch represents *sōphrosunē* and the idea of, specifically, what it means to be a *sōphrōn* woman or lover.[68] As Goldhill suggests, there is a tension between what is purported to happen in the situation involving Ismenodora (can kidnapping a potential husband ever be *sōphrōn*?), and what is stated in the debate, particularly by 'Plutarch',[69] whose speeches promote the idea of *sōphrōn* love in marriage to quite an extent (principally at 767c–f).[70] The statement put forward as part of the argument for the superiority of loving boys by Pisias, in which he claims that no *sōphrōn* woman can receive or bestow erotic love without impropriety (752c), is opposed by 'Plutarch' in the dialogue, who builds up to the question of whether there is anything wrong with a youth being ruled by an older wife (754d–e). Goldhill makes the sensible point that we should not read this as symbolic of Plutarch's own view, as Foucault does: rather it is a provocative question to which the standard response would be to provide many examples of how there are many things wrong with such a situation where the precedence of masculinity is threatened.[71] The narration by Autobulus of the actions of Ismenodora (providing detail which the friend who arrives from Thespiae with the message does not supply) soon after this comment from 'Plutarch', acts to put the theory of female dominance over a youth into practice. It also allows a change of direction in the debate, once the pederasts Pisias and Protogenes have left in a state of anger. At this point in the dialogue, there is some doubt over whether a woman can be *sōphrōn and* take the initiative in erotic matters, a problem which is solved potentially in the Greek novels by the mutuality of the protagonists' affection, in terms of equality of desire.

The debate moves on, following the exit of Protogenes and Pisias, to consider the role of *Erōs* and his status as a god (from 756a), and there are many references to Platonic ideas here, both from the *Symposium* and, more substantially, from the *Phaedrus*.[72] Plutarch's debt to Plato in this dialogue is an important factor to recognise, signalling how Plutarch represents Plato as an authority on the philosophy surrounding *erōs*, and adding weight to the idea that the novels are also indebted to these texts, something which I referred to earlier in this introduction and which will be expanded in later chapters.[73]

The way in which 'Plutarch' later argues for the importance of the role of *sōphrosunē* in heterosexual marriage is crucial:

Ἔπειτα σωφροσύνη πρὸς ἀλλήλους, ἧς μάλιστα δεῖται γάμος, ἡ μὲν ἔξωθεν καὶ νόμων ἕνεκα πλέον ἔχουσα τοῦ ἑκουσίου τὸ βεβιασμένον ὑπ' αἰσχύνης καὶ φόβων, πολλῶν χαλινῶν ἔργον οἰάκων θ' ἅμα,
διὰ χειρός ἐστιν ἀεὶ τοῖς συνοῦσιν· Ἔρωτι δ' ἐγκρατείας τοσοῦτον καὶ κόσμου καὶ πίστεως μέτεστιν, ὥστε, κἂν ἀκολάστου ποτὲ θίγῃ ψυχῆς, ἀπέστρεψε τῶν ἄλλων ἐραστῶν, ἐκκόψας δὲ τὸ θράσος καὶ κατακλάσας τὸ σοβαρὸν καὶ ἀνάγωγον, ἐμβαλὼν αἰδῶ καὶ σιωπὴν καὶ ἡσυχίαν καὶ σχῆμα περιθεὶς κόσμιον, ἑνὸς ἐπήκοον ἐποίησεν.

Next, *sōphrosunē* towards each other, which in marriage is particularly needed, the one sort comes from the outside, is on account of laws being brought about by force because of shame and fear, rather than being voluntary,
    The task of many a bit and many a rudder,
it is always to hand for those living together. The other sort, which Love has a share in, with such self-control, decorum and trust, so that, if he touches the soul of a profligate, he turns him away from other lovers, expelling insolence and breaking down pride and intractability, introducing modesty and silence and calm and, putting on him the robes of decorum, makes him listen to the one.

Mor. 767e–f: my translation[74]

The above passage suggests that Erōs can bring about a better kind of *sōphrosunē*, which is sincere, for the married couple, who, without his influence, would just be demonstrating a blind obedience to custom in their *sōphrōn* behaviour. The idea that Erōs causes desire for one person to the exclusion of other lovers is highly relevant when considering the Greek novels and their approach to 'exclusive' love between the protagonists. Further, this passage suggests that Erōs and *sōphrosunē* are not necessarily in conflict; indeed, here Erōs makes *sōphrosunē* part of the erotic experience in marriage, something which is a marked development of the Platonic ideas presented in the *Phaedrus*, which presents philosophical love involving *sōphrosunē* as conducive to giving the soul wings, but in a pederastic rather than heterosexual context. Again, this is important in terms of the Greek novels, where Erōs' role, while often represented as disruptive or mischievous, ultimately leads the hero and heroine to conventional marriage (whether the wedding is celebrated at the close, or the already married couple are allowed to enjoy their marriage together), and indeed prevents them from loving anyone other than their chosen beloved. The representation of married love and *sōphrosunē* in the *Amatorius* elucidates in philosophical terms the way in which *erōs* is represented in the novels. While one must be cautious in evaluating this equivalence in simplistic terms (the narrative complexity of the *Amatorius* implies that what is stated within the dialogue is not necessarily representative of the position of Plutarch, or of his contemporaries), it is clear that certain ideas and debates were developing in this period, and there is no reason to believe that the novels, with their approach to mutual desire and *sōphrōn* fulfilment, were not a part of this general trend.

Greek texts from the Imperial period

Two writers from this period whose work includes some reflection on sexuality (specifically involving prostitution), and demonstrate some contemporary views on the nature of *sōphrosunē* are Dio Chrysostom and Lucian. Dio's Seventh Oration or *Euboicus* is significant in this respect. The later emphasis on the dangers of prostitution for society as a whole, which is clearly designed to drive home the message concerning how urban life is in moral decline and requires ethical improvement, demonstrates an interest from Dio in *sōphrosunē* as sexual restraint or, broadly speaking, chastity, which is endangered by those practising sexual vice.

Lucian's *Dialogues of the Courtesans* approach the theme of prostitution in ways which diverge significantly from Dio Chrysostom in terms of style and content. Three of the *Dialogues* include σωφρ- root terms: 2, 7 and 10, where they indicate, in each instance, a lack of sexual decency. For example, in *Dialogi Meretricii* 2, a client (Pamphilus) of the courtesan, Myrtion, and the father of her unborn child, reassures her when she believes that he has married another woman and thus abandoned her. His mother reportedly complains that he continues to avoid marriage, unlike his friend, Charmides, whose wedding was mistaken for Pamphilus' own by Myrtion's slave girl, Doris. It is here that the term σωφρονεῖ is used in the reported speech of Pamphilus' mother to describe Charmides' behaviour in marrying, in contrast to Pamphilus' behaviour in continuing his relationship with Myrtion. The implication of this terminology in its context is to imply behaviour which is honourable or decent, demonstrated here by the act of marriage. It is also implied that not marrying and 'keeping' a courtesan are non-*sōphrōn* forms of behaviour for young men, indicating a lack of sexual self-control. There is also some irony in the idea that Pamphilus' mother would view her son as *sōphrōn* if he abandoned his pregnant lover.

It is clear that the use of such terminology in the *Dialogi Meretricii* reflects its context in each case, with the idea of sexual restraint being foremost in the minds of the characters who use the terms. These dialogues are layered with irony and invite a variety of responses from the reader, and, in his use of σωφρ- root terms, Lucian is humorously subverting conventions surrounding what constitutes a virtuous life and he is exploring how sex affects the possibility of being *sōphrōn*. While the tone and implications of Lucian's *Dialogues of the Courtesans* is considerably different from those of the ideal Greek novels, there is still the potential for perceiving connections in how *sōphrosunē* and sexual desire are represented in this text: σωφρ- root terms are primarily used to represent sexual restraint, although in places this is connected to a broader kind of moderation. Further, as an example of fiction from the period in which Longus and Achilles Tatius were writing, and as an example of fiction which approaches the themes of sexuality and desire, this text is particularly noteworthy for my purposes.[75]

Lucian/Ps.-Lucian's *Amores*'[76] general concern with erotic desire demonstrated by the character of Theomnestus in the frame dialogue, and demonstrated by the unrestrained sexual appetites of Charicles and Callicratidas (particularly emphasised in their reactions to the statue of Aphrodite of Cnidus) makes it important for this study. This dialogue also contains the kind of debate regarding the relative merits of homo- and heterosexual love present in both Plutarch's

Amatorius (see above), and, crucially, Achilles Tatius' *Leucippe and Clitophon*. While the composition of the *Amores* is in doubt due to its debated authorship, if it is the work of Lucian, as is likely, then it is potentially contemporaneous with Achilles Tatius. This makes its concern to provide a humorous slant on this philosophically charged theme, and its tendency to play with philosophy and eroticism in a way not dissimilar to that demonstrated by Achilles Tatius, very interesting indeed.

While this dialogue picks up on many elements present in both the *Amatorius* and *Leucippe and Clitophon*, it is also clear that the author of the *Amores* expands and develops those elements, sometimes for humorous purposes and sometimes in order to explore the prejudices of sexual preference more fully. The intention to act with sexual restraint as evoked in Callicratidas' speech (31–49) is rewarded by Lycinus, but it is then made a little ridiculous by Theomnestus' riposte (52–53). Of course, none of the characters taking part in the debate or in the framing dialogue, apart from Lycinus, seems to possess *sōphrosunē*, or at least this cannot be perceived in their behaviour, and this means that there is further irony in the representation of their views. Can we believe Callicratidas is capable of philosophical friendship with beautiful boys when we have seen him aroused to passion by the rear of the Aphrodite of Cnidus? Should one look to a promiscuous lover like Theomnestus for confirmation of the possibility of *sōphrōn* love? Like the Greek novels, this dialogue provides a view of erotic desire focalised through several different characters. The exploration of the erotic theme and the intensity and humour with which that theme is represented indicate that this text is crucial for an understanding of how sexual desire and the philosophical restraint of sexual desire both invite ironic and insightful responses in this period.

Christianity

North gives an overview of how those promoting the emerging faith of Christianity adapted and manipulated the virtue of *sōphrosunē*, so that its central meaning initially narrowed to that of 'chastity' or 'purity', while Augustine, with his original philosophical view, placed the emphasis on *temperantia* being a Christian virtue, namely that of moderation.[77] For the reader of the later Greek novels (Achilles Tatius and Heliodorus in particular), it is important to appreciate the inclusion of imagery which seems close in nature to that used in martyr accounts and in the apocryphal *Acts of Paul and Thecla*. This influences our reading of *sōphrosunē* in the novels to a certain extent too. The focus on the concept as it relates to chastity is crucial in the novels, and while this does not imply an exclusively Christian ideology, there is certainly the suggestion that there is a movement in these texts towards a view of the concept which adheres more to the Christian representation than to that of Classical philosophical Greek thought. Of course, it is imperative to point out here that the Christian view exploits the common thread running through Greek thought that *sōphrosunē* is representative of control of the passions or appetites, sexual or otherwise. In later chapters we will return to the question of Christian influence: it is enough here to recognise that this complex concept, *sōphrosunē*, retains its relevance despite the myriad cultural changes which impact upon it.

*

Now to turn to the aims and structure of the following chapters. In Chapter 1, focus will be on the representation of *sōphrosunē* in the characterization of the protagonists of the novels and how this differs according to their gender. There will also be analysis of the virtue in other characters where this is significant. This chapter will have five sections, each focusing on an individual novel, chronologically arranged. While this chronology is not firmly established in current scholarship, I have conformed to the consensus. Characterization has recently received some much-needed attention in scholarship:[78] a sustained focus on *sōphrosunē* in the psychological make-up of the protagonists and of other major characters offers new insight into techniques of characterization, and offers a new perspective on the differentiation of gender within these texts. It will become clear that each author has their own approach to the concept and virtue of *sōphrosunē*, which can be analysed through close reading. In places, the sophistication of the author will affect how he represents the virtue, but I will not attempt to establish any linear progression through the genre in this representation. This would be a highly fraught task: only five extant examples exist; and the aims and priorities of the authors of these five texts are not uniform. I agree that the texts belong to a genre, but this does not imply any restriction on how the five authors choose to treat their erotic subject matter or, indeed, *sōphrosunē*. Therefore, it is not the respective dating of their texts which necessarily causes a disparity in how these authors approach the concept of *sōphrosunē*, but rather their respective motives, which, although clearly affected by their literary and cultural context, are principally directed by individual imaginative ability and ethical concerns. The arrangement of the discussion according to relative chronology is intended to provide cogent narrative flow.

Chronological arrangement also allows those instances of the later novels' allusion to the earlier texts to be explored coherently.

I will explore in Chapter 1 whether the regularity of the occurrences of σωφρ-root terms in each novel indicates the importance of the concept in the characterizations within that novel. While the fact that Xenophon of Ephesus has a proportionally far higher count of these terms than the other novels seems to imply that he has the most *sōphrōn* protagonists (most of the instances of the words refer to Anthia and Habrocomes), this must be countered by the consideration of whether other protagonists, such as Heliodorus' Chariclea, demonstrate behaviour which is not necessarily always described by such terminology, but is consistently and determinedly *sōphrōn* nevertheless. The additional factor of considering usages of the terminology with a negative will also be considered. The frequency of the usage of *sōphrosunē* and its cognates in depictions of character will necessarily determine to some extent the proportion of my analysis dedicated to each text (so that the scarcity of such usage in Longus will be reflected in the discussion). However, it remains the case that where such usage is unusual or has complex implications it will necessitate in-depth discussion that may not be required for each instance of the term which follows the general trend within the respective text. Also, which characters/narrators use σωφρ- root terms, and to which characters/narrators they refer when doing so, will be under consideration.

In Chapters 2 and 3, the role of readerly *sōphrosunē* will be centre-stage. This aspect of *sōphrosunē* is largely unexplored,[79] but the work of scholars who have elucidated the nature of readerly 'erotic' desire informs sections of my discussion.[80] The centrality of *sōphrosunē* on the level of characterization as discussed in Chapter 1 is reflected in the centrality of *sōphrosunē* in the reading experience itself. Chapter 2 will focus on how readerly voyeurism is tempered by readerly *sōphrosunē*. The first four sections within Chapter 2 will isolate passages where readerly voyeurism is most prevalent, grouped chronologically according to the pattern of Chapter 1; the final section will look at the textual nature of the heroines of the novels, building on the ideas presented by König and Morgan,[81] and the resulting implications for readerly voyeurism and *sōphrosunē*. Chapter 3 will be concerned with how *sōphrosunē* is necessary as a resistance to the erotic drive of the novels. Within Chapter 3, the first few sections will be concerned with metanarrative drive and will progress chronologically, and the latter sections will focus on embedded narratives and internal narratees and how *erōs* and *sōphrosunē* act in these inset episodes to influence readerly reactions to the wider narratives.

As in Chapter 1, the results for each novel will be determined by the nature of that novel and the concerns of its author, rather than by its position in the relative chronology of these novels. It will become clear that there is a correlation between the sophistication of the text and its metaliterary complexity. It is likely that the nuances involved in reading Achilles Tatius' text, with its narrative and ethical complexity, will far outweigh those involved in reading Xenophon of Ephesus', and this will be reflected in the attention those texts receive in Chapters 2 and 3. However, while Longus' text may not receive the lion's share of the attention in these chapters, his usage of σωφρ- related terminology in his Prologue invites detailed consideration. Heliodorus' *Aethiopica*, with its famous and intriguing narratology, merits a sustained exploration of its readerly *sōphrosunē*: we will discover whether the text invites responses from its readers which reflect the *sōphrosunē* of its heroine.

1

Characterized *Sōphrosunē*

1.1 Chariton's *Callirhoe*

This section will be concerned with the role and representation of the term and concept of *sōphrosunē* in the characterization of several major characters in Chariton's novel. Male *sōphrosunē* is defined by individual characterization and social status, as demonstrated in the representation of three major male characters (Dionysius, Artaxerxes and Chaereas): how they are represented as regards their *sōphrosunē* or lack thereof will lead on to analysis of their individual struggles with intense passions, and the extent to which their submission to love or jealousy means a loss of *sōphrosunē* or self-control. Next, we will consider Callirhoe's *sōphrosunē*, and how its preservation is to her a central concern. She focuses on fidelity of the soul (towards Chaereas), rather than on absolute sexual chastity, thus gaining subjectivity and autonomy despite her outwardly passive persona.

1.1.1 Dionysius: Erōs, *Sōphrosunē* and reputation

Dionysius' possession of *sōphrosunē* and his ethical struggle regarding his erotic desire have complex implications for how Chariton approaches *sōphrosunē*, and this unusual antagonist's regard for *sōphrosunē* is a good place to start this discussion. Dionysius' internal struggle between *pathos* and *logismos* has been well analysed in recent scholarship.[1] This section will demonstrate the extent to which *sōphrosunē* is represented in direct opposition to Erōs, before focusing on how Dionysius' *sōphrosunē* is closely related to his reputation, and the consequences of this for his overall characterization.

At 2.4.5, following Dionysius' soliloquy in which he rails against himself for what he perceives as his immature passion, unworthy of a cultivated man, who is first among the Ionians, the narrator states that:

ἐφιλονίκει² δὲ ὁ Ἔρως βουλευομένῳ καλῶς καὶ ὕβριν ἐδόκει τὴν σωφροσύνην τὴν ἐκείνου· διὰ τοῦτο ἐπυρπόλει σφοδρότερον ψυχὴν ἐν ἔρωτι φιλοσοφοῦσαν.³

But Erōs struggled with these fine deliberations, considering his self-restraint an insult, and for that reason inflamed all the more a heart which attempted to philosophize with love.[4]

The way in which this is expressed through the focalization of Erōs, who transgressively aligns *sōphrosunē* with *hubris*,[5] suggests that this is not a straightforward narratorial statement, but is rather an indication of the dangerous, and anti-ethical potential of Erōs and the emotion he represents. Smith suggests that Chariton's portrayal of Dionysius' internalized struggle indicates the generic propensity for demonstrating Erōs' complete control over his victims.[6] Dionysius' internal *agōn* allows insight into the nature of his desire, represented by 'Erōs': while Dionysius is displaying *sōphrosunē* in his reasoned rejection of his erotic impulse, he is not *sōphrōn* enough to overcome his passion. Erōs' view of Dionysius' restraint as *hubris* also implies that it is not Dionysius' place to choose whether he succumbs to his desire: his surrender is a necessity imposed on him by Erōs. Dionysius' educated ability to act with *sōphrosunē* is therefore shown to be useless in the face of his emotion. Balot suggests that the end-result of Dionysius' loss of self-control is that he becomes selfish, dishonest, and calculating.[7] This is perhaps a little harsh: even though there is a marked deterioration in Dionysius' moral behaviour,[8] it is not altogether reprehensible, but rather indicates the flexibility of one's moral limits when Erōs is in control. Dionysius, as a man with a cultivated reputation, wishes to display his judgement, reason and *sōphrosunē*. However, Erōs, or the desire which he personifies, signifies the implacable power of Callirhoe's beauty over this male subject.

Dionysius claims, at 2.6.3, that he is famed for his *sōphrosunē*.[9] This self-definition is borne out by his behaviour and by his noble struggle against his passion for Callirhoe. He suggests that it is his *sōphrosunē* that stops him from violating Callirhoe:

… καὶ Διονύσιος ὁ ἐπὶ **σωφροσύνῃ** περιβόητος ἄκουσαν **ὑβριῶ**, ἣν οὐχ **ὕβρισεν** οὐδὲ Θήρων ὁ λῃστής;

… Shall I, Dionysius, famous in my self-restraint, violate an unwilling woman whom not even the pirate Theron violated?

Here *hubris* and *sōphrosunē* are in direct opposition. The iteration of *hubris* in this passage highlights this opposition, which directly contradicts Erōs' implication in their alignment discussed above:[10] Dionysius understands that *sōphrosunē* is crucial in overcoming any intention of committing *hubris* in the name of desire, and this ironizes Erōs' perspective and deliberate subversion of the virtue. However, while the use of the same terminology is surely significant, the meaning of *hubris* at these two junctures is different: at 2.4.5, Erōs sees Dionysius' *sōphrosunē* as *hubris* in that it is an affront to the god's unimpeachable power over his victim, whereas at 2.6.3, Dionysius' use of the term implies sexual violation, which can be avoided if one possesses *sōphrosunē*. The semantic range of *hubris* and its cognates allows both Erōs' and Dionysius' perspectives to be technically right, but the reader is encouraged to question whether these disparate representations of *hubris* and *sōphrosunē* suggest more about each character's motivation than about the concepts themselves. Jones argues that this scene is indicative of how important Dionysius' reputation is to him: his renown for *sōphrosunē* means he must not be worse than low-life individuals such as Theron.[11] There is the worrying implication that if Dionysius did not have a reputation to uphold, it might be acceptable, in his own view, for his behaviour to extend to sexual violence. *Sōphrosunē* has a crucial role to play in this situation, Dionysius implies: it acts as the tempering force on physical desire in those who have acquired it, because they have to live up to expectations. The fact that this suggestion is framed as a rhetorical question in a series of such questions directed at his slave Leonas, further complicates matters. The questions build in emotional intensity towards this final one, demonstrating that Dionysius' passion and his education succeed in producing good rhetoric. But this begs the question of whether he really believes what he is saying. Is there the subtle implication that Dionysius is trying to convince himself of what he claims? His reputation for *sōphrosunē* **should** prevent *hubris*, and he knows this, but maybe he doubts his own capacity for performing in the appropriate manner, for not committing a violation of Callirhoe's honour and his own.

The above discussion suggests that *sōphrosunē*, far from being a virtue held for its own sake by morally upstanding individuals, was intrinsically involved in the reputation and rhetorical self-definition of the elite male. This is not to claim that Chariton's picture of Dionysius necessarily reflects reality in the Imperial Greek world, which would be to deny the role of fantasy and imagination in this novel. However, the behaviour of this nobleman must be grounded in contemporary cultural attitudes to some extent. Chariton shows us how a man might react to *erōs*: but Dionysius does not display complete moral agency; rather he displays *sōphrosunē*, as befits a man of his social status and rhetorical ability. It is easy to see in Dionysius' behaviour a deeply held sense of right and wrong, and even a respectful chivalry. We must not be wrong-footed in this way. It is not Chariton's concern to demonstrate Dionysius' moral nature, but instead to convey the transgressive nature of illicit desire (represented by Erōs), and how a man in Dionysius' position must attempt to fight against that desire with *sōphrosunē*, or at least seem to do so.[12]

1.1.2 Royal restraint?

At 6.1.9, the King of Persia, Artaxerxes, in the throes of passion over Callirhoe, makes the following speech:

> σκέψαι τί σοι πρακτέον ἐστίν, ὦ ψυχή· κατὰ σαυτὴν γενοῦ· σύμβουλον οὐκ ἔχεις ἄλλον· ἐρῶντος σύμβουλός ἐστιν αὐτὸς ὁ Ἔρως.

> Consider, my soul, what you should do: become yourself again. You have no other counsellor: Erōs is the lover's counsellor.

It is noted that Artaxerxes' dilemma is in many ways a repeat of Dionysius', but also that his situation involves his power as much as his passion.[13] However, at this point the King articulates his dilemma with perspicacity: he will be proven right by subsequent events, when his obsequious eunuch fails to succeed in his efforts to assist him, so that it is indeed the case that unless his soul can overcome this passion, only Erōs can provide the cure. Power, then, is not enough to conquer Erōs, but it is the language of power over the self by which the King's self-control is depicted.[14] Artaxerxes' struggle is with himself: he tries to find a solution, and initially believes this is within his power. Although he knows Erōs can conquer the gods, he never believed that anyone could compete with him and win (6.3.2).

The eunuch Artaxates emphasizes the idea of the King's ubiquitous power, when he asks:

> ποῖον . . . κάλλος δύναται τῆς σῆς κρατῆσαι, δέσποτα, ψυχῆς, ᾧ τὰ καλὰ πάντα δουλεύει, χρυσός, ἄργυρος, ἐσθής, ἵπποι, πόλεις, ἔθνη;

> Master, what beauty can control your soul, when all that is beautiful is subject to you, gold, silver, clothes, horses, cities, peoples?

6.3.4

The language of power (κρατῆσαι) and slavery (δουλεύει) puts the King's world into sharp relief: he is master of everything and everyone is his slave. However, the focalization through the eunuch marks his character as much as the King's: it is Artaxates' sincere belief that everything is within his master's power; and he proves in his relentless pursuit of Callirhoe that he thinks that the slave closest to the omnipotent ruler has much of that power by default. The use of language which depicts power over self, rather than direct *sōphrosunē*, demonstrates how the narrator intends the King to be seen. The distinction between the two forms of self-control, *enkrateia* and *sōphrosunē*, is not so much in the result, as in the nuance of the motivation and the understanding of that motivation: so, whereas Dionysius prides himself on his cultivation and *paideia*, and the status that these bring him, the King is only concerned with his excessive power over the world, which includes his power over his own soul and its desires. Whether this is indicative of his ethnicity as a Persian rather than a Greek, in addition to it being indicative of his social position as a monarch rather than a nobleman, is debatable. However, Chariton's narrator implies at certain points the ethical inferiority of the Persians and their tendency to display arrogance: Artaxates is an example of an archetypal obsequious and cringing Eastern slave; and the Persian women are proved wrong in their assumption of their most beautiful woman's superiority over Callirhoe (5.3.1–9). Artaxerxes' lack of overt *sōphrosunē* could well fit with the narrator's general disdain for the Persians, but it is also clear that the King's characterization is drawn with a subtlety that goes beyond that of an ethnic stereotype. Furthermore, the King expresses himself in Aristotelian terms: as discussed in the introduction, as Book 7 of the *Nichomachean Ethics* makes clear, *enkrateia* is present when there is a struggle with the appetites; if one were *sōphrōn*, there would be no moral struggle and self-control would be present through habituation. It is not often that a clear connection with Aristotelian ethics is made in the Greek novels, but this is an occasion where we can perceive such a link.

Montiglio notes that the King's self-control is overcome by his desire, and this is betrayed by the eunuch's increasingly threatening speeches to Callirhoe, and, with her options narrowing to sex with the King or suicide, she is only saved by the interruption of war with Egypt brought about by Tychē.[15] Montiglio's reasoning is sound, but the King has not been completely overcome: his eunuch is not honest with him about the situation regarding Callirhoe's recalcitrance (6.6.6), and, although plagued by sleeplessness and night-fantasies (6.7.1–2), it is nowhere suggested that Artaxerxes would use force on Callirhoe. His morality may be becoming less rigid in the face of Erōs' onslaught, but it is not altogether lost. The King shows that he has not lost his *enkrateia* regarding Callirhoe after the war, as I will discuss below, and there is no concrete evidence that his statement at 6.3.8 (μηδεμίαν μου καταγνῷς ἀκρασίαν. οὐχ οὕτως ἑαλώκαμεν 'Do not accuse me of lacking self-control. I am not overcome to that extent') does not continue to hold true despite his suffering.

When he knows that he has lost all hope of ever having his desire for Callirhoe requited, and he learns of Chaereas' actions and their consequences in Book 8, Artaxerxes is said to be filled with envy (φθόνος), and states that Chaereas is luckier than him. However, in contrast to how erotic jealousy affects Chaereas, and to how Dionysius is covetous, the King here seems to regain his former self-control. He does nothing rash but rather seems to accept the situation and he expresses much relief at the return of his wife, Stateira. It could be argued that he has little choice but to do so, and this is Chariton's way of depicting how complete Chaereas' victory is: the King of Persia is subdued and has to settle for less than he would ideally want. While this is true, it is also the case that having just fought a war and nearly lost his wife to the enemy, Artaxerxes now counts his blessings and sees that morally and pragmatically he must now let go all hope of ever seeing Callirhoe again.[16] Chariton shows us in this one instance that Erōs cannot dominate all of the people all of the time: someone has to relent or there would never be a resolution. The characterization of Artaxerxes may never be couched in terms of *sōphrosunē*, but sexual self-restraint is certainly involved in his response to his desire for Callirhoe, and his situation is resolved not only through circumstances beyond his control, but also through his self-mastery and rationality.

The King of Persia's self-control in relation to his desire for Callirhoe hints at Chariton's homogenous world-view: although we do not have the same terminology for Dionysius' and Artaxerxes' responses to desire, their attitudes are essentially identical: neither wants to damage their reputation or social standing through a capitulation to erotic desire. Although Callirhoe is taken out of the Greek world during her adventures, she is never beyond its ethical sphere.

1.1.3 Chaereas: jealousy and latent *sōphrosunē*

At 1.3, Chaereas reacts angrily when his suspicions are aroused by the signs of partying outside Callirhoe's house, but here his anger is quickly reduced to sorrow, and then overcome by Callirhoe's defiant response and their mutual apologies. This episode acts as an inverse prolepsis of the consequences of Chaereas' jealous anger in the next chapter: here anger is easily assuaged; there it is deprived of such an opportunity. At 1.4, when Chaereas has been told that Callirhoe is committing adultery and he is shown the fraudulent evidence, the phrases οὐκέτι κατέσχεν and κρατούμενος δὲ ὑπὸ τῆς ὀργῆς clearly indicate the loss of self-mastery which is occurring.[17] The sight of the supposed lover entering the house causes the initial flare of jealous anger, and Chaereas' intention is to kill him in the act. On seeing his wife greet him with open arms, Chaereas' anger is reignited and results in him kicking her. His rage and loss of self-control are brought about directly by the sight of those whom he considers to be making him a cuckold. When Chaereas' is depicted with such a lack of restraint in his jealous rage, the reader has witnessed no other male character reacting to his erotic desire for Callirhoe: this flawed hero sets a precedent for the reader's expectations about male erotically related self-control, which is countered when Dionysius' concerted attempts at *sōphrosunē* feature.

The issue of whether Chaereas' jealousy is still a matter for concern at the close of the novel is one which deserves some attention in order to trace the hero's character development and whether this allows for any acquisition of *sōphrosunē*.[18] While it is clear that his jealousy is active enough to cause *hubris* only in the episodes considered above, it is still the case that it is for him an innate characteristic. At 8.1.15, when Callirhoe is narrating her adventures to him following their reunion, she falls modestly silent when reaching the part about Miletus and the following statement is made:

Χαιρέας δὲ τῆς ἐμφύτου ζηλοτυπίας ἀνεμνήσθη ...

Chaereas was reminded of his innate jealousy ...

This is picked up again at 8.4.4, when Callirhoe prepares to write to Dionysius, and she does so secretly and the reason is given: '... εἰδυῖα γὰρ αὐτοῦ τὴν ἔμφυτον ζηλοτυπίαν ...' ('... for she knew of his innate jealousy ...').[19] Given that Callirhoe has not witnessed any instance of jealousy other than that which precipitated her *Scheintod*, it is obvious that she, through whom the last statement is focalized, judges her husband to a certain extent on his former behaviour. However, the statement that the narrator makes at 8.1.15 depicts Chaereas' own feeling of jealousy on hearing about Dionysius, so this is not a case of misjudgement on Callirhoe's part. Clearly, the jealousy that Chaereas possesses is still perceived as a threat by Callirhoe, and she feels compelled to act, if not deceitfully, then at least with due caution. Thus, Chaereas is not given the opportunity to show that he has changed: his jealousy is not sufficiently aroused for him to be *sōphrōn* in response. There is irony in this. His jealous rage in Book 1 was grounded in falsehood: Callirhoe had not betrayed him in any way. Now, however, in the final book, the reader is aware, along with Chaereas, that Callirhoe has been remarried. Putting aside the strong argument that can be made in her defence, it is not beyond the bounds of possibility that Chaereas could be roused to jealous anger by this: he would be more justified in reacting with anger at this point than he was when he kicked his faithful wife. The reader's (and Callirhoe's) fears about Chaereas' jealousy and lack of self-control in response to that jealousy are thus allayed, not by any real assurance that he has changed, but by calculated manoeuvring on Callirhoe's part. His jealousy is in his nature, it is suggested, and this begs the question of whether his lack of self-control is also in his nature.

Scourfield and De Temmerman both argue that part of Chaereas' personal growth is displayed by his *sōphrosunē* in the sphere of battle (7.4.9),[20] but is it the case that he also retains that sense of restraint as far as Callirhoe is concerned? Jones suggests that Chaereas is only able to display his latent *andreia* when no longer a slave to Callirhoe (he loses all hope of recovering her), and no longer a literal slave.[21] If this is the case, the reader must be right to worry for the consequences of Chaereas' reunion with his wife: will he lose his new-found manly *sōphrōn* persona and revert to type at some point beyond the close of this narrative? If Callirhoe's and Chaereas' erotic relationship is, at least in part, defined by intensity of passion, then how can the reader see a calm and contented future for the couple? It is distinctly possible that, as we have seen where Dionysius is concerned, part of Erōs' plan is to dismiss *sōphrosunē* as *hubris*: maybe Chaereas will always be readily jealous over his divinely beautiful wife, and it will perhaps be her awareness of this that will prevent future disaster, rather than any real self-mastery on his part.

There is only one instance where Chaereas' *sōphrosunē* is referred to, which is pertinent to his overall character development at this stage of the narrative:

Ἐν δὲ τῷ ἀδιηγήτῳ τούτῳ ταράχῳ μόνος ἐσωφρόνησε Χαιρέας …

In this indescribable confusion Chaereas alone kept control …

7.4.9

While this seems to mark Chaereas out as particularly self-possessed in comparison with both his comrades and enemies, it is especially important to consider the context of this one reference to the hero's *sōphrosunē*. It is noticeable that erotic self-control is not involved here, but rather the emphasis is on how Chaereas is able to retain calmness of mind in the midst of adrenalin-fuelled violence, where he is able to demonstrate his military prowess including his ability to be detached and objective, which clearly requires *sōphrosunē*. This causes the reader to reflect on how far he has come since he was duped by the suitors into an act of *hubris* against his wife. However, to return to the point made above about how the reader does not witness any similar demonstration of self-mastery in the sphere of his relationship with Callirhoe: it is only when she is not in the picture and when he perceives her as utterly lost to him that he shows his *sōphrosunē*. For Chaereas, the ultimate masculine sphere of war holds less danger than the sphere of love: he can be cool and collected in battle, but not in regard to his wife.

At 8.7.4, there is the suggestion that Chaereas flinches at having to recount his adventures. He is αἰδούμενος at the prospect.[22] The embarrassment which Chaereas feels is reiterated by Hermocrates' solicitude: μηδὲν αἰδεσθῇς. Before looking at how Chaereas' *aidōs* is represented, I will briefly discuss how the term itself is defined and how it is related to *sōphrosunē*. *Aidōs*, like *sōphrosunē*, is notoriously difficult to translate into an equivalent English term. Cairns states that it can be provisionally defined as '... an inhibitory emotion based on sensitivity to and protectiveness of one's self-image ...' with *aideomai* conveying '... a recognition that one's self-image is vulnerable in some way, a reaction in which one focuses on the conspicuousness of the self.'[23] Although, as Cairns acknowledges, these definitions are provisional and by no means represent the full semantic range of these multi-faceted terms in Greek literature, they are helpful in the present context of Chariton's text in that the instances of *aideomai* which are present do fit within the latter definition put forward by Cairns. There is an implicit relationship between *aidōs* and *sōphrosunē* which stems from Euripides, particularly the *Hippolytus*, where there is close alignment of the two concepts.[24] This semantic proximity is also evoked in Plato's *Charmides*, in which one of Charmides' early definitions of *sōphrosunē* is *aidōs*: this definition is rejected by Socrates but it potentially indicates a popular view of the virtue as intrinsically related to *aidōs*.[25] I suggest that within the Greek novels this strong association between the emotional condition of *aidōs* and the 'higher' virtue of *sōphrosunē* continues to be important.

At Chariton 8.7.4, what it is that causes Chaereas' *aidōs* is not made absolutely clear, but, given that Hermocrates proceeds to narrate the part everyone is already aware of, including Chaereas' violence against Callirhoe, it is surely the memory of his jealous rage that causes Chaereas to baulk at the prospect of voicing the episode and its consequences. That Chaereas feels remorse for his act of *hubris* is nothing new: he condemned himself to death when he thought he had killed Callirhoe (1.5.4–5). However, in displaying *aidōs* here there is a humility in his attitude which could indicate that, despite his military glory and Aphrodite's forgiveness, Chaereas is not revelling in his new-found good fortune to the extent that he forgets what has gone before. His shame suggests an emotional awareness which could lead to *sōphrosunē*. Thus, although it is not guaranteed by the time we reach narrative closure,[26] there is the subtle suggestion that Callirhoe's worldliness and Chaereas' *aidōs* could combine in order to produce *sōphrosunē* in this complex hero. So, while Chaereas is not completely absolved of his past offence by the narrator, and has not yet proven that he can be *sōphrōn* as far as Callirhoe is concerned, the way in which he is subtly characterized in the final book by his *aidōs* gives the reader hope for this flawed hero.

1.1.4 Callirhoe: passive *sōphrosunē* subverted?

Whereas *sōphrosunē* in the male characters is consistently challenged due to Callirhoe's beauty and its impact, for Callirhoe herself the virtue is present in her emotional fidelity to Chaereas, and she expresses this in her first reference to her own *sōphrosunē* (at 1.14.10): the men who desire her sexually threaten her physical chastity, but not her *sōphrosunē*. Universally in the extant genre, the female protagonist has no desire for anyone but the male protagonist: Callirhoe is no different in this. The one distinct diversion from the generic norm as far as the heroine is concerned is her motherhood and her second marriage, which, unsurprisingly, has generated considerable debate.[27]

The scene where Callirhoe discovers that she is pregnant and considers her options is crucial for understanding her motivation in re-marrying. Tychē is said to plot against Callirhoe's *sōphrosunē* (2.8.4) by creating this situation, so the entire episode is extremely important in considering how the soliloquy virtue is represented in our heroine. During her soliloquy where she debates with herself whether she should kill or keep the child, Callirhoe says:

> βουλεύῃ τεκνοκτονῆσαι; πασῶν ἀσεβ<εστάτη, μ>αίνῃ καὶ Μηδείας λαμβάνεις λογισμούς. ἀλλὰ καὶ τῆς Σκυθίδος ἀγριωτέρα δόξεις· ἐκείνη μὲν γὰρ ἐχθρὸν εἶχε τὸν ἄνδρα, σὺ δὲ τὸ Χαιρέου τέκνον θέλεις ἀποκτεῖναι καὶ μηδὲ ὑπόμνημα τοῦ περιβοήτου γάμου καταλιπεῖν.

> Are you planning to kill your child? You wicked woman, you are mad and thinking like a Medea. But you will seem even more barbaric than the Scythian for it was her husband she hated while you want to kill Chaereas' child and not even leave behind any memorial of that famous marriage.

> 2.9.3–4

By evoking Medea, Callirhoe immediately contextualizes the idea of child-murder in a mythological framework, and also assigns a clear moral code to the question of abortion.[28] The language used suggests a certain perspective on

Medea's actions, clearly seeing her reasoning as madness (μαίνῃ καὶ Μηδείας λαμβάνεις λογισμούς). Trzaskoma sees the Medean allusion as part of Callirhoe's strong impulse towards the abortion, and that the thought of being like Medea does not actually dissuade Callirhoe from this impulse.[29] While this is true (Callirhoe does not turn away completely from the decision until Chaereas' appearance in her dream), I suggest that this allusion to Medea raises an alternative image of female transgression which precludes consideration of Chaereas' feelings, and gives Callirhoe's reasoning a sharper edge. Her understanding of her own motivation as being more savage than Medea's is suggestive of how she perceives the situation not in terms of the child's right to live, but in terms of the child's status as the product of her and Chaereas' union, as something which commemorates that 'famous marriage'. This actually underlines a similarity between Medea's reasoning and Callirhoe's. Their children are indicative of their status as married women. For Medea, once the marriage is destroyed, she can conceive destruction of her children, despite the emotional hurt to herself. Callirhoe's motivation in keeping her child will revolve around her feelings for her husband, rather than be based on her own. She also considers the child's future in terms of its maleness, and associates him with Hermocrates in addition to Chaereas (2.9.1; 2.9.5; 2.11.2).[30]

On witnessing Callirhoe's struggle and the Medean allusion, readers familiar with Euripides may recall that Jason states towards the close of the play that a sexually-slighted woman would not act like Medea if she was *sōphrōn* (1369). Callirhoe's choice is clearly demarcated as being between child and *sōphrosunē* (by Plangon at 2.9.1 and 2.10.8; by Callirhoe at 2.10.7 and borne out by her statement at 2.11.5–6), but this allusion to Medea subtly suggests that Callirhoe's decision to go through with the pregnancy is in itself *sōphrōn*. If Medea is not *sōphrōn* as is suggested by Euripides' Jason, and if her actions are mad, as suggested here by Callirhoe, then to act contrary to Medea implies Callirhoe's possession of *sōphrosunē*. Further, Callirhoe's preservation of her child's life is not self-interested: she is motivated by her love for Chaereas and this adds weight to the idea that she maintains her *sōphrosunē*, which represents her fidelity to her husband, in the very act of apparently giving it up. Callirhoe's status as a high-born Greek is also emphasized by her rejection of the alluded-to actions of Medea, an archetypal barbarian female figure.

Callirhoe inadvertently defines her own *sōphrosunē* most succinctly at 2.11.5:

δέδοικα δὲ μή, κἂν ὑπομείνω τὴν ὕβριν, Διονύσιός μου καταφρονήσῃ τῆς τύχης καὶ ὡς παλλακὴν μᾶλλον ἢ γυναῖκα νομίσας οὐ θρέψῃ τὸ ἐξ ἄλλου γεννώμενον κἀγὼ μάτην ἀπολέσω τὴν σωφροσύνην.

> But I am afraid that even if I submit to his lust, Dionysius may look down on my misfortune and, thinking me a concubine rather than a wife, refuse to rear another man's child. Thus I shall have surrendered my chastity for nothing.

This follows on from Callirhoe's earlier stark statement that she must choose ἤ σωφροσύνης ἤ τέκνου, and Plangon's cunning re-emphasis of this in suggesting either decision is justified (2.10.8). On a surface-level reading, the passage at 2.11.5 seems to reinforce Callirhoe's passivity as regards her *sōphrosunē*: it will be taken from her and she risks being treated with disrespect because of her situation. However, this is not really what she is saying. She is consciously surrendering the virtue and is motivated to do so following much soul-searching and logical reasoning (see 2.11.1–3). So the fear she expresses here could be read as another careful move: this will prompt Plangon to work on her behalf and ensure her status as wife and respectable mother. However, what is also significant is the way in which she perceives *sōphrosunē* itself. As Chaereas' wife and Hermocrates' daughter, Callirhoe is often represented in relation to the men in her life: they bestow status on her and her *sōphrosunē* seems to be deeply involved in this, not only from the perspective of the narrator, but, markedly, from her own perspective. It is this status which ensures Dionysius treats her with respect, as discussed above. Again, in this passage, she links her *sōphrosunē* with status: it is only worth surrendering if she is guaranteed a similar status to that which she has lost, and this is expressed through her male connections. *Sōphrosunē* for Callirhoe is not something which she has acquired for herself as a status symbol, like it is, at least in part, for Dionysius, but it is directly linked to a paternalistic framework which projects certain modes of behaviour on women, in order to ensure social cohesion and the continuation of high-status bloodlines. However, what Callirhoe achieves in this narrative is the direct subversion of this framework. She remarries and successfully convinces Dionysius that the baby is his. Does she really lose her *sōphrosunē* by doing this? Not really. In Book 6, when the persistent eunuch is about to pester her on the King's behalf, we are told that he did not have any idea of 'the pride and nobility of a Greek and especially of the chaste (σώφρονος) and faithful Callirhoe.' (6.4.10). Callirhoe's subsequent manoeuvres and outright rejection of the King prove this description true, as she plans suicide to escape his attentions. Callirhoe has, it seems, had her cake and eaten it: she is *sōphrōn* despite her bigamy. She has subverted male expectations and by never faltering in her faithful feelings towards Chaereas she maintains *sōphrosunē*. Chariton's heroine is finely-tuned to the dangers of the male world and she acts with outward passivity which belies her inner strength of purpose. Therefore, while her *sōphrosunē* is part of her identity in terms of her social status and familial connections, by her own definition her possession of the virtue primarily represents her fidelity to Chaereas, and, in regard to her emotional commitment, this is never in doubt.

*

Chariton offers several differentiated approaches to the concept of *sōphrosunē*, which he represents in several of his major characters. Dionysius is the male character in whom the virtue is most evident, and he is the only male character to define himself as *sōphrōn*. It is in his representation that the conflict between erotic passion and rational *sōphrosunē* is most clearly displayed. Erōs easily triumphs over Dionysius' virtuous efforts to resist his desire, so that *sōphrosunē* is presented as an affront against the god. While the virtue is firmly placed in the erotic sphere and is the impetus behind an effort at sexual self-restraint in Dionysius, there is also the interconnected factor of *sōphrosunē* acting as the rationalized response to an irrational passion.

Passion must be restrained in the most politically powerful character in the novel, the Persian King, Artaxerxes. The absence of σωφρ- root terms in relation to Artaxerxes, whose self-control is instead described by κρατ- root terms, suggests that it is monarchical control which is important for one who has such power over his world, rather than any virtue acquired through education, as in the case of Dionysius. The Persian King fears a loss of control rather than any lapse in sexual virtue or a lack of propriety, and this is reflected in the language which is used. However, it is also clear that Artaxerxes' fears are similar in tone to Dionysius' and both characters display an adherence to external expectations of how they should behave: reputation is central for both of them, although this is nuanced according to their ethnic and social status.

Chaereas matures over the course of the novel, following a distinctly unrestrained jealous action from which he clearly learns. His marked character development is demonstrated by a new-found self-control and *aidōs*, which allows the reader to hope that he has acquired *sōphrosunē* by the close of the novel.

Despite her second marriage to Dionysius, Callirhoe retains her *sōphrosunē*, which is consistently presented in relation to her emotional fidelity to Chaereas. Callirhoe's erotic passion for her first lover is inextricably connected to *sōphrosunē*, so that in his female protagonist, Chariton creates a woman who falls in love once and is consequently consistently *sōphrōn* in her commitment to her initial lover.

In subsequent chapters, the extent to which this idea of *sōphrosunē* as emotional fidelity between hero and heroine is consistent within this genre will be central. A complex picture of *sōphrosunē* and how it is gendered emerges from Chariton's text. For the male characters, *sōphrosunē* is both sexual self-restraint and a more generalized and rationalized self-control, which is closely associated with social status and reputation. Callirhoe represents her own *sōphrosunē* in terms of her fidelity to Chaereas, but the way the virtue is nuanced according to the situations in which Callirhoe finds herself suggests that Chariton allows flexibility in how Callirhoe is *sōphrōn*, but he never allows her possession of the virtue to lapse.

1.2 Xenophon of Ephesus' *Ephesiaca*[31]

Xenophon of Ephesus' *Ephesiaca* is rich in references to *sōphrosunē*, with more occurrences of the term and its cognates proportionally than in any of the extant Greek novels.[32] *Sōphrosunē* and its cognate terms are applied almost exclusively to Habrocomes and Anthia,[33] and the virtue is implied in relation to them, even when alternative terms are used. Moreover, they each frequently define themselves using σωφρ- root terms. The intense focus on the virtue is nuanced by the respective characterization of the protagonists, which is ultimately governed by a generic ideal involving focus on gender roles. Anthia and Habrocomes are described in terms of their *sōphrosunē* close to their introductions, and this is where this discussion starts. Consideration of the oath-swearing scene will follow, before analysis of the role of morbidity in relation to *sōphrosunē*. Anthia's strategies for defending her *sōphrosunē*, and the role of narrative in these strategies will be discussed next, before we finally turn to look at how Hippothous' narrative stands in contrast to the primary narrative and throws light on to how Habrocomes is represented in terms of his *sōphrosunē*, a concept which is markedly absent from Hippothous' characterization.

1.2.1 Introducing *sōphrosunē*

Although Habrocomes is the first to be introduced, it is Anthia who first receives the implied accolade of *sōphrosunē*. To be clear, she is not said to be *sōphrōn* directly, but at 1.2.6 it is stated that:

ὀφθαλμοὶ γοργοί, φαιδροὶ μὲν ὡς καλῆς, φοβεροὶ δὲ ὡς σώφρονος·

Her eyes were vivacious, bright like a beauty's, but forbidding like a chaste girl's.[34]

This is clearly ambiguous: is Anthia actually a 'beauty' *and* a 'chaste girl'? Or does she just have eyes which are evocative of both? Her beauty is central, of course, and this description of her eyes marks the culmination of a passage focused on how she looks. Does this description of her eyes imply a frisson of conflict in the girl's composition, given the use of the μὲν/δὲ clause? Or is there an implied unity between beauty and *sōphrosunē* in this burgeoning heroine?[35] The remainder of the initial book will to a certain extent show the result of Anthia's beauty (along with Erōs' power), but the remainder of the novel supports the idea that she does not lose her *sōphrosunē* because of men's reactions to her beauty, although it takes all her resourcefulness to retain it. This phrase is quite significant, not only introducing terms which are very important in relation to how Anthia is represented, but also introducing two central themes for this novel. In addition, the phrase points to the interrelation of κάλλος and σωφροσύνη. As has been noted, the male gaze is invited here, and Anthia is also presented as conforming to patriarchal mores,[36] which the narrator perpetuates, and this is programmatic for much of Anthia's representation in this novel, although this is not the whole story, as I will discuss later (section 1.2.4).

To look a little more closely at this phrase, there is some ambiguity in the original, which is not conveyed by Henderson's translation: 'φοβεροὶ' is not necessarily active.[37] While the term is used consistently elsewhere in the text in its active sense,[38] the context in this instance does not dictate that the adjective must be active. So, the *sōphrōn* girl's eyes could either inspire fear in others or be expressing her own fear. This dilemma in interpretation has significant implications for understanding female *sōphrosunē* in the text. It is either a virtue with which the possessor can frighten potential suitors or it implies the passivity and vulnerability of the girl who possesses it. Anthia's eyes are also described with the adjective 'γοργοί', which seems to imply an inherent danger (relating to the Gorgon) in addition to the vivacity which is conveyed by Henderson's translation.[39] This might favour the interpretation of 'φοβεροὶ' as being 'forbidding' in line with Henderson's translation. However, I think there is the potential for reading this phrase as deliberately ambiguous, thus adding duality to the way in which Anthia's connection with *sōphrosunē* is represented at this early stage in the narrative. Notably, this is the only instance before Anthia's and Habrocomes' wedding at which *sōphrosunē* and Anthia are connected, and in her behaviour after seeing Habrocomes, Anthia acts with little restraint:[40] it is the potentiality of her possession of the virtue which is indicated by the use of the adjective at 1.2.6, rather than her present possession of it.

Habrocomes is not initially described in terms of *sōphrosunē* by the narrator, although his resistance to *Erōs* is described (1.1.4–6) and implies an extreme Hippolytus-like chastity.[41] He is introduced first through his parentage, thus emphasizing his aristocratic status, and then by his astonishing beauty, and subsequently his educational and sporting achievements (1.1.1–3). This introduction, by preceding the female protagonist's, and by giving details other than parentage and beauty, seems to go beyond what we find in Chariton regarding Chaereas.[42] The possible invitation to compare Habrocomes' introduction not necessarily with Chaereas', but rather with Callirhoe's, is encouraged by Xenophon's use of the phrase '... μέγα δή τι χρῆμα ... κάλλους ...' ('... a paragon of handsomeness ...' 1.1.1). This echoes Chariton's description of Callirhoe,[43] which includes the phrase, '... θαυμαστόν τι χρῆμα παρθένου ...' ('... a marvel of a girl ...' 1.1.1: trans. Goold 1995). Given that Chariton introduces his female protagonist first and implies her extraordinariness in the very first lines of his text, Xenophon is deliberately reacting to this technique by introducing his male protagonist first and using similar terminology, in the same textual position, again to imply the unique nature of his creation. The similar objectification of Callirhoe and Habrocomes emphasizes their respective powers of attraction. This leads on to the introduction of Callirhoe's many suitors (1.1.2), and, conversely, to Habrocomes' rejection of Erōs (1.1.4–6).

Xenophon has Habrocomes and Anthia define themselves as *sōphrōn* on fifteen occasions, thirteen of which occur in direct speech: Habrocomes' five direct uses of this self-definition come in the first two books; while Anthia's eight direct usages occur in Books 4 and 5, with seven of these in the latter.[44] This suggests the primacy of the virtue for Habrocomes in the early stages of his and Anthia's relationship, whereas, for Anthia, the virtue must be claimed vigourously as she defends it in the latter sections of the narrative. It is Habrocomes who first defines himself as *sōphrōn*, when he realizes that Erōs has triumphed by causing him to fall in love with Anthia. The situation is as follows: Habrocomes attempts to resist his attraction to Anthia and talk himself out of submission, by alluding to his former resistance to such feelings and to the god, even trying to persuade himself to remain stronger than Erōs (1.4.1–3). The consequent intensification of Erōs' attack is described by the narrator in physical terms:

ταῦτα ἔλεγε καὶ ὁ θεὸς σφοδρότερος αὐτῷ ἐνέκειτο καὶ εἷλκεν ἀντιπίπτοντα καὶ ὠδύνα μὴ θέλοντα.

At these words the god attacked him the more determinedly, dragging him along as he resisted and tormenting him as he balked.

1.4.4

Following this, Habrocomes states in frustration at his predicament:

νενίκηκας … Ἔρως. μέγα σοι τρόπαιον ἐγήγερται κατὰ Ἀβροκόμου τοῦ σώφρονος

You win, Erōs! Here stands your great trophy over Habrocomes the Chaste.

1.4.4

The statement, with its self-definition in the third person, implies that he has a heightened awareness of the virtue which is now being vanquished by his new-found desire for Anthia. While Habrocomes is acknowledging that he has lost the battle against Erōs, he is also maintaining a degree of arrogance by furnishing himself with this epithet. He admits defeat by simultaneously indicating his ethical status, so that just as erotic desire takes control of him, his *sōphrosunē* is foregrounded. This positions *sōphrosunē* as a virtue which resists Erōs: as a part of Habrocomes' initial impiety towards the god, his reference to it at this point is surely a sign of Habrocomes' continuing self-assertion. Habrocomes could mention his pride in his beauty or in his social status or education, but instead he chooses to refer to the virtue which he perceives that he is losing as Erōs wins, as if to remind the god that his *sōphrosunē* was once strong enough to dismiss any thought of him as a deity. Habrocomes' view of *sōphrosunē* at this point is limited: he represents it exclusively as the force which acts against Erōs; it will become clear later in the novel that there is another role for *sōphrosunē* in Xenophon's characterization of Habrocomes, as I will discuss below.

The introduction of Habrocomes as a handsome youth who rejects love and sex, refusing to acknowledge Erōs as a god recalls Hippolytus' similar attitude and his rejection of Aphrodite in Euripides' tragedy.[45] The nature of Hippolytus' *sōphrosunē*, which is part of his self-definition (79–81) as it is for Habrocomes, is represented as extreme from the beginning of the play, where Aphrodite condemns the youth for his impiety in rejecting her as a goddess and in rejecting the marriage-bed (13–14). While the attitude of Habrocomes is presented as similarly extreme, the way in which Aphrodite wreaks her revenge is not programmatic for how Erōs wreaks his in the *Ephesiaca*: Hippolytus' attitude is fixed, whereas Habrocomes' is reversed. The fate suffered by Hippolytus is the result of the onslaught of desire on Phaedra and her vengeful final act in accusing Hippolytus of rape, while Habrocomes' suffering springs from his own desire for

Anthia, and the subsequent trials and tribulations the couple endure. The generic emphasis on love, its fulfilment and the resulting happiness it brings is obviously crucial when considering how the tragedy is subverted in this novel: the initial *sōphrosunē* of Habrocomes looks very similar to Hippolytus', but the way in which Erōs punishes Habrocomes allows a differently nuanced *sōphrosunē* to survive in this protagonist, and allows mutual desire to be rewarded in the end.

In introducing terms related to *sōphrosunē* early in the representation of the male and female protagonist the author does not adhere to any particular 'gendered' form of the virtue in terms of how it is defined: in both Anthia and Habrocomes at this introductory stage the virtue is a form of sexual restraint, or the motivation behind chastity. However, Anthia's implied maidenly status and her related or potential *sōphrosunē* are presented in terms which suggest that these enhance her feminine beauty and charm. Conversely, Habrocomes' resistance to Erōs and his excessive arrogance can be perceived as problematic: the virtue plays its part in Habrocomes' masculine self-definition which allowed him to reject Erōs. In the opening chapters of the first book, the import and significance of *sōphrosunē* is clearly emphasized, but the gender of the agent is also relevant and colours the virtue to a certain extent.

1.2.2 Swearing *sōphrosunē*?

At 1.11.4–6, Habrocomes and Anthia each swear their fidelity to one another. Before focusing in depth on this scene and its implications for *sōphrosunē* as the couple face their first ordeal following their marriage, I will look at an earlier passage (1.9.3), which contains a reference which can be read as an anticipation of the oath:

> ὦ φωτὸς ἡδίων ἐμοὶ κόρη καὶ τῶν πώποτε λαλουμένων εὐτυχεστέρα, τὸν ἐραστὴν ἔχεις ἄνδρα μεθ' οὗ ζῆν καὶ ἀποθανεῖν ὑπάρξαι γυναικὶ σώφρονι.

> Girl sweeter to me than the light of day, and luckier than any girl they talk about in stories, you have your lover as a husband: may it be yours to live and die with him as a chaste wife.

These are the words of Habrocomes on his and Anthia's wedding night and form part of his first speech to his beloved. Before concentrating on the use of the term σώφρονι and its implications, consideration must be given to the tone of these words and how they characterize Habrocomes in order to appreciate the nuances at work here. He begins charmingly enough, expressing Anthia's sweetness in comparison to the light of day, but this compliment is couched in terms which relate to how he values her, rather than in terms of her own objective qualities. Tagliabue has discussed how this scene emphasizes the representation of Anthia's dominance over Habrocomes in certain respects, thus drawing attention to Habrocomes' passivity, which is belied by the self-definition of Habrocomes as *erastēs*.[46] However, the passivity which commentators note is not sexual, but emotional, so his presentation here as an *erastēs* is not necessarily misleading: he has never, as far as the reader is aware, been anyone's *erōmenos* in the sexual sense. It is also important to appreciate the focalization of the term: Habrocomes is to be a lover to Anthia, and it is feasible to suggest that he is preparing her for sex with this term. Sex and marriage are aligned in this speech, so that, while there is the potential to see arrogance in Habrocomes' assertion of Anthia's good fortune, it is also clear that he is defining his role in relation to her with these words.

So how does all this influence his use of the term σώφρονι? If Habrocomes is taking the active role here, prior to the consummation of his and Anthia's desire, then what does this reference to Anthia's *sōphrosunē* imply in this context? The narrator is emphasizing Anthia's *sōphrosunē*, rather than Habrocomes', by foregrounding the hero's encouragement of Anthia's possession of it. However, Anthia is defined as *sōphrōn* not by her own words, or even directly through the voice of the narrator, but via Habrocomes' focalization. This echoes the earlier use of the ὡς clause (1.2.6: see above), which while hinting at Anthia's *sōphrosunē*, did not directly assert it as a fact. While I acknowledge that this phrase at 1.9.3 is proleptic of the oath-swearing scene a couple of chapters later, it is also clear that, by taking the active role not only regarding sex, but also regarding the moral restraints of marriage, Habrocomes asserts a degree of dominance over Anthia to the extent that he imposes an anxiety on her which she herself seems not to possess. At this stage, there is a conflict in the representation of the couple: Anthia seems dominant in terms of the quantity of her speech later in the passage, as noted by Tagliabue;[47] however, Habrocomes is represented as the dominant force as he describes himself as an *erastēs*, and as he enacts a gendered role in relation to his wife's fidelity.

To turn to the oath-swearing scene itself, Habrocomes is the intitiator, which picks up on his suggested anxiety at 1.9.3. The language which he uses to refer to Anthia is significant. He suggests that he and Anthia swear that:

... σὺ μὲν ἐμοὶ μενεῖς ἁγνὴ καὶ ἄλλον ἄνδρα οὐχ ὑπομενεῖς, ἐγὼ δὲ ὅτι οὐκ <ἂν> ἄλλῃ γυναικὶ συνοικήσαιμι.

... you will stay chaste for me and not submit to another man, and that I will not live with another woman.

1.11.4

Henderson uses the term 'chaste' to translate ἁγνός, as he does to translate σώφρων: ἁγνός is unusual in the extant corpus of Greek novels, but fairly frequent in Xenophon, where it is used only of Anthia.[48] For Habrocomes to use this term in the oath rather than refer to *sōphrosunē* as he did at 1.9.3, implies that ἁγνός perhaps has stronger connotations than σώφρων when associated with female sexual mores. There is the overtone of religious or ritual purity in this term, which makes its use in this text seem indicative of an extreme preoccupation with female chastity,[49] beyond what is usual in the corpus. It is perhaps also significant that ἁγνός is used of Anthia only after the consummation of her marriage: could Habrocomes be suggesting that their union is in someway sacred, and not to be defiled? If so, Anthia's purity is directly related to her relationship with Habrocomes.

Once more Habrocomes imposes a role on Anthia, who, in her response, seems not a little perturbed by his evident need for reassurance on this front (1.11.5). While oath-swearing either to fidelity or to maintaining chastity until marriage is a device used in later Greek novels,[50] it is there initiated by the female protagonist, demonstrating a maidenly concern for the behaviour of their lover: in the extant corpus, it is only in Xenophon that the oath-swearing is initiated by the male protagonist. While his active stance in initiating the oath could also be read as an example of him taking control of the situation, something which is further borne out by the fact that he achieves his goal of making Anthia swear fidelity to him, it is still the case that, as at 1.9.3, his focus on the potential for infidelity on Anthia's part suggests that his love for her is coloured by an image of a devoted, pure wife. While this is not an unrealistic prospect in this novel, or in the genre as a whole, Habrocomes' emphasis on both *sōphrosunē* and *hagneia* in these two scenes conveys differently nuanced ideas of fidelity, and his iteration of the idea of a 'chaste wife' hints at a lack of firm belief in the constancy of her love, which could be read as a somewhat emasculating fear.

1.2.3 *Sōphrōn* unto death and beyond

There are several places in Xenophon's text where the protagonists refer to their own deaths or their own corpses. While a preoccupation with the potential for suicide if things go wrong is not unusual in the genre, the emphasis on morbidity is here very strong. Moreover, it is in several places linked with *sōphrosunē*, so that the idea of sexual infidelity is directly connected with the demise of the speaker, and the desire to remain *sōphrōn* is preferred to life itself. Again, this is not generically unusual, but it deserves some careful analysis in order to fully engage with the overtones at work here.

Anthia, in response to her husband's initiation of the oath-swearing as discussed above, strongly emphasizes the depth of her loyalty to him by promising that she would rather die than be without him (1.11.5). The iteration in her oath (οὐδε ζήσομαι . . . οὔτε ζήσομαι) drives home her absolute conviction and contrasts with Habrocomes' weaker '. . . οὐκ <ἂν> ἄλλῃ γυναικὶ συνοικήσαιμι' (1.11.4), which, coupled with the fact that we are not given the content of Habrocomes' actual oath (1.11.6), indicates the different tone and import of their respective fidelity. While it is clearly important for Habrocomes to remain faithful, the way in which Anthia's oath is prioritized and emphasized in terms of life and death implies that without the presence of Habrocomes she is lost. While *sōphrosunē* is not present as a term in this section of dialogue, the primacy of fidelity and the manner in which chastity is gendered are clearly indicators of the centrality of these issues for the protagonists of this novel. Moreover, Anthia's oath and the emphasis on death are echoed elsewhere in relation to *sōphrosunē* and this will be discussed below.

Following their enslavement at sea, the couple learn of their pirate masters' love for each of them, and they both lament their fate. Both Habrocomes and Anthia use allusions to death to emphasize the depth of their despair. Habrocomes' emphasis on *sōphrosunē* is clear:

εἰς τοῦτο ἄρα μέχρι νῦν σώφρων ἐτηρήθην ἵνα ἐμαυτὸν ὑποθῶ λῃστῇ ἐρῶντι τὴν αἰσχρὰν ἐπιθυμίαν;

Is it for this that until now I have kept myself chaste, only to submit to the sordid lust of an amorous pirate?

2.1.3

He continues in a similar strain a little further on:

ἀλλ' οὐ μὰ τὴν μέχρις ἄρτι σωφροσύνην ἐκ παιδός μοι σύντροφον οὐκ ἂν ἐμαυτὸν ὑποθείην Κορύμβῳ, τεθνήξομαι δὲ πρότερον καὶ φανοῦμαι <καὶ> νεκρὸς σώφρων.

No, I swear by the chastity that has been my companion since childhood that I will not submit to Corymbus! I will die first and be revealed chaste even as a corpse!

2.1.4

This is the first time since his marriage that Habrocomes has referred to his *sōphrosunē*, which suggests that implicit in his despair is a continuing self-definition which precedes his love for Anthia. Despite the change in his status, Habrocomes still regards his original stance vis-à-vis sexual virtue as a pre-condition for avoiding illicit carnal contact with a pirate. While his marriage to Anthia and his love for her are significant contributing factors (2.1.3), they do not stand as the only considerations here, and this is an unusual situation in the genre, where resistance to the lust of antagonists is always based firmly in the central relationship between the protagonists. Habrocomes' determination to preserve his *sōphrosunē* echoes Anthia's earlier oath to die rather than be separated from him (1.11.5), but the emphasis here is not on physical separation, but rather avoidance of a pederastic affair. It is worth noting that, as far as the reader is aware, Habrocomes has not sworn to keep free of sexual contact with men, only with other women. It is clear that the idea of submitting to the lust of a pirate is not only problematic due to his oath of fidelity, but is distasteful to Habrocomes because it would make him a passive and feminized object of desire for someone far beneath him in social status. Whereas Jones sees Habrocomes' refusal to submit to Corymbus' sexual advances as stemming solely from his new status as a married, and therefore 'active' man, his rejection of pederasty is also connected to Habrocomes' original anti-erotic behaviour: he has always resisted male lovers, and now he is not about to change this.[51] There could also be the implication that while technically no longer completely chaste in sexual terms (he has had sex with Anthia), he replaces his former absolute *sōphrosunē* with extreme fidelity to Anthia. This could be read as a teenage reaction to fast-moving events and to the significant upsets to his original, childish approach to the concept. So, he prefers to die and be a 'νεκρὸς σώφρων'. The death-wish theme is taken into new territory with this phrase, and implies once more that Habrocomes has an obsessive and rather eccentric need to maintain his *sōphrōn* reputation even as a dead body.[52]

Anthia's focus on death is coloured by her need to remain with Habrocomes. After the recognition that this is the first test for her oath (2.1.5), she envisages dying as a means to an end. She will be reunited with her lover beyond the grave, untroubled by any other sexual attentions:

δεδόχθω ταῦτα· ἀποθνήσκωμεν, Ἀβροκόμη. ἕξομεν ἀλλήλους μετὰ θάνατον ὑπ' οὐδενὸς ἐνοχλούμενοι.

Let this be our decision: that we die, Habrocomes. After death we will have each other and be molested by no one.

2.1.6

It is surely significant that each of the lovers wishes for death, but for Habrocomes to be a *sōphrōn* corpse is the ultimate accolade, while for Anthia, death is an escape from violation, and the only way she can conceivably remain with Habrocomes. The way in which they view *sōphrosunē* unto death is not, at least in this passage, the same for both lovers, and this indicates how they each have individual characteristics which continue to be significant. Xenophon uses Habrocomes' intitial obsessive resistance to Erōs beyond the first book: we are reminded of the god's role in events at 2.1.2, and Habrocomes' continuing, although altered (he is now *sōphrōn* in his resistance to extra-marital sex, rather than in his resistance to all sex) *sōphrosunē* is evident from his words at 2.1.4. Meanwhile, Anthia, who from the beginning has only been defined by how she is viewed by others, and by Habrocomes in particular, continues by her own volition to be defined by her relationship to her husband. The repeated focus on morbidity re-emphasizes how both protagonists' *sōphrosunē* and fidelity is differentiated.

While I do not argue for a great deal of sustained characterization in Xenophon's text, the couple, particularly Anthia, do retain their focus on death throughout their various ordeals.[53] One of the places where this is important for a discussion on *sōphrosunē* is at 4.3.3–4, when Anthia prays to Isis in Memphis, prior to her proposed journey to India with the lustful Psammis. Her language, when she refers to the prospect of dying, mirrors that of Habrocomes at 2.1.4. Here, she finishes her prayer with:

> ... εἰ πάντως εἵμαρται χωρὶς ἀλλήλων ἀποθανεῖν ἔργασαι τοῦτο· μεῖναί με σωφρονοῦσαν τῷ νεκρῷ.

> ...if it is absolutely fated that we die apart, contrive this: that I remain chaste for his corpse.

> 4.3.4

While Habrocomes wanted his corpse to be chaste, Anthia wishes to be chaste for his corpse. They both emphasize their own *sōphrosunē* in relation to Habrocomes' corpse, and it is not absolutely clear whether Anthia wishes to die chaste for his corpse, or live chastely in his memory. She has previously reiterated her desire to die rather than be violated or remarry (3.5.6; 3.6.2–3), and she will state this wish again (4.5.3; 5.5.6; 5.8.8–9), and this would seem to imply that the likely implication of her prayer is to die rather than betray Habrocomes. However, she proceeds on her journey following this prayer and makes no attempt to kill herself, which suggests that she wants to live on, or that she leaves matters entirely in the goddess's hands. Whether or not she wants to die, thus guaranteeing she remain *sōphrōn* for Habrocomes' corpse, the implication of her prayer in terms of how she relates her situation to her husband dead or alive is clear: she not only prioritizes her *sōphrosunē*, she also aligns it with death, in a similar way to Habrocomes at 2.4.4. Her language earlier in the prayer also echoes her husband's way of describing her at 1.11.4: she uses the term ἀγνὴ and describes her marriage as γάμον ἄχραντον (4.3.3). The intensity of her focus on a near-ritual sexual purity, connected with a desire to maintain this unto death, aligns Anthia with Habrocomes, and demonstrates that she conforms to his early expectations of her, and to the conditions of her oath. The passage at 4.3 quoted above is the first occasion on which Anthia defines herself by use of σωφρ- root terms in direct speech, and it is clear that not only is *sōphrosunē* central to Anthia's self-representation at this point, but it is also intrinsic to how she maintains her identity as Habrocomes' wife during her separation from Habrocomes, even should that separation become permanent through death.[54]

1.2.4 Desperate measures? Anthia's strategies for *sōphrosunē*

There are several places in the narrative where Anthia finds herself in situations which threaten her *sōphrosunē*: she must resist attempts on her virtue by suitors of varying degrees of depravity. For the purposes of this discussion, I shall focus on two instances where she uses differing methods in order to maintain her *sōphrosunē*. The first will be where she intends suicide in reaction to having to marry Perilaus. The second will be her fake epilepsy when facing a life of prostitution. Both of these passages will illustrate how Anthia's behaviour *in extremis* is demonstrative not only of her resourcefulness, but also of the way in which the constant challenges to her sexual virtue provide an insight into how that virtue is gendered in Xenophon's novel.

To give some context to the first episode for consideration in this section: Anthia has been rescued from Hippothous' gang of brigands by Perilaus, the foremost man in Cilicia (2.13.5). He takes her back with him to Tarsus, where he promptly falls in love with her, and declares this to her, promising that she will be everything to him (2.13.7). Anthia feels pressured into agreeing to marry him, and begs for a thirty-day delay, to which Perilaus agrees (2.13.8). This is a curious passage, where Anthia's excuse in requesting this delay is not specified:

> ... καὶ σκήπτεται <μέν τι>, ὁ δὲ Περίλαος πείθεται ...

> ... She offered some sort of excuse, and Perilaus acquiesced ...

However, Anthia's delaying tactics are effective, here as elsewhere,[55] but it takes a graver method to completely avoid Perilaus' ardour. When the thirty days have elapsed and preparations are underway for her marriage to Perilaus, Anthia is despondent at the prospect and resorts to an extreme solution. She has made the acquaintance of an Ephesian physician, Eudoxus, who comforts her by reminding her of home. It is to him that she turns, when she decides on her strategy. She resolves to kill herself rather than submit to a man other than Habrocomes, and this is revealed via her speech to Eudoxus, when she requests he acquire for her some fatal drug, and then report her own and Habrocomes' deaths in Ephesus (3.5.6–9). The narrator then tells us that the doctor agrees to do all she asks, but in fact procures a harmless sleeping draught for her (3.5.11).

The process which results in Anthia's decision to take her own life is simple enough: she remembers her oaths; she imagines Habrocomes suffering in his imprisonment, even possibly dead because of his determination to remain her husband; she pictures her new wedding night with Perilaus (3.5.2–3).[56] All these imaginings lead her further into despair, and result in her decision. She refers to her oaths and 'σωφροσύνης συνθήκας' again when explaining her plight to Eudoxus (3.5.6). The reiterated mention of her 'pact' (συνθήκας) with Habrocomes in her direct speech to Eudoxus (3.5.7), strengthens her request for help. The doctor is faced not just with an emotional plea for assistance, but with a situation which involves religious oaths which cannot be broken. Is her emphasis on her oaths meant as a persuasive technique, then? Or does she genuinely believe it is these oaths which mean she must die? Anthia seems to genuinely desire death rather than her coming wedding to Perilaus, and this would likely hold true whether she had sworn fidelity or not: her emotional attachment to Habrocomes is clearly at the root of her despair. The oaths allow her to express clearly to this stranger how genuine and deeply held is her need to remain *sōphrōn* for Habrocomes, and they carry a gravitas which is part of her persuasive strategy. On the extradiegetic level, the oaths function effectively as devices which ensure that the sustained focus on *sōphrosunē* is not lost.

In Book 5, Anthia refers to her own *sōphrosunē* seven times, mostly as a response to direct threats to her chastity (5.4.6; 5.5.5; 5.5.6; 5.7.2), but also as a part of her reaction to her troubling dream of Habrocomes (5.8.7; 5.8.9), and on her reunion with Habrocomes towards the close of the novel (5.14.2). In this final book, Anthia is the only character to use σωφρ- root terms: on one occasion this is indirectly conveyed by the narrator (5.9.10), but this is a negative analeptic usage (μὴ σωφρονοῦντα) referring to Anchialus' behaviour; the other instances are all in her direct speeches, and only one refers to Habrocomes, rather than to herself. A significant factor which Anthia's self-definition in this book conveys is how she is resourceful in defending her *sōphrosunē*, particularly in one situation which is more extremely challenging than those in which she has already found herself. Although she frequently laments her fate in this book, she is simultaneously able to conceive and act on defensive strategies for preserving her sexual virtue.

Anthia is sold to a pimp in Tarentum (5.5.7). Prior to this, aware that this is to be her fate, she laments the misfortune which her beauty brings her, and begs to be killed rather than become a prostitute (5.5.5–6). In this speech, she refers to the *sōphrosunē* she has been able to preserve for Habrocomes, and emphasizes the fact that she has always been *sōphrōn*, in an attempt to persuade the servant charged with selling her to a pimp to show mercy and kill her. Here, then, we have Anthia's direct recognition of how her beauty threatens her *sōphrosunē*. This subtly picks up on the dichotomy which is highlighted in the initial description of the heroine at 1.2.6, as discussed above (section 1.2.1). This lament is close in its emphasis on the misfortune brought about by beauty to Callirhoe's in Chariton's novel (5.5.3), indeed, the terminology is identical: '... κάλλος ἐπίβουλον ...'. Callirhoe also lists her previous misfortunes in a similar manner to Anthia (Chariton, 5.5.2: Xenophon, 5.5.5) The situation facing both protagonists is worth comparing. Callirhoe has just discovered she is to be involved in a trial in Babylon regarding adultery; Anthia, as we have seen, is to be sold into prostitution. Callirhoe laments the fact that her beauty has brought her fame, while Anthia fears that her beauty directly threatens her *sōphrosunē*. It is clear then, that the situations are not identical, but the fears of the two women are close in how they are expressed. There is much debate about which text was composed first,[57] and this instance of allusion, as with the one discussed above at 1.2.1, contributes to the argument for Chariton's precedence. The comparison of these two scenes is important when considering the relative emphasis on beauty, misfortune and the results for *sōphrosunē*. While Callirhoe does not mention the virtue specifically in her speech at 5.5.2, the trial is concerned with adultery, so the reputation she laments is strongly associated with her sexuality. Anthia's clear focus on how this new misfortune brought about by her beauty threatens her *sōphrōn* devotion to Habrocomes seems highly focused on the personal rather than the public, which contrasts with Callirhoe's view. Xenophon is playing with Callirhoe's anticipation of the trial. By making Anthia's situation more base he is deliberately inviting consideration of the most extreme threat to female *sōphrosunē* imaginable: Anthia's beauty makes her a commodity. Whereas Callirhoe is famed for her beauty and her attractiveness has brought about a trial before the King of Persia, Anthia's beauty results in a descent into a world of vice. The stark contrast in the context succeeds in conveying how, despite the differences, essential similarities in how the protagonists understand their misfortunes remain. Further, Anthia's sustained preoccupation with *sōphrosunē* indicates how, in this text, sexual virtue is always the most important consideration. Also, how Anthia defends this virtue is crucial to the trajectory of the narrative. The comparison with Chariton's text gives the reader the sense that where Callirhoe is concerned with reputation, Anthia is concerned with only Habrocomes at this juncture, and her *sōphrosunē* is essential to this relationship.

At 5.7.2, having been dressed-up and placed in front of a stall by the pimp who has bought her, Anthia repeats in her lament the disadvantage her beauty brings, and then turns to think pragmatically about how she can guard her *sōphrosunē*. After narrating how Anthia is taken to the brothel and put on display in front of an eager crowd of men, the narrator states:

ἡ δὲ ἐν ἀμηχάνῳ γενομένη κακῷ εὑρίσκει τέκνην ἀποφυγῆς· πίπτει μὲν γὰρ εἰς γῆν καὶ παρεῖται τὸ σῶμα καὶ ἐμιμεῖτο τοὺς νοσοῦντας τὴν ἐκ θεῶν καλουμένην νόσον ...

But in her impossible predicament she found a means of escape: she fell to the ground, let her body go limp, and imitated the victims of the so-called sacred disease.

5.7.4

Anthia's innovative solution is further enhanced by the tale she tells the pimp when he demands an explanation. She relates how the disease was cast into her by a being which leaped out of a grave and attacked her during a nightlong festival, which she attended as a girl (5.7.7–8). Anthia's ingenuity here underlines not only her resourcefulness which arises out of a crisis, but also the necessity of her skill and imagination at this point. Her solution not only ensures the immediate avoidance of sex, but also means that the pimp will be forced to relinquish her: a girl afflicted with this disease in this context is a liability rather than an asset. Indeed, at 5.9.4, the pimp decides to sell Anthia, which, although not ideal, is a preferable alternative to being prostituted, and proves fortuitous when she is bought by Hippothous.

Schmeling has noted the parallel between this episode and *Apollonius King of Tyre*, Chapter 34, where the King's daughter, Tarsia, having been sold to a pimp, avoids sexual transactions by telling her story to the men who come to her, and gaining their sympathy.[58] In agreement with Schmeling, I think this is indicative not of direct allusion, but of a common generic store, which suggests that the heroines' respective defence of their chastity in a brothel is a *topos*. This does not, however, detract from the significance of both episodes. While Anthia's scheme stems from a heightened state of emotion, and Tarsia calmly uses her intellect, both women succeed in duping both potential clients and pimps by means of narrative. While Anthia's false narrative requires support from her imitative skills, and Tarsia succeeds by rhetoric alone, the parallel is clear, and the emphasis on preservation of sexual virtue indicates a generic preoccupation with the issue, enacted in this context for maximum effect.

It is repeatedly the case that Anthia persuades various men either to change their intentions or do her bidding by means of storytelling.[59] In the case of Eudoxus the doctor, it is her actual life-story that encourages his obedience to her will. The pimp, who by definition of his profession is unlikely to be swayed by sentiment, is persuaded to change his actions by a false narrative. This connection between these examples, which ostensibly demonstrate how Anthia uses different methods to retain *sōphrosunē*, show that this female protagonist is masterful in manipulating situations by means of narrative. Anthia's resourcefulness is directly influenced by her relationship with Habrocomes and her consequent fervent commitment to *sōphrosunē*. While the episodes which display Anthia as desirable to all male onlookers imply her objectification by the narrator, it is also true that her innovative methods of escape from her suitors attentions mark her out as able to go 'beyond a woman's means' (as she remarks herself at 5.8.7), and these abilities stem from her determined *sōphrosunē*.[60] Thus, the virtue for Anthia supersedes any passivity which might be considered a female 'norm', and the representation of her gender is destabilized by her resourcefulness and self-assertion. Barbara Gold discusses the idea that destabalization of gendered roles in ancient texts (she focuses on Propertius) allows a glimpse beyond the traditional representation of the female.[61] While Anthia is constantly exposed to the male gaze, and the danger of becoming a prostitute can be read as an inherently masculine ploy aimed at a degree of titilation for the male reader, her resistance to the plots of antagonistic male characters endows her characterization with considerable nuance, which reacts against a purely traditional gender role.[62] Her narrative strategies form a significant part of this resistance, and these will be explored further in Chapter 3 (section 3.5).

1.2.5 Hippothous' narrative

The role of Hippothous is one which has received considerable attention,[63] but continues to defy analysis. My concern here is with the inset narrative at 3.2, in which Hippothous tells Habrocomes of his doomed love affair with Hyperanthes.

It is widely agreed that his tale stands as an alternative or comparable narrative to the central one.[64] The parallels are clear: the story involves a high-status hero who has a reciprocal love affair, temporary separation and travel. The contrasts are also evident: there is a pederastic relationship rather than a heterosexual one, which, it is subtly suggested, is covert due to the respective ages of the lovers; a murder performed by the narrator; and the death of the beloved. Hippothous begins to tell his tale after being persuaded to do so by Habrocomes, who promises to narrate his own story in return.

In the inset narrative, *sōphrosunē* is not mentioned, something which sets it apart from the wider narrative, where the virtue is central. This immediately sets up a contrast between Hippothous and Habrocomes and their respective tales, and, given the unhappy outcome of Hippothous' love affair, suggests that a lack of *sōphrosunē* could spell disaster. Further, the affair with Hyperanthes is covert, which contrasts with the very public marriage of Habrocomes and Anthia.[65] Hippothous' potential for transgression is evident in this tale, and is clearly borne out by his previous and subsequent behaviour.[66] While his banditry has been attributed to his traumatic love affair, and particularly his mistreatment by society,[67] the narrative regarding the love affair suggests an inherent flaw which results in his misfortune. To elaborate, there are several instances in Hippothous' narrative where a loss of self-control is highlighted: Hippothous loses control when seeing Hyperanthes wrestling (3.2.2: 'οὐκ ἐκαρτέρησα'); Aristomachus is said to be unable to restrain his desire for Hyperanthes (3.2.7 '… οὐκέτι μετρίως κατεῖχε τὸν ἔρωτα …'); Hippothous again loses self-control when facing separation from Hyperanthes who is in the possession of Aristomachus (3.2.10 '… οὐκέτι καρτερῶν ἐμαυτὸν …'). While Aristomachus is clearly the villain of the piece, it is obvious from Hippothous' own admission that self-control is not his strong point.[68] The emotion which causes his loss of control is *erōs*: love at first sight in the first instance, and erotic jealousy in the second. Thus, as is the case with his rival Aristomachus, the loss of self-control is distinctly sexual, and so indicates an inherent lack of *sōphrosunē* in his behaviour.

No judgement on the story is given: Habrocomes' reaction is not narrated and he moves straight into his own tale (3.3.1), encouraged by Hippothous. The external narratee is left to make up his own mind about Hippothous. While sympathy is surely invited by the emotive nature of the story and the reciprocal affection between its protagonists,[69] it is also true that Hippothous' complexity is evident and the absence of *sōphrosunē* is marked. In this inset narrative *erōs* controls the main characters and no restraint is permitted. It should also be noted that Hippothous suggests that his and Hyperanthes' affair offends 'some divinity' (δαίμων: 3.2.4), which marks the change in their fortune. This detail of course makes the parallel with the wider narrative more concrete: Habrocomes offends Erōs. Whether the *daimōn* referred to is Erōs is unclear, but unlikely, given that Hippothous is not displaying *hubris* by resisting his desire, and that when Erōs is referred to it is as a *theos*,[70] rather than a *daimōn* in this text, but this could be put down to focalization. So, this seems to be a narrative where the offence to a divinity is an excess of happiness, contrasting with Habrocomes' impiety, in being overtly and extremely *sōphrōn* (at least in his own view). Both Hippothous' lack of *sōphrosunē* and Habrocomes' excessive *sōphrosunē* (emphasized by his rejection of and contempt for Erōs) are represented as problems: a balance is needed, which neither character achieves, but which the narrative succeeds in bringing about through the trials and punishments enacted on the characters and their eventual redemption. There is also the question of whether Hippothous' sexual orientation is a factor which the author views as excluding him from the possession of *sophrosyne*. This could be a ploy on the author's part to claim an ethical superiority for the central, heterosexual relationship. As we see in Achilles Tatius and Longus, with the representations of Clinias and Gnathon repectively, pederastic love affairs do not end well, and are sidelined in favour of the prioritized boy/girl alliance. They are also indicative of a lack of sexual restraint encompassed in the generic model of *sōphrosunē*, which is borne out in the embedded Hippothous narrative.

*

While the *Ephesiaca* lacks complex characterization and is not as sophisticated a text as Chariton's or as the later extant novels, the sustained emphasis on the protagonists' *sōphrosunē* invites a detailed exploration of how the virtue is represented and gendered. Both protagonists repeatedly define themselves in terms of *sōphrosunē*. For Anthia, *sōphrosunē* is consistently a factor in her characterization and is defined by her absolute emotional and sexual devotion to Habrocomes, almost exclusively.[71] Habrocomes' *sōphrosunē* is initially the motivating factor behind his rejection of Erōs, but later comes into line with Anthia's, and symbolizes his fidelity to her.[72] Both protagonists strive against the odds to maintain their *sōphrosunē*, but Anthia seems to use more intelligence than Habrocomes to do so. I think that, overall, Anthia's sustained focus on *sōphrosunē* and the various methods she employs to retain the virtue imply that hers is a more determined and unimpeachable *sōphrosunē* than Habrocomes'.

While this can be read as part of an authorial strategy to indulge male tastes for a *sōphrōn* beauty who must constantly be put in sexually charged situations which challenge her *sōphrosunē*, it is significant that Anthia uses innovative and intelligent skills to preserve her virtue while Habrocomes seems to submit to fate, which always results in the preservation of his *sōphrosunē*, but his passivity in comparison to Anthia is clear. However, Habrocomes cannot be said to be anything other than *sōphrōn* in his devotion to Anthia, and his sexual restraint is brought sharply into focus when implicitly compared with the marked lack of self-control displayed by Hippothous in his narrative. In the case of Habrocomes, there is no subtle gradation of *sōphrosunē* similar to that found in the male characters in *Callirhoe*, but the emotional fidelity that we see in Chariton's heroine is mirrored in both protagonists in Xenophon's text.

1.3 Longus' *Daphnis and Chloe*

Sōphrosunē is mentioned at two strategic points in *Daphnis and Chloe*: in the prayer at the close of the Prologue, which will be discussed in Chapter 2 (section 2.2), and when the servant who abandoned Daphnis, 'Sōphrosunē', is referred to by his mother, Cleariste at 4.21.[73] When the terminology is used, it is used by, or about, the urban, educated elite. The Prologue narrator is clearly an educated urbanite, and so is Cleariste. The only other occurrence of a term relating to *sōphrosunē* is that which refers to the behaviour of the Methymnaeans at 3.2.3: these are urban invaders of a rustic, pastoral landscape and their lack of *sōphrosunē* is surely mentioned in order to draw attention to their awareness of the virtue, even if they do not practise it. All of this does not suggest that Longus ignores the virtue: it is rather the case that his use of focalization allows the term to be used at two significant points in the novel, while its absence elsewhere reflects the innocence and rustic simplicity of his central characters. Therefore, it is necessary for an understanding of exactly how Longus represents the virtue regarding characterization and gender to analyse the use of the term at 4.21, and discussion of how this usage relates to the wider narrative will also be important. The reference to the name of Daphnis' nurse has consequences for Daphnis' characterization and maturation, rather than for Chloe's. In order to explore the extent to which Chloe's education in sexual and social convention implies the acquisition of *sōphrosunē*, Chloe's *aidōs* will be key: this provides the basis for her gradual acceptance of her place as a high-status aristocrat and allows her to comply with her role as Daphnis' wife.

1.3.1 Sōphrosunē: what's in a name?

At Longus 4.21, Clearistē, Daphnis' mother, recognizes the tokens she and her husband sent with the serving-woman whom they entrusted with the task of abandoning their baby. This servant is named either 'Sōphronē', as has been conjectured, or, as the manuscript tradition has it, 'Sōphrosunē'. Either naming is significant for my purposes, but, it is also important to note that any naming of such a figure is unusual. The archetypal tale of child-exposure is that which is represented by Sophocles in his *Oedipus the King*: the herdsman who is charged with the task of abandoning Laius' son is never named, although his pity for the baby results in the situation which develops in the tragedy. In the genre of the Greek novel, there is one instance of child-exposure other than the two found in *Daphnis and Chloe*: in Heliodorus' *Aethiopica*, Persinna is solely responsible for the abandonment of her daughter, Chariclea (Hld. 4.8). It is significant that Longus chooses to have Clearistē mention and name this serving-woman at all (the narrative does not require this: it would suffice to state that Clearistē recognized the tokens sent when Daphnis was exposed), and the name Sōphrosunē is surely meant to capture the reader's attention. Her role is not of crucial importance for the plot: the act of abandonment is not subverted by the servant, as in the case of Oedipus' exposure. The important thing seems to be the name itself.[74]

Daphnis is abandoned by Sōphrosunē and comes under the care of Erōs (1.7.2) who shepherds him and Chloe towards their sexual union. Herrmann notes that, in other examples of the genre, the author sends his protagonists out into the world so that the reader can observe their *sōphrosunē*: many of the challenges they face are connected with the virtue.[75] There is an inherent tension between the role of Erōs and *sōphrosunē* in other examples of the genre: for example, in Achilles Tatius' novel, Clitophon demonstrates how in order to submit to Erōs he must ignore his *sōphrosunē*.[76] Here, in *Daphnis and Chloe*, Daphnis' abandonment by Sōphrosunē acts metaphorically to draw attention to how Erōs is able to take the youth's education in hand. With more subtlety than Achilles Tatius, Longus potentially implies that there is a tension between *sōphrosunē* and Erōs, specifically in their nurturing and educational roles, by using this name for the servant who abandoned Daphnis. However, and the revelation of this name towards the close of the novel requires us to ask this question, is *sōphrosunē* absent in Daphnis' characterization? Through learning about Erōs, does Daphnis' *sōphrosunē* emerge naturally? I will provide answers to these questions in the next sub-sections.

1.3.2 Non-*sōphrōn* stories?

Herrmann highlights the Platonic claims in the *Republic* that *sōphrosunē* is the first virtue attained by young children through *mimēsis* of the right sort of stories and is the only one attainable by all.[77] But what types of stories are told to Daphnis and are they the right sort? Are they conducive to *sōphrosunē*?

Longus' narrative contains four inset tales within it. Two of the tales are told by Daphnis to Chloe: the story of the *phatta* at 1.27, and the story of Echo at 3.23. Philetas tells his autobiographical account to the teenagers, which they enjoy as if it was a *mythos* rather than a *logos* (2.7).[78] The narrative concerning Pan and Syrinx is told to Daphnis and Chloe by Lamon (2.34). As only the latter two tales are told to Daphnis, rather than told by him, they will be my main concern here.[79]

Philetas' role as *praeceptor amoris* is central to the plot: he teaches the innocent teenagers the name of Erōs and tells them of his universal power. Also, he tries to provide them with the cure for love, but this is too euphemistic for Daphnis and Chloe to comprehend.[80] When considering this tale from the perspective of the discussion regarding the right sort of stories in the *Republic*, a few issues arise. First, there is a god 'misbehaving' in Philetas' garden; second, the teacher himself is shown to be susceptible to the charms of this god (albeit before he knew of his identity); third, the aim of the story is to allow the consummation of sexual desire, and the content of the story is designed to demonstrate the futility of any other option. When discussing the types of stories that should be avoided when trying to teach *sōphrosunē* and *enkrateia*, Socrates introduces examples which deal directly with sexual matters: the unbridled lust of Zeus for Hera and the narration of the sexual liaison between Ares and Aphrodite, from the *Iliad* (14.293 ff.) and the *Odyssey* (8.266 ff.) respectively (*Rep.* 390b–c). Socrates suggests through his use of these examples that figures which have authority, such as divinities, should not be represented to children as ethically unsound, because there is the danger that children will think it right to imitate their behaviour. In Philetas' story, Erōs is mischievous and coy rather than lustful, but there is the suggestion that, before the old man was told of the boy's identity, Philetas felt attracted to him and asked for a kiss, and the boy expressed a wish to kiss him which was stronger than Philetas' desire to be young again (2.4.4–2.5.1). Kissing is again encouraged when Philetas states at the close of his lesson:

> Ἔρωτος γὰρ οὐδὲν φάρμακον, οὐ πινόμενον, οὐκ ἐσθιόμενον, οὐκ ἐν ᾠδαῖς λαλούμενον, ὅτι μὴ φίλημα καὶ περιβολὴ καὶ συγκατακλιθῆναι γυμνοῖς σώμασι.

> Indeed, there is no cure for love, nothing to be drunk or eaten or chanted in song, except a kiss and an embrace and lying down together with naked bodies.
>
> 2.7.7[81]

The first mention of kisses by Philetas might strike a chord with Daphnis in particular because his love was initiated with a kiss from Chloe, but it is the direct reference at the close of Philetas' lesson which inspires subsequent kissing (they kiss on meeting the next day (2.9.1)). Of course, Philetas' advice hints at sex, but the young couple will only manage the kissing and cuddling. In contrast to Socrates' concern in the *Republic*, in response to Philetas' narrative, Daphnis and Chloe do not imitate Erōs or Philetas: they act on Philetas' instructions instead.[82]

There is nothing to encourage *sōphrosunē* in Philetas' story: this is not the aim of this lesson. Philetas' aim is to explain what Erōs is and to show them of what the god is capable. Erōs is shepherding the couple, and it is implied in the reported conversation between the god and the old man that this should have a similar result to the god's earlier management of Philetas and Amaryllis, which brought about 'fine sons' for the cowherd (2.5.3–4). While Erōs is eventually successful in uniting the couple sexually, Philetas does not say enough at this stage to bring about that union. This is fortunate in terms of the plot (an early sexual act would disrupt the generic trajectory), but it also gives *sōphrosunē* a chance in that Daphnis' and Chloe's sexual ignorance gives them time to acquire the virtue, even though they are not aware of its existence.

The story of Pan and Syrinx, which is told to Daphnis and Chloe by Lamon while the rustics are celebrating the rescue of Chloe by Pan from the Methymnaeans (2.34), inspires the pair to imitate the god and the nymph in response (2.37). This story, in contrast to the one told by Philetas, is not intended to be didactic, yet it produces a direct mimetic response from the young couple, whereas, as we have seen, Philetas' lesson results in them trying to follow instructions rather than imitate actions from within the narrative.

This story, in representing the unbridled lust of a god (Pan) towards an unwilling female (Syrinx) seems emblematic of the type of story that Socrates would reject as inappropriate for the training of youths in the *Republic*, particularly as regards their *sōphrosunē* or *enkrateia*. However, during the narration of the story the sexual intention of Pan is somewhat obscured, at least for an audience who are not cognisant of what the act involves. Pan is introduced as follows:

Πὰν ταύτης . . . προσελθὼν ἔπειθεν ἐς ὅ τι ἔχρῃζε . . .

Pan approaching her . . . tried to persuade her into doing what he wanted . . .

2.34.1

Daphnis and Chloe do not know what this is. That it is related to *Erōs* soon becomes clear, when the nymph laughs at 'τὸν ἔρωτα'. Pan is then moved to chase her and use force (ἐς βίαν), and the nymph flees from him into the reeds. Again, by suggesting 'force', Lamon is not being specific: the innocent teenagers' comprehension of this story must be limited, and their re-enactment of the story does not suggest otherwise. When Daphnis takes Pan's role, the language of imitation is clear (Ὁ Δάφνις Πᾶνα ἐμιμεῖτο (2.37.1)), and it is clear also that Daphnis imitates exactly what he has just heard, and, importantly, exactly what he has understood. So, he begs (ἱκέτευε) trying to persuade (πείθων: which picks up on Lamon's use of ἔπειθεν). Chloe, mimicking Syrinx, smiles indifferently (ἀμελοῦσα ἐμειδία). There is much comic mileage to be had from this naïve interpretation, as the boy and girl who are desperate to have sex, without knowing what it is, impersonate a rapist god and his contemptuous victim. The message of the *Republic* about unsuitable stories is subtly undermined here: this couple's *sōphrosunē* should be at risk following on from the story, but their sexual ignorance remains intact, along with their ignorance of *sōphrosunē*. They are incapable of imitating their mythical models here: Daphnis possesses none of Pan's amorous aggression at this point partly because he lacks the basic knowledge of how to be sexually impetuous;[83] Chloe is not an example of a sexually resistant female like Syrinx because she is not aware of exactly what it is she is rejecting. Pan's lack of success in his rape attempt is also significant, but his success in possessing the pipes suggests an implicit victory over Syrinx: again, due to their limited outlook, Daphnis' and Chloe's appreciation of this irony is doubtful.

It is clear that the stories told to Daphnis (and Chloe) are not conducive to *sōphrosunē*, but neither do they hinder it. Philetas' lesson is incomplete but successful in its aim of making the youths aware of Erōs and his power: there is no encouragement to be *sōphrōn*, but neither does the lesson completely undermine any future acquisition of the virtue by allowing sex to take place. Lamon's narration of the myth of Pan and Syrinx obscures Pan's sexual intentions to the extent that Daphnis and Chloe imitate the story in dance without fully comprehending its central theme: *sōphrosunē* should be at risk here, but the lack of sexual awareness excludes any danger. Daphnis' and Chloe's *sōphrosunē* is not put at risk directly from hearing the wrong type of stories as is suggested in the *Republic*: they learn only the name and power of Erōs from Philetas, whose euphemistic instructions allow their sexual innocence to continue. Their mimetic response to the tale of Pan and Syrinx proves that teenagers will imitate what they hear in myths, but the ethical risk is humorously undermined.

Therefore, while Herrmann's observations are relevant in that mimetic education as defined in the *Republic* is central to *Daphnis and Chloe*, there is much humour in how this is nuanced and subverted. When Sōphrosunē is named I would argue that Daphnis' education is finally complete, and there is one more episode which is crucial to this *paideia*, which I discuss next.

1.3.3 Daphnis' restraint

Lycaenion's lesson at 3.18–19 relieves Daphnis of one anxiety only to replace it with another. He now knows the mechanics of sexual intercourse, but his love for Chloe prevents him from performing the act with her because of the warning Lycaenion gives him about the painful and bloody consequences of taking a girl's virginity (3.19.2). It is necessary to see what the sexual act with Lycaenion means for Daphnis, and what issues it raises for his potential *sōphrosunē*.[84]

His desperation to know how to be 'cured' in line with Philetas' tuition at 2.7.7, and his trust in Lycaenion's motivation, mean that Daphnis eagerly engages in the act with someone whom he does not desire, at least not in the way he desires Chloe. Is he unaware of sexual jealousy? It has never been taught to him, so could conceivably be outside his knowledge. The only factor that suggests that this may not be the case is this: Chloe has only recently displayed anxiety about fidelity when, after the pair have already sworn oaths to one another, she insists that Daphnis swear a second oath, this time not by Pan, because of her worries regarding that god's promiscuity ('Οὗτος μὲν οὖν ἀμεληθεὶς ἐν τοῖς ὅρκοις ἀμελήσει σε κολάσαι κἂν ἐπὶ πλείονας ἔλθῃς γυναῖκας τῶν ἐν τῇ σύριγγι καλάμων.' 'So if you do not care to keep your oaths, he will not care to punish you even if you go after more women than there are reeds in your pipe.' 2.39.3). However, Daphnis' second oath is given in indirect speech and its content does not suggest that by having sex with Lycaenion he breaks it:

> Ἥδετο ὁ Δάφνις ἀπιστούμενος καὶ στὰς εἰς μέσον τὸ αἰπόλιον καὶ τῇ μὲν τῶν χειρῶν αἰγός, τῇ δὲ τράγου λαβόμενος ὤμνυε Χλόην φιλήσειν φιλοῦσαν, κἂν ἕτερον δὲ προκρίνῃ Δάφνιδος ἀντ' ἐκείνης αὐτὸν ἀποκτεῖναι.

> Daphnis enjoyed being mistrusted and standing in the middle of the flock and taking a nanny-goat and a billy-goat in his hands he swore to love Chloe, loving him, and if she preferred another to Daphnis to kill himself instead of her.
>
> 2.39.5

The implications of Daphnis' lack of direct speech here are that while he enjoys Chloe's mistrust because it illustrates her desire for him, he does not fully address her concern which is about potential promiscuity on his part inspired by Pan. He makes no promise regarding exclusivity in his and Chloe's relationship, which is clearly what she is anxious about. He is promising always to love Chloe while she loves him, and this oath is not broken when he experiences sex with Lycaenion. There is, then, despite an apparent appreciation of how Chloe has the potential to be jealous, a sustained ignorance about how the sexual act is involved in this jealousy. Chloe's worries are based on the stories she has heard concerning Pan and how he chases nymphs, but she is also unaware of what he chases them for. The couple are aware that Erōs drives their desire and Pan's, but until Lycaenion performs sex with Daphnis, the lack of practical sexual knowledge has consequences for how Daphnis and Chloe perceive fidelity.[85]

Although in terms of fidelity Daphnis' encounter with Lycaenion is not presented as a problem, and is not perceived by Daphnis as problematic, the results of his experience of the act and its pleasure, along with Lycaenion's subsequent warnings, do cause a conflict in Daphnis' mind, which comes to involve *sōphrosunē*. The way in which the sexual act itself is narrated leaves room for manoeuvre as far as interpreting Daphnis' engagement and enjoyment goes.[86] His feelings are effaced once the act is underway. However, there is a subtle suggestion at 3.20.2 that he did enjoy sex with Lycaenion: he is said to embrace and kiss Chloe as he had kissed Lycaenion at the height of his pleasure (… περιφὺς ἐφίλησεν οἷον ἐν τῇ τέρψει Λυκαίνιον …).[87] Is Daphnis kissing Chloe differently now, perhaps with the passion which stems from his knowing where kisses can now lead? This has implications for his restraint in not seducing her: he has had an experience of pleasurable sex but he does not wish to harm Chloe and so demonstrates self-restraint, a form of *sōphrosunē*, in his behaviour. His decency towards Chloe stands as an example of mature, responsible, protective masculinity in opposition to the sexual aggressors in the text: Dorcon, Pan, Gnathon and Lampis.[88] This development in his characterization comes to the fore at 3.24.2–3:

Ἤδη ποτὲ καὶ γυμνοὶ συγκατεκλίθησαν καὶ ἓν δέρμα αἰγὸς ἐπεσύραντο, καὶ ἐγένετο ἄν γυνὴ Χλόη ῥᾳδίως εἰ μὴ Δάφνιν ἐτάραξε τὸ αἷμα. Ἀμέλει καὶ δεδοικὼς μὴ νικηθῇ τὸν λογισμόν ποτε πολλὰ γυμνοῦσθαι τὴν Χλόην οὐκ ἐπέτρεπεν, ὥστε ἐθαύμαζε μὲν ἡ Χλόη, τὴν δὲ αἰτίαν ᾐδεῖτο πυνθάνεσθαι.

One day they even lay down naked together, and drew a single goatskin over themselves, and Chloe might easily have become a woman, had not the thought of blood scared Daphnis. In fact, for fear that one day his logic would prove unequal to the test, he did not let Chloe take her clothes off very often. Chloe was surprised, but too modest to ask why.

While Daphnis' behaviour can be put down to fear born of compassion for Chloe, he is clearly demonstrating the ability to use sexual self-restraint, which could be termed *sōphrosunē*.[89] Repath points out that that there is intertextuality with Chariton (specifically with the use of the term λογισμός), at work in this passage, along with Platonic intertextuality: Alcibiades' comments regarding his failure to seduce Socrates in the *Symposium* are recalled by the couple laying down naked under a single blanket.[90] Repath's comments on the results of this intertextuality highlight the changing nature of Daphnis' awareness about the nature of love and life,[91] and I would add that the Platonic echo recalls Socrates' *sōphrosunē* in a sexual context, which reinforces the idea that this is what Daphnis is demonstrating at this juncture. There is humour in this passage as Platonic echoes are juxtaposed with the impulses of sexual desire, as noted by Repath.[92] This humour also works to highlight the author's concern to imbue his representation of Daphnis with a *sōphrosunē* that the youth cannot be aware of, but which is generically necessary in order to prevent the narrative from coming to an untimely end. Lycaenion's role as an 'educator' is not limited to her practical lesson: her warning to Daphnis is not aimed at teaching him about *sōphrosunē*, but it nevertheless leads to an acquisition of a sexual self-restraint which is simultaneous with his potentially generically dangerous, new-found sexual knowledge.

The dynamics of Daphnis' and Chloe's relationship change again once Daphnis has gained permission to marry Chloe, following his negotiations with Dryas, her adoptive father. The scene at 3.34, where Daphnis plucks the highest and most desirable apple against Chloe's wishes, is demonstrative of his new-found mastery over Chloe as his wife-to-be. As Morgan discusses, the apple-plucking is a metaphor for Daphnis taking Chloe's virginity,[93] which as we have seen above, he restrains himself from doing until their wedding night. While this figurative act suggests that *sōphrosunē* is overcome by Daphnis' desire for Chloe, the very fact that the metaphor replaces the sexual act demonstrates that Longus is keen to demonstrate that Daphnis is no ordinary goatherd, and he is able to restrain his desires even as he displays his new-found sexual confidence. Daphnis' subsequent allusion to the Judgement of Paris illustrates a certain level of mythological knowledge in the young man as he seeks to flatter his fiancé by comparing her to Aphrodite, which again suggests that he is represented as a sophistic lover, rather than merely a country lad in love. Consequently, Daphnis' increasing knowledge about his role as a masculine lover and future husband of Chloe is tempered by his burgeoning *sōphrosunē*, and the fact that the act of sex is transferred to a metaphor in the apple-plucking scene underlines this nuance.

*

While Daphnis' abandonment by Sōphrosunē and by his educated, socially elite family might have resulted in a dearth of proper education, Longus demonstrates how Erōs' influence over the youth allows him to learn how to be *sōphrōn*: the mention of the nurse's name acts to reinforce the fundamental importance of the virtue. Now, as Daphnis is reunited with his birth-parents, the story has come full circle: the baby abandoned by Sōphrosunē returns to his parents having received an erotic education, but one which allows the virtue of *sōphrosunē* to be evident in this young man, although the term can only come from his mother, whose status as an elite urbanite allows her to use it. It seems that, regarding *sōphrosunē*, focalization must be consistent, and this is perhaps why Daphnis and Chloe never use the term and are never described by its use.[94] Their education is not explicit in relation to how they might acquire *sōphrosunē*, but their possession of the virtue by the close of the novel is implicitly hinted at. Sōphrosunē is behind the scenes, but, like that of the concept itself, her role is essential to this narrative.[95]

1.3.4 Chloe's *aidōs*

The noun *aidōs* itself does not occur in *Daphnis and Chloe*, but its verb, *aideomai*, occurs eight times,[96] with *aischunomai* (semantically close to *aideomai*) also appearing once.[97] Three out of the eight occurrences of the verb *aideomai* refer to Chloe's behaviour: at 1.31.2, Chloe does not tell Daphnis about the kiss she gave to Dorcon on his deathbed, a decision governed by her embarrassment; at 3.24.3, following on from the one occasion where they lie down together naked, her *aidōs* prevents her asking Daphnis why he no longer wishes for her to be naked, when he is scared because of the warning given by Lycaenion regarding the pain and blood suffered by a girl on losing her virginity; and, at 4.14.1, Chloe's *aidōs* is brought about by the arrival of strangers from the city.[98] Given the reiterated usage of *aideomai* in relation to Chloe, which outweighs its usage in relation to any other character, it is necessary to look at how the use of this verb affects Chloe's representation, and how that usage emphasizes a particular aspect of Longus' ethical motivation which is potentially connected to *sōphrosunē*.

At 1.31.2, Chloe's silence regarding Dorcon's dying kiss is explained by the narrator by her embarrassment or inherent shyness at recalling it:

Μόνον αἰδεσθεῖσα τὸ φίλημα οὐκ εἶπεν.

The kiss was the only thing she did not mention, feeling embarrassed.

Is this silence brought about by some kind of shame over the kiss, or is her embarrassment the result of her understanding that she provided pleasure for Dorcon, while she does not reciprocate his desire for her?[99] Chloe does not comprehend what sexual desire is, but she is aware that a kiss is pleasurable if one feels what she feels for Daphnis (she has desired to kiss him for a long time, the narrator states at 1.17.1): it follows that she can appreciate that Dorcon felt something similar for her, and her embarrassment could stem from knowing that she provided Dorcon with pleasure, which she wants only to provide for Daphnis. This feeling of having committed some slight impropriety can be seen as a development of Chloe's erotic awareness: although she does not know what this desire she feels for Daphnis is called or how she can satisfy it, she has a burgeoning understanding of how these emotions cause certain behaviours and physical needs. Similarly, even though she has not acquired *sōphrosunē* through education or experience, her natural *aidōs* stands in for the virtue and ensures that her behaviour does not become inappropriate or licentious: her emotional response to Dorcon's death allowed her to kiss him, but the kiss was one of pity, rather than desire, and Chloe's modest silence regarding the kiss demonstrates that she behaves in a manner which is socially and ethically appropriate for a *parthenos*.

I have already discussed the passage at 3.24 regarding its consequences for how Daphnis' restraint is viewed: here my concern is with Chloe's response to Daphnis apparently not wanting her to be naked as often. Here is how the narrator describes Chloe's emotions:

> ... ὥστε ἐθαύμαζε μὲν ἡ Χλόη, τὴν δὲ αἰτίαν ᾐδεῖτο πυθέσθαι.

> ... Chloe was surprised, but too modest to ask why.

3.24.3

Just as in the use of *aideomai* at 1.31.2, Chloe's reticence in speaking is attributed to her modesty. Daphnis' recent acquirement of sexual knowledge which surpasses Chloe's is behind his new-found reluctance to see his beloved naked, and, as De Temmerman suggests, this situation is a reversal of that at 1.31: there, Chloe restricted Daphnis' access to information; here, her access to information is controlled by Daphnis.[100] However, I would argue that there is significance in the fact that it is Chloe's reluctance to ask questions, rather than Daphnis' reluctance to offer information, which is emphasized at 3.24. What precisely is the emotion which prevents Chloe's curiosity getting the better of her? The translation from Morgan suggests that modesty is behind her silence, which perhaps implies an understanding on Chloe's part that to speak about nudity would somehow involve crossing a boundary which she is not comfortable with. Her *aidōs* is evidence of a growing sexual awareness and self-consciousness: *sōphrosunē* would involve the same behavioural limitations, but it cannot be present in Chloe's psychology at this point, and, in *sōphrosunē*'s place, *aidōs* restrains Chloe's actions and speech.

The final place where Chloe's actions are governed by her *aidōs* is at 4.14.1:

Χλόη μὲν οὖν εἰς τὴν ὕλην ἔφυγεν ὄχλον τοσοῦτον αἰδεσθεῖσα καὶ φοβηθεῖσα, ὁ δὲ Δάφνις εἱστήκει . . .

Chloe ran away into the forest, because she was shy and frightened of such a crowd, but Daphnis stood there . . .

The contrast between the fleeing Chloe and the stationary Daphnis is clear (emphasized by the μὲν/δὲ clause) and this is a good example of how Daphnis can demonstrate greater confidence than Chloe in the presence of the wealthy landowners, something which is possible not just because of his masculinity, but also because he knows more than Chloe about the world, and particularly about sex. His worldliness is something which places him closer to the urbanites who have arrived in the pastoral setting, whereas Chloe is uncomfortable with this invasion, which threatens her innocence. While Chloe cannot understand precisely how these newcomers threaten her idyllic existence, it is clear that her need to flee from their presence is indicative of an unease which is related to her earlier emotional reactions to sexually nuanced events (Dorcon's kiss, and her own nudity in front of Daphnis). On a second reading, it becomes clear that Chloe's embarrassment and fear of the newcomers is potentially connected to the fact that the arrival of the urbanites signals the new world that Daphnis and Chloe will become a part of. Further, the discoveries of Daphnis' and Chloe's true parentage (which can be guessed at even on an initial reading by readers with their knowledge of the youths' abandonment) will lead to their union in marriage, socially sanctioned as an elite match, and to their sexual union, at which point Chloe's innocence is truly lost (see 4.40.3). Thus, the inclusion of Chloe's *aidōs* at 4.14 indicates an intrinsic emotional shying away from the realities which will inevitably encroach on her pastoral world, and one of these realities is that she will lose her virginity, and her idyllic girlhood with it.

This survey of Chloe's *aidōs* shows that as she gradually learns about love, Chloe's behaviour and speech are governed by a propriety which is brought about by an inherent modesty and by a growing emotional awareness of the erotic world. Her *aidōs* is demonstrated at significant junctures in the novel, which mark her movement from sexual innocence towards complete sexual knowledge. Her *aidōs* is not a virtue, but rather a response to a fear regarding how her actions will be perceived: however, it has the result that Chloe acts in a virtuous manner. We never witness Chloe's *sōphrosunē*: this is something of which she remains unaware within the confines of the novel, but it is implied that the married, aristocratic Chloe, with her evident modest demeanour, will easily acquire knowledge of and adherence to *sōphrosunē*. In this text, it is the *aidōs* of the maidenly heroine which leads us to believe in the importance of her restricted behaviour which would, in another novel, be the result of *sōphrosunē*.

*

Sōphrosunē as a term is elusive in *Daphnis and Chloe*: focalization through the protagonists, which allows their gradual erotic maturation to be fully appreciated, also prevents the couple from being described as *sōphrōn*, and prevents them defining their own behaviour in such terms, which would imply a level of ethical and social awareness with which they are not endowed. Despite this, through the naming of the serving-woman who abandoned Daphnis, and through the repeated representation of Chloe in terms of her *aidōs*, Longus introduces hints at how his protagonists are heading towards a knowledge of *sōphrosunē* and are clearly receptive to that virtue. Daphnis' superior sexual knowledge allows him to acquire certain aspects of *sōphrosunē* during the latter part of the narrative. Chloe, on the other hand, although modest and vulnerable to feelings of sexual self-consciousness, does not display overt *sōphrosunē* within the narrative, but the reader has a clear sense that she is capable of possessing the virtue. Longus' treatment of *sōphrosunē* in his protagonists is markedly removed from the earlier treatments of Chariton and Xenophon of Ephesus, and demonstrates the innovation of the author in how he playfully manipulates generic themes for his own purposes. Daphnis demonstrates an independently acquired *sōphrosunē*, which is indicative of his greater level of control over events in comparison with that of Chloe; Chloe's actions and words are governed by her *aidōs*, so that her autonomy is somewhat reduced as she moves towards acculturation. *Sōphrosunē*, although obscured because of the ruralized idyll which envelops his protagonists for the majority of the narrative, is a clear marker of the sophistication which emerges as a crucial part of a proper response to *erōs* by elite youths.

1.4 Achilles Tatius' *Leucippe and Clitophon*[101]

The technique of ego-narration in Achilles Tatius' *Leucippe and Clitophon* restricts the reader's access to the events and characters which are portrayed, and this must be a central consideration in this analysis of how certain characters' *sōphrosunē* (or lack thereof) is represented and how this is affected by their respective gender. Clitophon's perspective on his own *sōphrosunē* and on that of other characters is necessarily nuanced by his motivation to present a certain type of narrative, and to promote himself and his story as he wishes.[102] My first concern in this chapter will be to look at how Clitophon represents his own *sōphrosunē* and fidelity and to discuss the extent to which the reader can read beyond Clitophon's narrative, and perceive authorial irony at the narrator's expense. The way in which the idea of male virginity is introduced by Clitophon will be considered, along with how this affects our view of the narrating-hero and his sexual ethics. The final section on male *sōphrosunē* will contain analysis of how male characters other than Clitophon are portrayed regarding the virtue. Next the focus will be on Leucippe and the extent to which she is characterized by her *sōphrosunē* or by its absence, considering the consequences and implications of Clitophon's limited representation of his beloved, and how this affects our view of her.

1.4.1 Clitophon's *sōphrosunē*[103]

The first place in the text where *sōphrosunē* is mentioned comes at 1.5.6, when Clitophon narrates how, following on from his initial viewing of Leucippe, he heard a slave sing about Apollo's pursuit of Daphne. His reaction to this song is described from the dual perspective of narrator and character.[104] First, here is the narrator's statement:

> Τοῦτό μου μᾶλλον ᾀσθὲν τὴν ψυχὴν ἐξέκαυσεν· ὑπέκκαυμα γὰρ ἐπιθυμίας λόγος ἐρωτικός. Κἂν εἰς σωφροσύνην τις ἑαυτὸν νουθετῇ, τῷ παραδείγματι πρὸς τὴν μίμησιν ἐρεθίζεται, μάλισθ' ὅταν ἐκ τοῦ κρείττονος ᾖ τὸ παράδειγμα· ἡ γὰρ ὧν ἁμαρτάνει τις αἰδὼς τῷ τοῦ βελτίονος ἀξιώματι παρρησία γίνεται ...

> The song inflamed my soul all the more, for an erotic story is the fuel of desire. Even if someone steers his mind towards self-control, he is roused towards imitation by an example, especially when that example is a divine one; in which case, any shame that you feel at your moral errors becomes an outspoken affront to the reputation of a higher being ...

> 1.5.6

While the sententious nature of this statement is clear (and, as narrator, Clitophon often expresses himself by using generalizations),[105] there is the implicit suggestion that this statement reflects Clitophon the narrator's view of himself: he believes he had practised *sōphrosunē* up until this point, something which the narratee must take on trust. Clitophon shifts the responsibility for any transgression on to the divinity that he suggests must be imitated. Also, by connecting *sōphrosunē* with the *aidōs* one might feel at any *hamartia*, Clitophon implies a view of the virtue as something which regulates ethical behaviour by causing shame.[106] This is a somewhat oblique view of *sōphrosunē*, tailored to Clitophon's needs as narrator at this point. If *sōphrosunē* is practised, it should, theoretically, ensure that *hamartia* might be avoided along with the consequent *aidōs*. In this statement, then, Clitophon as narrator suggests that *hamartia* can be acceptable if one errs by following a badly-behaved god's example, and that any feeling of *aidōs* should be avoided in view of the potential for insulting that divine example and, consequently, *sōphrosunē* becomes unnecessary.

Much of the terminology in this passage suggests some engagement with Platonic ideas. The idea of the imitation of divine examples recalls Socrates' warnings in *Republic*, Book 3 about only providing the youth with positive examples of divine behaviour. Clitophon somewhat misses the point of this discussion, by advocating the *mimēsis* of any type of divine behaviour. This indicates the veracity of Socrates' fears, particularly those voiced at 390b–c, where the 'bad' examples from Homer which are not conducive to *sōphrosunē* and *enkrateia* are provided, including those which are erotic, very much like the version of Apollo presented in this song.

The mention of ἐπιθυμίας, νουθετῇ and *sōphrosunē* suggests wider engagement with Platonic ideas. While I am not suggesting that this terminology acts as a direct allusion to any specific discussion in the *Republic*, I will offer an example from that dialogue where such terminology is central to show how Achilles Tatius strengthens implicit connections between the Platonic text and his own. The discussion of the parts of the soul which occurs in the *Republic*, Book 4 is one such example. The initial discussion, which focuses on how the better part of the soul or city governs the worse part, which makes the soul *sōphrōn*, includes the following statement from Socrates, when he is expanding on his summary of the different types of desires (ἐπιθυμίας) and of who possesses them:

> Then there are the moderate and temperate kinds, which are led with sense (νοῦ) and with regard to correct belief (λογισμῷ), and you will come

across them in a few people who are naturally very good or have been well taught.

431c5–7[107]

This leads on to the conclusion that the city which Glaucon and Socrates conceive is *sōphrōn* because those few who are in possession of these superior desires can control the many who are not. Thus, the roles of νοῦς and λογισμός are intrinsic to the control and management of τὰς ἐπιθυμίας, and the ultimate consequence of this control is *sōphrosunē*. There is a similar relationship between νοῦς and *sōphrosunē* in Clitophon's speech, with ἐπιθυμία represented as the impetus which is nourished by erotic stories, and which is therefore acting against the efforts of the agent to be *sōphrōn*. This particular kind of ἐπιθυμία is erotic, and directly sexual as signalled by Apollo's pursuit of Daphne and its purpose, and this type of desire is deemed 'unnecessary' (οὐκ ἀναγκαία) at *Republic*, Book 8 (559e4).[108] It is possible that Clitophon is deliberately recalling Platonic ideas through his language, but it is clear that he is trying to justify his behaviour in this passage, and this involves either a fundamental misunderstanding of the implications of the central educational theories expressed in the *Republic*, or a challenge to those theories.

Clitophon the character's comments follow on from those he makes as narrator:

Ἰδοὺ καὶ Ἀπόλλων ἐρᾷ, κἀκεῖνος παρθένου, καὶ ἐρῶν οὐκ αἰσχύνεται, ἀλλὰ διώκει τὴν παρθένον· σὺ δὲ ὀκνεῖς καὶ αἰδῇ καὶ ἀκαίρως σωφρονεῖς· μὴ κρείττων εἶ τοῦ θεοῦ;

You see, Apollo too loves, and he too loves a maiden. *He* feels no shame at his love but chases the maiden; whereas *you*, you are hesitant and embarrassed, and you practise an untimely self-control. Do you think yourself superior to a god?

1.5.7

Like the narratorial comment which precedes it, this presents a view of *sōphrosunē* as something which should be disregarded in view of divine examples and which can be dropped depending on opportunity. It is simple to see this as demonstrative of Clitophon the character's erotic desire and his wish to pursue it, but it is significant that both as narrator and as character, Clitophon appears to manipulate the concept of *sōphrosunē*. I would argue that the alignment between the narratorial comments and the direct speech from the character implies that Clitophon has not developed in terms of *sōphrosunē* during the time that has elapsed from when he heard the song of Apollo and Daphne up to the time of his narration. While the passages quoted above could be read as Clitophon's misunderstanding of Plato, there is also another perspective to consider: is Achilles Tatius challenging Plato's ideas about imitation and education? The censorship of poetry and the resulting narrowness of the 'education' of youth which is promoted in the *Republic* is something which an author such as Achilles might well rail against. Clitophon, as a young man reacting to desire, has no real reason to follow Platonic theory around not imitating the 'bad' behaviour of Apollo, and this illustrates the limitations of the theory. Whether Clitophon is aware of the discussion in the *Republic* is debatable. However, Achilles demonstrates that Plato's approach can be questioned and is easily undermined by those who wish to represent characters who follow, rather than deny their desires.

While the episode at 1.5 illustrates how Clitophon argues with himself to present a show of *sōphrosunē*, there are two occasions where he represents his moral dilemma in terms of internal *agōnes*, at 1.11.3 and at 2.5.2. First, at 1.11.3, in a speech to Clinias which follows the latter's erotic advice, Clitophon imagines his father's opposition to his pursuit of Leucippe. He expresses this conflict in metaphorical terms, picturing his father and Erōs at war:

> Ἐν μεθορίῳ κεῖμαι δύο ἐναντίων· Ἔρως ἀνταγωνίζεται καὶ πατήρ. Ὁ μὲν ἕστηκεν αἰδοῖ κρατῶν, ὁ δὲ κάθηται πυρπολῶν. Πῶς κρίνω τὴν δίκην; Ἀνάγκη μάχεται καὶ φύσις. Θέλω μὲν σοὶ δικάσαι, πάτερ, ἀλλ᾿ ἀντίδικον ἔχω χαλεπώτερον. Βασανίζει τὸν δικαστήν, ἕστηκε μετὰ βελῶν, κρίνεται μετὰ πυρός. Ἂν ἀπειθήσω, πάτερ, αὐτῷ καίομαι τῷ πυρί.

> I am on the border between two countries at war: Erōs is marshalled against my father. The one is standing, and his weapon is shame; the other lounges, brandishing his torch. How am I to deliver my verdict? Fate and nature are at war. I want to judge in your favour, father; but I have a more dangerous adversary; he is torturing the judge, he stands fully armed in the dock, he wields his torch as he is being tried! If I disobey him, father, his very flames consume me!

This passage can be directly compared to that which appears at 2.5.2, when Clitophon argues with himself about his erotic *andreia* in opposition to his *sōphrosunē*, when his fear around pursuing Leucippe is still restraining his advances towards her, despite the clear encouragement from Clinias, and from Clitophon's slave, Satyrus:

> Μέχρι τίνος, ἄνανδρε, σιγᾷς; Τί δὲ δειλὸς εἶ στρατιώτης ἀνδρείου θεοῦ; Τὴν κόρην προσελθεῖν σοὶ περιμένεις;᾿ Εἶτα προσετίθην· ᾿Τί γάρ, ὦ κακόδαιμον, οὐ

σωφρονεῖς; Τί δὲ οὐκ ἐρᾷς ὧν σε δεῖ; Παρθένον ἔνδον ἔχεις ἄλλην καλήν·
ταύτης ἔρα, ταύτην βλέπε, ταύτην ἔξεστί σοι γαμεῖν.' Ἐδόκουν πεπεῖσθαι·
κάτωθεν δὲ ὥσπερ ἐκ τῆς καρδίας ὁ Ἔρως ἀντεφθέγγετο· 'Ναί, τολμηρέ, κατ'
ἐμοῦ στρατεύῃ καὶ ἀντιπαρατάττῃ; Ἵπταμαι καὶ τοξεύω καὶ φλέγω· πῶς δυνήσῃ
φυγεῖν; Ἂν φυλάξῃ μου τὸ τόξον, οὐκ ἔχεις φυλάξασθαι τὸ πῦρ. Ἂν δὲ καὶ
ταύτην κατασβέσῃς σωφροσύνῃ τὴν φλόγα, αὐτῷ σε καταλήψομαι τῷ πτερῷ.

How long will your silence last, O man without manhood? Why this cowardice
in a soldier in the service of a manly god? Are you biding your time until the girl
makes an attack upon you?' Then, however, I rejoindered: 'Why do you show no
self-control, you wretch? Why does your desire not follow your duty? There is
another beautiful maiden inside for you: *she* is the one you should be desiring,
she the one you should be beholding, and *she* the one it is open to you to wed.' I
thought myself persuaded; but Erōs spoke up in opposition, as if from the depths
of my heart: 'So you really are arming yourself to resist me, my daredevil friend?
I can fly, I can shoot and burn: how can you escape? If you shield yourself against
my bow, you will be unable to do so against my flame; and even if you should
extinguish that flame with your self-control, I shall use my very wings to catch
up with you.

2.5.2[109]

In both passages, Erōs is represented as armed and determined to win: any effort
to resist him is clearly futile. At 1.11.3, Clitophon's metaphor arms his father with
aidōs, whereas it is *sōphrosunē* which is the clear ethical antithesis to Erōs at
2.5.2. This is illustrative of the differing metaphorical struggles which Clitophon
is using: his father's *aidōs* is his weapon of choice because it is designed to shame
Clitophon into conforming to his parent's wishes, whereas in the internalized
debate at 2.5.2, it is Clitophon's own *sōphrosunē* which resists his desire to pursue
Leucippe. By placing both *aidōs* and *sōphrosunē* in opposition to Erōs at these
junctures in the text, Clitophon aligns the two concepts, but he also implicitly
reduces them to the level of anti-erotic imperatives. De Temmerman highlights
the fact that *sōphrosunē* is aligned with cowardice at 2.5.2,[110] and this is a
significant factor in Clitophon's representation of *sōphrosunē*, which is couched
repeatedly in terms which marginalize the virtue and make it a mere hindrance
to the protagonist's prevailing desire. By consistently positing *sōphrosunē* in
opposition to Erōs, and by implying that it is cowardly and aligning it with *aidōs*,
Clitophon, both as narrator and character, seems to be determined to dismiss
this virtue, perhaps as something which is feminizing, in order to succeed in his
pursuit of Leucippe and in his narration of that pursuit. The implied link between
sōphrosunē and cowardly behaviour is, in fact, flawed when considering what

motivates Clitophon to make his erotic attack on Leucippe: his fear of Erōs, or, in more prosaic terms, his fear of the emotional suffering brought about by resisting his desires, is what really motivates him, despite his efforts to dress this up as manly courage.

Clitophon's perspective on *sōphrosunē* is fairly clear from the above passages: he claims to possess it, but it must be overcome in order for him to succeed in his seduction of Leucippe. I suggest that Achilles Tatius could be working to undermine Clitophon by emphasizing his limited display of *sōphrosunē*. One way to explore this idea is to consider potential influences from earlier novels. First, I will look at how the *agōn* between Erōs and Clitophon's *sōphrosunē* depicted in *Leucippe and Clitophon* (2.5.2) alludes to Chariton's use of the same device in regard to Dionysius at *Callirhoe* 2.4.5.[111] Dionysius' dilemma demonstrates his wish to remain loyal to his recently deceased wife's memory which is in opposition to his passionate desire for Callirhoe. In his emotional turmoil he tries to talk himself out of his passion with rational argument, as befits a man of his social status and noble character. The narrator follows this argument with the following comment:

> ἐφιλονίκει δὲ ὁ Ἔρως βουλευομένῳ καλῶς καὶ ὕβριν ἐδόκει τὴν σωφροσύνην τὴν ἐκείνου· διὰ τοῦτο ἐπυρπόλει σφοδρότερον ψυχὴν ἐν ἔρωτι φιλοσοφοῦσαν.

> But Erōs struggled with these fine deliberations, considering his self-restraint an insult, and for that reason inflamed all the more a heart which attempted to philosophize with love.[112]

If it were not for the differing narratological situations between the above passage and that presented at *Leucippe and Clitophon* 2.5.2, the role of Erōs can be seen as almost identical, particularly in regard to his view of *sōphrosunē*.[113] The verb διαλέγω is used closely following the two exchanges (Char. 2.4.6; Ach. Tat. 2.6.1), and both Dionysius and Clitophon are joined by a third party after the depiction of the *agōnes*, moving the action on and thus clearly marking out the soliloquies as distinctly private. The allusive use of Dionysius' *agōn* in Clitophon's soliloquy highlights that there is a markedly different result for each character. Dionysius' struggle is depicted sympathetically by the omniscient narrator, and the character's efforts to overcome his passion are genuine. Moreover, his eventual marriage to Callirhoe is not due to his own efforts at seduction, but to external circumstances (she is pregnant with Chaereas' child) which force her to marry him. Compare this with Clitophon, who at 2.6.1, immediately sets about getting a kiss from Leucippe, which he will build upon by overt sexual propositioning later (2.19.1): the question of marriage only comes into the picture at 3.10. This intertextuality is surely intended to undermine Clitophon's self-serving representation of *sōphrosunē*, by drawing a comparison with a generic antagonist who is ethically superior to this protagonist.[114] On the other hand, Dionysius, despite his status and ethical integrity and despite his marriage to Callirhoe, is not her beloved and will not keep Callirhoe as his wife. By being implicitly compared to Dionysius, Clitophon's status as the right man for Leucippe is called into question.

De Temmerman has recognized some 'intertextual play' between Clitophon's question of whether to give in to his erotic desire and Habrocomes' similar dilemma at Xenophon of Ephesus 1.4.1–2 and 1.4.4–5.[115] De Temmerman makes some valid points about how Achilles Tatius 'reworks' Xenophon, particularly regarding how each author's use of daring in relation to Erōs is nuanced.[116] My priority here is to explore how this instance of intertextuality affects Clitophon's position vis-à-vis *sōphrosunē*.[117] Clitophon's stance on *sōphrosunē*, as discussed above, is marked out as being in opposition to the will of Erōs, and in this respect, follows Habrocomes' perspective. However, while Habrocomes' *sōphrosunē*, as De Temmerman notes, stems from a renunciation of Erōs and his power, Clitophon's stems from his betrothal to another girl.[118] This shows us that Clitophon has no deeply held conviction which leads him to be *sōphrōn*: his is a pragmatic self-restraint, so is not really *sōphrosunē* at all. It could be argued that Habrocomes' conviction is misguided and morally questionable too: his impiety is clear and seems to be rooted in excessive pride and arrogance. However, the presence of conviction in Habrocomes' characterization draws attention to the marked lack of conviction in Achilles Tatius' characterization of Clitophon. Not only is the alignment between courage and *sōphrosunē* which is implied by Habrocomes reversed by Clitophon at 2.5,[119] but also the integrity of Achilles Tatius' secondary narrator is endangered by the echo from the *Ephesiaca*. Clitophon's struggle to master himself is distinctly hollow in comparison to Habrocomes' *agōn* with Erōs. Despite these marked differences in the motivation behind these two novelistic protagonists, there are also factors that align their approach to the virtue. Habrocomes may have a more profound aversion to obeying Erōs' power, but Clitophon's situation illustrates that whatever the reason for erotic reticence, any *sōphrosunē* will be overcome by the god. So, while Clitophon and Habrocomes both claim to possess *sōphrosunē*, they also both possess the virtue to a limited and ineffectual extent. Both protagonists, by pitting their supposed *sōphrosunē* against the will of Erōs, invite the reader to consider the value of a virtue which seems to act in opposition to the main emotional drive of these characters.[120] Erōs is unchallengeable in these narratives, but *sōphrosunē* continues to be a factor in the *Ephesiaca*, where it is involved in the couple's mutual fidelity, and I shall now consider whether fidelity in Achilles Tatius' text, particularly in regard to Clitophon, carries the same ethical weight.

1.4.2 Clitophon's fidelity

There is a glaring problem with Clitophon's fidelity: he voluntarily has sex with a woman other than his beloved. *Sōphrosunē* is represented in the earliest two extant examples of the genre (Chariton, Xenophon of Ephesus) as being closely linked to marital fidelity: the couples are married at the beginning of each novel and must remain faithful to one another while separated and while undergoing various misfortunes, many of which are brought about by their sexual attractiveness to other characters. In the later novels (Achilles Tatius, Longus, Heliodorus), marriage comes at the end, so that any fidelity performed in these novels is not dictated by marital convention but springs from the mutual desire of the protagonists and their lack of interest in sex with anyone else. Despite these generic rules, fidelity is not represented consistently in the examples of the genre. Chariton's heroine Callirhoe remarries; Longus' Daphnis has a sexual tutorial from Lycaenion. In this novel, Clitophon 'cures' the excessive sexual desire of Melite by consummating their marriage, which is shown to be a sham by the return of Melite's husband Thersander; moreover, this consummation occurs after Clitophon learns of his beloved Leucippe's survival (5.27), making his behaviour in surrendering to Melite's advances at this juncture seem either decidedly cynical or ridiculously naïve.[121]

In relation to Melite, Clitophon displays sexual abstinence from choice for the majority of their 'marriage'. He determinedly fends off her equally determined advances at several junctures in the text (5.14.1; 5.16.1–2; 5.16.7–8; 5.21.3–7). While this abstinence is never said to be governed by *sōphrosunē* on Clitophon's part at the points when he refuses sex, the virtue is emphasized in regard to Melite in Book 8 (8.5.2), when Clitophon narrates his doctored version of events to Sostratus. Clitophon recognizes his lack of *sōphrosunē* when he did submit to Melite's wishes, but, what is also clear is that he views the rejection of sex as demonstrative of the virtue. There are two related comments from Clitophon regarding his sexual self-restraint with regard to Melite at 8.5:

Ἐπεὶ δὲ κατὰ τὴν Μελίτην ἐγενόμην, ἐξῆρον τὸ πρᾶγμα ἐμαυτοῦ πρὸς σωφροσύνην μεταποιῶν καὶ οὐδὲν ἐψευδόμην, τὸν Μελίτης ἔρωτα καὶ τὴν σωφροσύνην τὴν ἐμήν . . . διηγησάμην . . .

When I came to the part about Melite, I elevated my part in the deed remoulding it into one of self-restraint, although I told no actual lies: I narrated Melite's desire, and my self-restraint . . .

8.5.2

Ἓν μόνον παρῆκα τῶν ἐμαυτοῦ δραμάτων, τὴν μετὰ ταῦτα πρὸς Μελίτην αἰδῶ· . . .

Only one of my actions in this drama did I pass over, my subsequent shame with Melite . . .

8.5.3[122]

Clitophon's representation of events to Sostratus (and to Leucippe and the priest) is not doctored in any other respect (according to his wider narration) except in regard to his eventual submission to Melite, which the reader witnesses at 5.27. The details about the rest of this relationship, which are referred to between the two excerpts above, are in line with the rest of his narrative. This makes the importance of this lapse clear: although Clitophon submits, he clearly recognizes that this submission is not ideal in terms of how he wishes himself to be perceived by his audience at 8.5.

At 5.27, Clitophon's capitulation is difficult to comprehend. He is fully aware of the altered circumstances of his and Melite's situation. They are not really married because Melite's husband, Thersander, is alive and has returned to Ephesus. Moreover, Clitophon has discovered that Leucippe is alive and enslaved on Melite's estate, and Melite has reacted angrily to both of these changes of circumstance (5.25). It is worth also noting that other characters at various points believe that Clitophon and Melite have already consummated their marriage (at 5.18, Leucippe is accusatory towards Clitophon and his new marriage in her letter and stresses her own virginity; at 5.20, Satyrus is incredulous at the news that Clitophon has refused Melite's advances; at 5.23, Thersander accuses Clitophon of being an adulterer). Also, Clitophon, having read Leucippe's letter and being struck with conflicting emotions, says that he feels like an adulterer caught in the act (5.19.6).[123] Thus, a picture is created, before Clitophon gives in to Melite's advances, that it is expected that he will have had sexual relations with his 'wife'. Clitophon, as narrator, seems to imply that his continuing refusal to do so is beyond the bounds of 'normal' behaviour, emphasizing how morally staunch he is in regard to Leucippe, but also, paradoxically, perhaps laying the ground for his imminent sexual capitulation. It could be argued that once aware of Leucippe's survival and Melite's marital status, his behaviour in abstaining from sex with Melite becomes normal: now it is perfectly understandable and reasonable to expect him to abstain, where

formerly it could be seen to have been extraordinary, according to those within
the text, at least as Clitophon as narrator represents their views.

Melite gives a very long and impassioned speech, first remonstrating
with Clitophon, then begging him to allow her one sexual experience with him
(5.25–26). Clitophon responds, as narrator, with the following comment:

Ταῦτα φιλοσοφήσασα - διδάσκει γὰρ ὁ Ἔρως καὶ λόγους - . . .

With this philosophical exposition done (Erōs even teaches eloquence) . . .

                                                                                5.27.1

The slippage in meaning of terms relating to philosophy in this text is recognized
by Goldhill.[124] Melite's 'philosophizing' is aimed squarely at seduction, while
formerly (5.16.7), Clitophon used the same verb to refer to the practice of
abstinence.[125] Is there irony at work here from the author suggesting the
malleability of this terminology, and, ultimately, aimed at undermining the use
of philosophy as a form of sexual restraint?[126] The mention of Erōs' role is also
important: Clitophon does not credit Melite with her own words here, rather
implying that the god is responsible for her speeches. Erōs' role is emphasized
three more times within this chapter, first when Clitophon is claiming that fear
of Erōs makes him submit (5.27.2), then when everything happens as Erōs wants
(5.27.3), and finally as Clitophon eulogizes on the god's ability to turn any
environment into an erotic one, and sophistry is emphasized here:

Αὐτουργὸς γὰρ ὁ Ἔρως καὶ αὐτοσχέδιος σοφιστὴς καὶ πάντα τόπον αὐτῷ
τιθέμενος μυστήριον . . .

Erōs is a resourceful, improvising sophist, who can turn any place into a temple
for his mysteries . . .

                                                                           5.27.4[127]

In this passage, philosophy and sophistry seem to have a common aim,[128] and
Erōs' power over both disciplines is implied by Clitophon as narrator. As
elsewhere (1.5.6; 1.11.3; 2.5.2), Erōs is presented as an agent who can influence
Clitophon's behaviour, and this is perhaps intended as a way of shifting the blame
for this generically shocking turn of events.[129]

1.4.3 Male virginity

In this section, I will look at how the concept of male virginity is exploited by
Clitophon as he attempts, on two occasions, to use this term as a form of self-

definition in order to promote a certain view of masculine sexual identity.[130] Recent studies focus on how *parthenia* and *parthenos* in the context of the Greek novel are not absolutely equivalent to the English terms 'virginity' and 'virgin', but are rather more semantically complex, implying the state of a young female being ready for marriage, but not yet married, or implying a state of not having declared any experience of the sexual act.[131] While this argument, based primarily on the work of Sissa,[132] can be successfully borne out by the majority of usages in these texts, it could also be argued that absolute lack of sexual experience is also implied in each of these usages, so that the distinction becomes somewhat arbitrary. Also, in Achilles Tatius' text, when Leucippe describes her dream to Clitophon at 4.1, it is in direct response to his overt sexual advances that she suggests that Artemis has insisted she remain a *parthenos* until she should marry Clitophon (4.1.4), so that it is the sexual act that will compromise her status as *parthenos*, rather than the marriage itself, or the sexual act within marriage. While this study is not directed at an evaluation of the terms *parthenos* and *parthenia* in this novel, it is important to examine these concepts regarding sexual status in order to arrive at an understanding of how they relate to *sōphrosunē* as it is represented in the text.

With the above considerations in mind, I will look at how Clitophon uses terms relating to his 'virginity' on two occasions. The first is in response to Leucippe's letter (5.18), where she emphasizes her own status as *parthenos*, aware that Clitophon is now married to Melite. In his reply, Clitophon states the following:

... Εἰ μὲν οὖν τὴν ἀλήθειαν περιμενεῖς,[133] μηδὲν προκαταγινώσκουσά μου, μαθήσῃ τὴν σήν με παρθενίαν μεμιμημένον, εἴ τις ἔστι καὶ ἐν τοῖς ἀνδράσι παρθενία ...

... If you will wait for the truth, not condemning me first, you will learn that I have imitated your virginity, if there be a male equivalent of virginity ...

5.20.5

Repath notes that this epistolary response from Clitophon demonstrates his self-obsession and, in contrast to Leucippe's emotional *tour de force*, falls somewhat flat.[134] Indeed, he is focused firmly on his own reputation in Leucippe's view, and his comments about his virginity are at the physical and emotional centre of the letter, so that his use of this terminology is distinctly bound up with his self-representation as faithful and devoted to Leucippe. But the question remains, why use this terminology specifically? The conditional clause 'εἴ τις ἔστι καὶ ἐν τοῖς ἀνδράσι παρθενία' clearly emphasizes that there might not be such a thing as male virginity,[135] so why not express more clearly the fact, that so far, he has not had sex with his new wife, Melite? While Clitophon is trying to mirror Leucippe's language in her letter, as Repath suggests,[136] it is clear that his manipulation of her statement regarding her status as *parthenos* is not ideally suited to the letter's purpose, given its slippery nature as a 'male' concept. Clitophon is shown to have limited understanding of how to persuade with language, and how to ensure that his own letter has its intended effect upon Leucippe. Moreover, his focus on the idea of male virginity does not emphasize his motivation: he omits to explain why he has remained 'virginal' and he does not refer to the emotional duress under which his marriage to Melite has placed him. The inclusion of some indication of his continuing desire for Leucippe and the apparent *sōphrosunē* which this has encouraged in him would surely drive his point home more successfully than this rather vague use of male *parthenia*. The fact that this letter never seems to be received by Leucippe renders it irrelevant in terms of the narrative drive, but it is entirely relevant when considering how Clitophon misses an opportunity to represent his behaviour in the best possible light, when this is exactly what he thinks he is doing.

In view of the above, while we can explain that instance away by seeing it as an attempt to reflect the language of Leucippe's missive, it is surprising that this is not the only occasion where Clitophon uses this terminology. At 8.5.7, when narrating his experiences to Leucippe's father, Sostratus, Clitophon makes the following comment:

> ... Εἴ τις ἄρα ἔστιν ἀνδρὸς παρθενία, ταύτην κἀγὼ μέχρι τοῦ παρόντος πρὸς Λευκίππην ἔχω ...

> ... If there be such a thing as virginity in a man, I have retained it up to the present day, as far as Leucippe is concerned ...

> 8.5.7

While I agree with Jones' suggestions regarding Clitophon's tailoring of the idea of virginity to suit his specific situation,[137] what is particularly significant when considering the use of this terminology is how Clitophon returns to this idea of male *parthenia* when it is unnecessary: he could easily represent his sexual abstinence with regard to Leucippe in other terms, and indeed does so in this very section. He could also emphasize his respect for *her* virginity more strongly. So why does he choose to express himself in this manner? Is it the case that he envies the ability of Leucippe to claim virginity? Does he regard the specific terminology relating to this kind of abstinence as more impressive to his narratee, Sostratus? In both cases, he is directing his comments towards those whom he is keen to impress, and it is worth noting that Leucippe is present at 8.5.7, so that his use of the terminology he used in his letter could be directed at her specifically. He is perhaps ensuring that the claim in his letter should appear validated by the repetition of it here, unaware as he is that Leucippe did not receive the missive anyway. It is significant that his claims of virginity are separated by the one sexual act that he engages in during his narrated adventures, namely that with Melite: any moral highground he could claim when composing his letter is now rendered void. While the narratees of Clitophon the character at 8.5.7 cannot be aware of this lapse, the narratee of Clitophon the ego-narrator is. Thus, Clitophon, who seeks to present himself in the opening frame as a victim of Erōs and continues to emphasize his own sufferings and viewpoint throughout his narrative, seems to invite his narratee to perceive his sophistic skill in papering over the cracks in his story when narrating his experiences to Sostratus. By referring once more to his *parthenia*, although he does qualify it as being in regard to Leucippe, I maintain that he is undermined by the authorial irony with which this term is imbued at this point. He tries so desperately to convince those present of his *sōphrosunē* that he seems to overplay his hand: the gullibility of his audience at the time should not distract the reader from the implications of his toying with virginal terminology. There is the subtle message that Clitophon understands that male virginity is debatable, but he does not understand that in claiming it for himself and tailoring its meaning he entirely deprives the term of any real ethical force, and his claims for *sōphrosunē* can be read with the awareness that this narrator-character is not to be trusted with moral concepts.

Male virginity, however, is not a concept which is unique to Achilles Tatius. In the earlier novels, the virginity of the heroes at the outset of their adventures is key to their characterization. While Daphnis loses his virginity to Lycaenion, Chaereas and Habrocomes both have their initial sexual experiences with their beloved wives. In Heliodorus' *Aethiopica*, Theagenes is just as virginal as Chariclea up to their marriage. In each of the novels apart from *Leucippe and Clitophon*, the hero's attraction is exclusively for the heroine, and their respective virginity reflects this idea (Daphnis' 'education' by Lycaenion is only present in order to facilitate consummation for Daphnis and Chloe). It is fascinating that it is only Achilles Tatius who foregrounds the issue of male virginity and simultaneously undermines it: he allows Clitophon's experience with prostitutes and his sexual encounter with Melite to detract from the veracity of the character's adherence to the idea. Whether Achilles has some awareness of the emergence of Christian views on the importance of virginity for both sexes, along with Stoic ideals around the benefit of abstinence for one's virtuous life is up for debate, but it is clear that virginity as a concept is not limited to the representation of women in the novel.

1.4.4 Minor male *sōphrosunē*

The term *sōphrōn* and its derivatives only occur in relation to male characters other than Clitophon on three occasions: twice in relation to Thersander, both in the trial scene in Book 8, first in the priest's speech (8.9.2), in order to denigrate the antagonist's display of *sōphrosunē*,[138] and then in the counter speech, where Thersander's lawyer claims that his client possesses the virtue (8.10.7); and once regarding Callisthenes, who is a changed man in Sostratus' view, now behaving in a *sōphrōn* manner (8.17.5), where previously, in Clitophon's version of events, he was a dissolute profligate, with malign erotic intentions (2.13). It is significant that none of these instances is narrated by Clitophon alone, but appear in the speeches of other characters. In regard to Thersander, each comment is motivated by clear prejudice on the side of the speaker, who is attempting to, respectively, denigrate and elevate Thersander's morals. The reader, having 'witnessed' Thersander's abhorrent behaviour towards Leucippe at 6.20–21, can easily recognize that he demonstrates a lack of *sōphrosunē* unequalled by any other character in this novel, which makes the fact that two out of the seventeen instances of *sōphrosunē* and its cognates are applied to this antagonist all the more ironic. To look a little closer at these occurrences, the priest's speech is said to be like a comic performance by Aristophanes (8.9.1), which immediately presents what follows in a somewhat dubious light: the speech is, at least in part, designed to entertain Thersander's enemies, rather than offer a truthful picture of his character. Many of the accusations the priest levels at Thersander refer to his sexual submission to males in his youth, so that his pretence at *sōphrosunē* is related to his association with older men under the guise of his desire for *paideia*. It is worth noting that Thersander's faults, as the reader perceives them so far, are not mentioned: his excessive aggression and violence in seeking an extra-marital liaison are not used in evidence against him, suggesting, perhaps, that he has not previously behaved in this way, or that accusations of sexual misconduct relating to actively sought pederastic liaisons are more damaging to a man's character (because of the implicit emasculation) than accusations relating to the pursuit of attractive women.

While the priest's speech presents a pretence of *sōphrosunē* in Thersander's past, the advocate's response, which begins with an invective against the priest, claims that Thersander has always possessed *sōphrosunē* (8.10.7). This directly counters the priest's claims, and the emphasis on this virtue is intended to imply a clear contrast with Melite's behaviour, and the allegations pertaining to her which follow bear this out. There is nobody present, apart from possibly Thersander and Sopater (the advocate) who believe in the veracity of this claim for *sōphrosunē*. While the priest's representation of Thersander's lack of *sōphrosunē* could be completely fabricated, the advocate's claim is even less reliable, and the guilt of Melite does nothing to raise her husband's moral status. The way in which these disparate representations are technically irrelevant to the trial emphasizes how conjecture and arbitrary judgements are introduced in this final book with a destabilizing effect on the reader: *sōphrosunē* is manipulated here, as different semblances of fictive reality are presented. This emotive, sophistic use of terminology related to *sōphrosunē* not only implies doubt regarding the characterization of Thersander, but also implies doubt regarding the way in which *sōphrosunē* is presented in the wider narrative.

This slippage in the use of the virtue is similarly borne out by Sostratus' representation of Callisthenes. There is much room for scepticism regarding Callisthenes' character transformation, as Repath suggests.[139] Sostratus shows himself to be not altogether perceptive and somewhat gullible in the naïve way in which he receives Clitophon's version of events (8.5.9), so that the reader is left with the impression that Callisthenes might easily have fooled the old man into believing he is an entirely reformed character. In this inset narrative, Sostratus' description of Callisthenes as *sōphrōn* (8.17.5) is unreliable so that again the virtue is misrepresented in its application to a character who cannot be judged objectively. While Kasprzyk sees Callisthenes' role reversal as a part of the ironic strategy employed by Achilles vis-à-vis *sōphrosunē* which is aimed at belittling the virtue,[140] this is to ignore the nature of the narrator of this role reversal and the nature of the wider ego-narration. While both Clitophon and Sostratus (along with the priest and Sopater regarding Thersander) apply *sōphrosunē* in a somewhat haphazard fashion, which effectively undermines the virtue on the surface-level reading, on further consideration it becomes clear that theirs is an invalid viewpoint. Their very unreliability as moral authorities and narrators conveys how this concept which is central to the genre and to male ethical status is misunderstood by Achilles' male characters. However, Achilles does not employ this strategy to belittle the concept, but rather to belittle his narrators and characters. The implicit questions about reliability and authority invite a consideration of how a concept as generically important as *sōphrosunē* is inevitably subject to the same destabilizing forces which affect all aspects of this novel, yet it still remains at the centre of how male identity is conceptualized within this text.

1.4.5 Leucippe: for virtue or virginity?

It is important to note at the outset of this discussion of Leucippe and how she is represented by Clitophon regarding her *sōphrosunē* that there is only one occasion in the narrative where the term is used in reference to the heroine and where it refers directly to sexual restraint or chastity.[141] This is at 8.7.1, where the priest praises her *sōphrosunē* along with her good fortune, having just heard about her successful defence of her virginity from Clitophon's account. As Kasprzyk notes, Leucippe herself is mute on the virtue, something which is unique in the extant examples of the genre (except in the case of Longus' protagonists).[142] In this section, I will explore whether *sōphrosunē*, in the sense of sexual restraint, is possessed by Leucippe at all, and the extent to which Clitophon presents his heroine as an idealized, chaste maiden.

Before analysing Achilles Tatius' technique of blurring Leucippe's characterization by filtering our view of her through Clitophon's ego-narration, consideration of how the female character can emerge from a male authored and narrated text is needed. Alice Jardine coined the word 'gynesis' to denote the way in which the valorization of 'woman' in contemporary discourse emerges through space in that discourse.[143] This theory can be mapped onto ancient narrative contexts too, as Barbara Gold has emphasized: 'Jardine proposes for modernity, and I propose for antiquity, that we look in our texts for what is hidden, deemphasized, left out, or denied articulation, and try to make evident the spaces produced in these texts over which the writer has no control and in which 'woman' can be found.'[144] When reading a text as self-conscious as *Leucippe and Clitophon*, and when seeking the 'real' Leucippe within such a text, theories such as Jardine's can help immensely. Achilles Tatius invites highly evolved modes of reading and interpretation through his narrative structure and rhetorical style, and these aspects allow for reading 'against the grain' or 'between the lines', so that a reading involving 'gynesis' is not excluded. Where Leucippe is silent or only visible through Clitophon's lens, we can react by using the space created by her obscuration to perceive the potential for this female character's agency.

While Leucippe's apparent willingness to have sex up to the beginning of Book 4 has received some attention, along with the implication that the heroine is perhaps just as interested in sex as Clitophon is,[145] her lack of direct speech in the relevant passages (2.19.2; 2.23.3–5) and the almost exclusive focus on Clitophon's feelings and actions throughout mean that it is very difficult to assert with any certainty exactly what Leucippe agrees to or intends.[146] Her marginalized status at this point is further emphasized by the fact that she is not named for the entirety of 2.23, emphasizing Clitophon's self-absorption which constantly prevents a clear picture of Leucippe from emerging. Clitophon's 'Leucippe' is silent as he attempts this seduction: she is not allowed a direct reaction to this most anti-generic situation, so that to claim she is fully cognisant of what Clitophon intends is an assumption rather than an obvious conclusion. However, it is fair to say that her behaviour following on from the attempted tryst does indicate a willingness to lie to her mother and to elope, both of which indicate that Leucippe is not a complete innocent, and that there is a danger that she will be further corrupted by Clitophon, and that the narrative will be derailed; that is, until the events at 4.1.

Leucippe's new-found commitment to virginity, brought about by her dream of Artemis at 4.1, is one of the major turning points in the text, correcting the generically acceptable trajectory, which is endangered by Clitophon's sexual advances, and casting Leucippe as a typical novelistic heroine.[147] Clitophon presents this dream in tandem with his own, less easily interpreted one involving the statue of Aphrodite (4.1.5–7),[148] and it is the combination of these two dreams, rather than just Leucippe's, which persuades Clitophon to relent and stop trying to 'force' his beloved into sex:

Καταλέγω δὴ τοῦτο τῇ Λευκίππῃ τὸ ἐνύπνιον καὶ οὐκέτι ἐπεχείρουν βιάζεσθαι.

I recounted this dream to Leucippe, and subsequently refrained from my attempts to coerce her.

4.1.8

So, while, for Leucippe, it is ostensibly Artemis' divine intervention which prevents her from submitting to Clitophon's sexual advances, it is both dreams which realign the narrative trajectory and allow Leucippe to preserve her virginity. The role of *sōphrosunē* is perhaps implied by Leucippe's new devotion to the will of Artemis, but it is somewhat undercut by her comment regarding her reaction to the dream:

Ἐγὼ δὲ τὴν μὲν ἀναβολὴν ἠχθόμην, ταῖς δὲ τοῦ μέλλοντος ἐλπίσιν ἡδόμην.

I was certainly irritated by the delay, but was delighted by hopes for the future.

4.1.5

This remark could be spoken by Leucippe to pacify the frustrated Clitophon, by aligning her feelings of desire with his own, or this could act as part of Clitophon's representation of Leucippe as just as eager for sex as he is. Either way, the result is that Leucippe's adherence to Artemis' will is not presented as unequivocally *sōphrōn*: hers is a willingness to comply rather than an ethical transformation. However, this is to suppose that the dream is not an invention of Leucippe's. It is conceivable that the characterization of Leucippe is made more complex at this juncture: is it plausible for the reader to assume that she realizes the precarious predicament in which she now finds herself, having eloped with Clitophon and already having suffered misfortunes? Perhaps now she needs to find a way to ensure her future stability and social status: this could cause her to create this convenient dream. If her motivation in resisting sex and waiting for marriage is not merely to obey Artemis' will, but is rooted in a more complex set of factors aimed at ensuring a socially sanctioned future, then how does this reflect on her *sōphrosunē* or lack thereof? I suggest that while the concept must involve social and emotional factors, it is not entirely divorced from circumstances. There is space opened up within the text for readers to perceive that Leucippe's motivation is not based primarily on a *sōphrōn* approach to sexual relationships, but is based on an attitude which is much more pragmatic and, one could argue, cynical.

Leucippe is represented as zealous in the defence of her virginity at 6.21–22, and this picks up on her appearance in the guise of the slave girl Lacaena at 5.17, where she displays her wounds which she has received as the result of her refusal to become Sosthenes' sex slave, and also picks up on the detail of her letter to Clitophon at 5.18, where she emphasizes her physical sufferings and her virginity. Morales suggests that the explicit invitation to inflict violence on her body at 6.21–22 casts Leucippe as an example of Roman and Stoic ideal femininity and also aligns her with female Christian martyrs. This implies that this particular representation is fundamentally connected to the novel's contemporary literary and social context, something which needs to be considered before deciding if Leucippe exemplifies a *sōphrōn* novel heroine at this point.[149] I find the argument for Stoic and Roman influence less convincing than that suggesting connections with Christian literature. Morales suggests connections with Stoic and Roman values which are somewhat tenuous: Leucippe's emphasis on virginity specifically means that her sexual integrity is important on a physical level in a way which does not resonate with Stoicism, where any suffering should be borne with fortitude and should not have an emotional impact. Similarly, Morales' suggestion that Leucippe celebrates the model of purity exemplified by Livy's Lucretia is flawed: Lucretia is sexually violated but her mind remains innocent; Leucippe successfully avoids violation, and it could be argued, in line with Chew's comment, that her mind is not as *sōphrōn* as her body.[150] The early Christian emphasis on suffering as something to be sought after is a significant move away from the Stoic idea of enduring or avoiding pain, as Chew notes,[151] which further indicates that the representation of Leucippe as actively seeking tortures is more in line with Christian ideals than those of Stoicism. Chew also suggests that Leucippe's resolute defence of her virginity at 6.21 prefigures the martyrs'colourful defiance in the face of sexualized violence, and she aligns the novel heroine's display of chastity with the martyrs' commitment to Christian principles.[152] While the adherence to virginity is evident from Leucippe's behaviour at 6.21, and while I accept that her fervour and invitation of tortures does seem markedly similar to accounts of Christian martyrs, it does not follow that Leucippe necessarily acts from a deeply held commitment to principles based on *sōphrosunē*, and this will be explored below.

While *sōphrosunē* could be said to be a part of Leucippe's zealous defence of her virginity in that she demonstrates a determination to remain chaste at all costs, to attribute this virtue to Leucippe at this point is mistaken, and it is important to recognize the nuanced implications of how she is represented by Clitophon here. Clitophon, as the narrator, is concerned to present Leucippe as faithful to him and consequently fervently opposed to sex with anyone else. Preceding the scene at 6.21–22, Leucippe's soliloquy at 6.16 demonstrates this clearly, by first addressing Clitophon and expressing concern about him (6.16.1– 2), then naming him as her husband twice (6.16.3; 6.16.6), before deciding against revealing her identity in case it brings about danger for Clitophon (6.16.6). On hearing all of this, Thersander is then said to voice his wish to be Clitophon (6.17.2), and Leucippe reproaches his increasingly aggressive advances by telling him he will only succeed if he becomes Clitophon (6.18.6). The continuing emphases on Clitophon in this section of the text clearly evoke an image of the narrator/protagonist which he wishes us to see: Leucippe's commitment to him and Thersander's jealousy of him both indicate that Clitophon, despite his present predicament, is the perfect example of a novel hero. Leucippe, who is given the rare opportunity to speak directly at 6.21–22,[153] does so only in order to reinforce that she is absolutely committed to Clitophon, to the extent that she will suffer tortures for him. This colours whether the reader can take this scene completely seriously: can we really trust Clitophon's self-laudatory representation of his beloved? Further, any *sōphrosunē* which could be recognized as a part of Leucippe's speech is devalued as her zealous defence of virginity either springs from her intense desire for Clitophon, or from a deliberate fabrication of that desire by Clitophon.[154]

The fact that Leucippe refers to herself as a *parthenos* repeatedly in the passage discussed above (6.21.2; 6.22.1; 6.22.2 (three times); 6.22.3), and never claims *sōphrosunē* for herself on this occasion or elsewhere, emphasizes how it is the state of being virginal rather than the motivation behind the continuation of that state that is important to Leucippe, or at least, to Clitophon's representation of her. However, I would not argue that this implies a negation of the virtue of *sōphrosunē* regarding females in this novel: it is rather the case that Leucippe is Clitophon's creation and as such she is limited by his control over her words and actions. Therefore, 'Leucippe' as a distinct, fictional entity is not an objectively produced example of a *sōphrōn* heroine such as that which we see in the *Ephesiaca, Callirhoe* or the *Aethiopica*, but is rather a construct of Clitophon's, and as such she reflects his concerns and priorities. All that matters to Clitophon is that he demonstrates how devoted his girlfriend is to him, and displays the trials that she endures for him. The emphasis on Leucippe as a *parthenos* is almost on a fetishistic level, and Clitophon's obsession is satisfied by this representation.

The events in Book 8 further bolster this emphasis on Leucippe's virginity as opposed to her *sōphrosunē*: while the priest praises her *sōphrosunē* and her *tychē*, this is not so much a sign that the virtue is present in Leucippe, but rather creates irony by implying that good luck has allowed Leucippe to remain virginal, at least as much as *sōphrosunē* has (8.7.1). Clitophon also emphasizes the couple's mutual sexual abstinence when he narrates their experiences to Sostratus (8.5). It is, I think, significant how Clitophon represents Leucippe's behaviour here. After drawing attention to those sufferings she has endured without him (slavery, tilling the earth, having her head shaved: 8.5.4), Clitophon then moves on to relate, in indirect speech, Leucippe's resistance to Sosthenes and Thersander:

> Κἀν τῷδε κατὰ τὸν Σωσθένην καὶ Θέρσανδρον γενόμενος ἐξῆρον καὶ τὰ αὐτῆς ἔτι μᾶλλον ἢ τἀμά, ἐρωτικῶς αὐτῇ χαριούμενος ἀκούοντος τοῦ πατρός· ὡς πᾶσαν αἰκίαν ἤνεγκεν εἰς τὸ σῶμα καὶ ὕβριν πλὴν μιᾶς, ὑπὲρ δὲ ταύτης τὰς ἄλλας πάσας ὑπέστη·

> Then, when I reached the part about Sosthenes and Thersander, I exaggerated her story even more than I had done mine, in an amorous attempt to gratify her, given that her father was listening. I told of how she had endured having every kind of violent outrage inflicted upon her body except one, and that it was for the sake of the last-mentioned that she had tolerated all the others.

> 8.5.5

This admission that he elaborates Leucippe's story alerts the reader to the danger that he might have done the same when narrating these events in Book 6 to the primary narratee, a narration which is later than that represented at 8.5.5.[155] Clitophon's edited account means that we do not know exactly what outrages he claims Leucippe underwent. Also, the one outrage she did not endure is not named, which could be explained by Clitophon's awareness that his narratee already knows that it is rape which Leucippe avoids, or, alternatively, could be explained by the need for euphemistic description in front of her father. While Clitophon's exaggeration of his own sexual restraint is aimed at representing his *sōphrosunē* (8.5.2), here the term is not used although similar exaggeration is said to be taking place. Leucippe's resistance to sexual *hubris* is clearly intended by Clitophon to flatter his girlfriend and assure her father of the preservation of her virginity, but the virtue's absence from this account is perhaps alerting us to the role of chance in this preservation.

Later in his narration to Sostratus, which by now has switched back into direct speech, Clitophon uses phraseology which is familiar from elsewhere in the text, and which I have already discussed above (section 1.4.2):

Ἐφιλοσοφήσαμεν, πάτερ, τὴν ἀποδημίαν· ἐδίωξε γὰρ ἡμᾶς ἔρως, καὶ ἦν ἐραστοῦ καὶ ἐρωμένης φυγή· ἀποδημήσαντες γεγόναμεν ἀλλήλων ἀδελφοί. Εἴ τις ἄρα ἔστιν ἀνδρὸς παρθενία, ταύτην κἀγὼ μέχρι τοῦ παρόντος πρὸς Λευκίππην ἔχω· ἡ μὲν γὰρ ἦρα ἐκ πολλοῦ τοῦ τῆς Ἀρτέμιδος ἱεροῦ.

Our peregrination bespoke philosophical moderation. For Erōs chased us: the escape was of a lover and a beloved. During our travels, we became like brother and sister. If there be such a thing as virginity in a man, I have retained it up to the present day, as far as Leucippe is concerned. As for her, well she has desired for a long time now the temple of Artemis.

8.5.7

At this point, Clitophon refers to the relationship between himself and Leucippe, rather than to the sexual aggression of other men towards Leucippe. The terminology in this passage, which relates to philosophy and desire, lovers and siblings, male virginity and Artemis, emphasizes restraint between lovers, rather than avoidance of rape. While the term ἐφιλοσοφήσαμεν might be closely related to *sōphrosunē* in that it represents a philosophical sexual restraint, the semantic slippage of philosophical terms elsewhere in the text indicates that, even here, Clitophon does not depict their mutual sexual forbearance as involving *sōphrosunē* directly. Clitophon also emphasizes Leucippe's longing for Artemis (referring back to her dream at 4.1, and her wish for marriage) rather than describing her in terms relating to *sōphrosunē*: this may seem like an arbitrary distinction at this point, but I suggest that the way in which the language of desire and restraint is manipulated by Clitophon to serve his own purposes and emphasize what is important for his narrative indicates that such language is never arbitrary. Clitophon could easily say that Leucippe is *sōphrōn* yet he fails to do so, which means that he does not recognize her as being virtuous in this respect or that he does not think that the virtue is important in his representation of her. He perhaps views the situation in pragmatic and somewhat simple terms: Leucippe did not have sex with him, although she wanted to, because Artemis told her not to in a dream, and Clitophon stopped pressurizing her. Clitophon is therefore honest in not attributing *sōphrosunē* to his beloved, and is consistent in this respect. Leucippe's virginity is at the heart of Clitophon's representation of her, but it has become clear that his representation of her motivation in preserving it is not based on the virtue of *sōphrosunē*.

To return to the idea of gynesis: Leucippe's apparent lack of *sōphrosunē* can be viewed not only as symptomatic of Clitophon's representation of her, but also as a somewhat liberating feature of her characterization. Leucippe does not completely conform to the generic ideal of femininity, and the way in which Clitophon omits to define her within the parameters of *sōphrosunē* allows the space within the text for that aspect of her characterization to emerge.

1.4.6 Leucippe and losing *sōphrosunē*

I argued in the last section that Leucippe is not defined in terms of her sexuality by *sōphrosunē*. In this section, I will look at part of the text where the term is used by Clitophon as a character in relation to Leucippe several times, but where it does not imply sexual self-restraint directly, but rather sanity. De Temmerman suggests that in this episode, where Leucippe is at the centre of the action, she is denied any autonomy and is 'literally not herself'.[156] It is unusual in the genre to find terminology related to *sōphrosunē* implying a non-sexual self-control,[157] and it is highly significant that in Clitophon's narrative, which often seems to contain subtle denigration or, at least, dismissal of this virtue, the term is used six times to denote the loss of reason in Leucippe.[158] First, at 4.9.7, as Clitophon witnesses Leucippe being bound because of her madness, following on from a lament regarding the couple's misfortunes thus far, he states:

Ἐγὼ μέν, ἂν σωφρονήσῃς, φιλτάτη, φοβοῦμαι πάλιν τὸν δαίμονα, μή τί σοι κακὸν ἐργάσηται. Τίς οὖν ἡμῶν κακοδαιμονέστερος, οἳ φοβούμεθα καὶ τὰ εὐτυχήματα; Ἀλλ᾽ εἰ μόνον μοι σωφονήσειας καὶ σεαυτὴν ἀπολάβοις, παιζέτω πάλιν ἡ Τύχη.

If your sanity returns, dearest, I fear that the god will once more devise some calamity for you. Who has suffered more divine persecution than us, who fear even good fortune? But may your sanity only return and may you come to yourself again, and let Fortune make sport again.

Next, at 4.10.6, Clitophon expresses regret that Leucippe must be bound in her sleep, and asks:

Ἆρα κἂν κατὰ τοὺς ὕπνους σωφρονεῖς, ἢ μαίνεταί σου καὶ τὰ ὀνείρατα;

Are you sane in your sleep at least, or are your dreams mad too?

At 4.17.2, after the cure for Leucippe's insanity is administered, Clitophon says to her:

Ἆρά μοι σωφρονήσεις ἀληθῶς; Ἆρα μέ ποτε γνωρίσεις; Ἆρα σου τὴν φωνὴν ἐκείνην ἀπολήψομαι;

Will your sanity really return? Will you ever recognize me? Will I hear that voice of yours?

He follows this with another comment referring to her dreams:

γρηγοροῦσα μὲν γὰρ μανίαν δυστυχεῖς, τὰ δὲ ἐνύπνιά σου σωφρονεῖ.

When you are awake this unhappy madness grips you, but your dreams are sane.

4.17.3

Then, when Leucippe's sanity is restored, Clitophon, this time as narrator, states:

Ἐγὼ δὲ ἰδὼν σωφρονοῦσαν ὑπὸ πολλῆς χαρᾶς ἔλυον μὲν μετὰ θορύβου τὰ δεσμά, μετὰ ταῦτα δὲ ἤδη τὸ πᾶν αὐτῇ διηγοῦμαι.

I was overjoyed to see her sane: I untied her excitedly and then told her the whole story.

4.17.5

It is clear both from the context of these usages of σωφρ- root terms and from the phrasing which is employed both by Clitophon as a character responding emotionally to the situation, and by Clitophon as narrator at 4.17.5, that the translations of sanity/sane are appropriate. But it is crucial to state that no other instance of such terminology in this novel can be translated in this way. Does Clitophon significantly alter his representation of this term in relation to Leucippe, implying perhaps that he thinks women (or is it just Leucippe?) incapable of *sōphrosunē* in the sense of sexual restraint? Or, alternatively, does the semantic range of the term allow Clitophon to mean sanity *and* moral restraint, so that he presents Leucippe at these points as bereft of both?

To consider the context of Leucippe's *mania*: following on from Leucippe's and Clitophon's dreams at the beginning of Book 4, the general, Charmides, has expressed an intense desire for Leucippe to Menelaus, who has in turn told Clitophon about it (4.6). Menelaus has managed to delay matters by claiming that Leucippe has her period, but Charmides has requested her presence anyway so that he can kiss and fondle the girl (4.7). Clitophon despairs at this and laments, and Menelaus then emphasizes the fact that they need a plan, and quickly (4.8). Leucippe's madness is then announced by a messenger (4.9). Leucippe, significantly, never gets the opportunity to display her *sōphrosunē* in relation to Charmides. While this could be explained by the need for her to be protected from his attentions by her male companions (his intentions are, after all, not honourable),[159] there is the result that we are left wondering about how she might have reacted, should she have been allowed a reaction. Repath notes the potential allusiveness of the name 'Charmides' to Plato's dialogue of the same name.[160] I agree with much of Repath's argument regarding how this allusion works, particularly concerning how Plato's Charmides is said to be *sōphrōn* which contrasts with Achilles' Charmides' conspicuous lack of the virtue. However, I would like to suggest a further level of engagement, involving Leucippe's *mania* which is interlinked with the scene of Charmides' infatuation with her and with the report of his death.

In the frame of Plato's *Charmides*, Socrates is introduced to the beautiful youth Charmides, and duly admires him. He is told by Chaerephon that if he could see Charmides' body, Socrates would think the boy faceless (ἀπρόσωπος), such is the beauty of his naked form (154d1-5). Chaerephon's comment about Charmides' unseen beauty proves proleptic when Socrates glimpses the boy's body beneath his cloak and is inflamed (ἐφλεγόμην) with desire and is 'beside himself'[161] (οὐκέτ' ἐν ἐμαυτοῦ ἦν: 155d). In *Leucippe and Clitophon*, when Leucippe's madness is described, one of the actions which, in additon to her violence towards Clitophon and Menelaus, betrays her absolute loss of self-control is when she exposes herself to all present:

ἡ δὲ προσεπάλαιεν ἡμῖν, οὐδὲν φροντίζουσα κρύπτειν ὅσα γυνὴ μὴ ὁρᾶσθαι θέλει.

She struggled with us, with no thought to conceal the parts that a woman would not wish to be seen.

4.9.2

While Morales notes that this self-exposure by Leucippe allows the male gaze to intrude and encourages voyeurism on the part of the reader,[162] these are not the only considerations, and, in addition, the context must be carefully considered. I suggest that there is a connection between Socrates' glimpse beneath Charmides' cloak in Plato's *Charmides* and this scene in which Achilles' Charmides and his desire for Leucippe is still very much in the mind of the reader. The beauty of Leucippe is constantly emphasized by Clitophon, and the reader can assume that it is not without a sexual frisson that he now sees what he should not, which aligns Clitophon with Socrates at this point. When Clitophon, as a character, subsequently laments about Leucippe's *mania* and asks when she might become *sōphrōn* again (4.9.7), surely there is dual meaning here: while Clitophon wishes for the return of her sanity, this also involves the return of her modesty, which has been diminished by her current state. The *sōphrosunē* that is conspicuously absent in the scenes involving Charmides is introduced repeatedly in the scenes of Leucippe's insanity which immediately follow, and it is possible that Achilles Tatius is juxtaposing the overtly non-*sōphrōn* Charmides with the presently non-*sōphrōn* Leucippe in order to encourage his readers to reflect on the different connotations of this terminology in a way which ironically picks up on the Platonic dialogue. While Charmides is the object of the older men's sexual desire in the Platonic dialogue and in Achilles' text Leucippe is the object of Charmides' (and, obviously, Clitophon's and also, we later discover, Gorgias') desire, this does not necessarily detract from the potential intertextuality, but rather demonstrates how Achilles toys with readerly expectations and recasts elements of pederastic desire in the *Charmides* as elements of heterosexual desire in this text.

The implications stemming from the above intertextuality for how we view Leucippe's *sōphrosunē* and its loss in this section of text are somewhat complex. While the focus on the titillating feature of her loss of sanity (which is picked up by her shame and embarrassment at hearing of her former actions when her soundness of mind returns at 4.17.5) and the connections with the frame of the Platonic dialogue imply that *sōphrosunē* is still related to sexual and moral restraint, the broader discussion in the *Charmides* and the generically unusual use of the term to denote mental health in these episodes of *Leucippe and Clitophon* imply that, for Clitophon's version of Leucippe, *sōphrosunē* is not exclusively concerned with sexual mores. In conclusion, when Clitophon as a character asks for Leucippe's *sōphrosunē* to return, he does so from a position of compassion and, ostensibly, he is merely desirous of her return to health, but, it is clear that, behind this innocent motivation, Achilles intends far more, and

Leucippe's *sōphrosunē* is consequently layered with allusion and, I suggest, sexuality is still at the heart of her representation.

*

In Achilles Tatius' text, *sōphrosunē* is subject to the whims of the secondary ego-narrator, Clitophon. Despite this, there is still a central role for the virtue. Clitophon's and other characters' manipulation of *sōphrosunē* for their own purposes is clear and their lack of ethical integrity is revealed by how they treat this virtue. Intertextuality with Plato's *Republic*, along with allusions to Chariton's and Xenophon of Ephesus' texts, help to elucidate how Clitophon represents *sōphrosunē* as a hindrance to his pursuit of Leucippe, and how Achilles Tatius represents Clitophon's approach to the virtue in contrast to its Platonic background. The clear transgression involved in Clitophon's eventual submission to Melite's sexual advances and the way in which Clitophon represents this, both as narrator and as character, indicates the dearth of *sōphrosunē* in the self-characterization of Clitophon. Clitophon attempts to provide his earlier self with ethical motivations for what were self-interested actions, and when he misrepresents his relationship with Melite to his immediate audience at 8.5, his pretence involves not the exaggeration of his *sōphrosunē*, which is how he perceives it, but the invention of his former possession of the virtue. Clitophon's misleading use of the idea of male virginity is a further indication of his flawed perspective on his own sexual ethics. The representation of minor male characters and their *sōphrosunē* demonstrates how the term is applied to those who do not possess the virtue on several occasions: *sōphrosunē* is deliberately and naively misapplied to certain male characters, inversely emphasizing the importance of the virtue to elite males within this text. My discussion regarding Leucippe explored how *sōphrosunē* is markedly absent from her characterization for the most part, which indicates the self-serving nature of Clitophon's representation of his beloved. The repeated usages of σωφρ- root terms in relation to the heroine in Book 4 demonstrate how Achilles Tatius uses Platonic allusion to play with the semantic range of these terms, with the result that sanity and sexual propriety are both lost in the characterization of Leucippe at this juncture. A complex picture of the layered representation of *sōphrosunē* in Achilles Tatius' characterizations emerges from this analysis, but the main conclusion is that the virtue is used to subvert and undermine the secondary narrator's representation of it, and that where characters seem to misapply the term this points to their ethical detriment. The resulting irony and humour is indicative of how Achilles Tatius approaches this serious concept with a typical lightness of touch: he upholds *sōphrosunē* while maintaining his subtle and playful approach.

1.5 Heliodorus' *Aethiopica*

Sōphrosunē and its cognates occur thirty-three times in the text of Heliodorus.[163] The frequency of this terminology indicates how central the concept is to the novel and to the characterizations within it. Out of these thirty-three, fourteen refer directly to the heroine, Chariclea,[164] and this consistent use of these terms in relation to the female protagonist will be reflected in the quantity of the analysis focusing on Chariclea which follows. Before I consider the way in which Chariclea is characterized by her *sōphrosunē*, I will focus on Theagenes and the extent to which he possesses *sōphrosunē*. Theagenes is described as possessing *sōphrosunē* on only two occasions (5.4.5; 8.6.4: he refers to *sōphrosunē* in general, implying his and Chariclea's mutual possession of the virtue, at 10.9.1), so I will explore how his attitude towards sexual restraint is implied and nuanced, even though the term is not often used of him. First, I will discuss some early representations of the male protagonist and of his implied *sōphrosunē*. Second, I will explore how Theagenes' restraint is perhaps subordinate to his desire for Chariclea. Third, I will focus on the ways in which Theagenes expresses some doubt over the value of *sōphrosunē*, and whether this significantly distances him from the overtly *sōphrōn* stance of Chariclea. I will then discuss how Calasiris and his son, Thyamis, are represented in terms of their *enkrateia* and *sōphrosunē* respectively. In the sections on Chariclea, I shall discuss her *sōphrosunē* from four different angles, which will allow a full picture of her *sōphrosunē* to emerge. I will explore her zeal and powers of manipulation in preserving her *sōphrosunē*, before I consider the role of emotion in challenging her possession of the virtue, and discuss how allusion to Plato's *Phaedrus* influences our view of her *sōphrosunē*.

1.5.1 Theagenes' *sōphrosunē*:[165] first impressions

In looking at Theagenes' *sōphrosunē*, it is important to consider how the reader becomes aware of the youth's character and his relationship with Chariclea. By establishing how the first impressions of Theagenes affect our reading of his approach to *sōphrosunē*, we can then continue to build on these initial findings in order to provide a clear picture of how this protagonist (the portrayal of whom is at times quite elusive) is represented in terms of the concept.

While Theagenes is introduced in the second chapter of the first book, the reader is left unaware of his identity until he is named by Chariclea in her first lament (first, that is, in terms of the *récit*: at 1.8.3). It is worth noting that Chariclea speaks first, but she names Theagenes before she herself is named in his reply. Her lament immediately emphasizes Chariclea's *sōphrosunē*, and, by implication, Theagenes' adherence to the virtue, at least in relation to Chariclea. I shall return to this passage in the section on Chariclea,[166] but for my present purposes it is enough to note that our very first impression of Theagenes involves his relationship to the *sōphrōn* girl who has stunned the bandits with her beauty. At this point, then, we are beginning to perceive generic conformity: two beautiful young people are apparently devoted to one another and *sōphrosunē* is central. However, Theagenes is represented through Chariclea's filter at this early stage, rather than via any self-representation. This representation is repeated at 1.25, when Theagenes' dismay regarding Chariclea's response to Thyamis' suit is quickly resolved by the heroine's explanation, which involves some crucial information regarding the central couple's back-story. The repetition in quick succession of terms related to *sōphrosunē* is clear evidence of how Chariclea values this virtue, but the speech is also indicative of how her relationship with Theagenes is couched in this narrative:

Ἐγὼ γὰρ δυστυχεῖν μὲν οὐκ ἀρνοῦμαι, μὴ σωφρονεῖν δὲ οὐδὲν οὕτω βίαιον ὥστε με μεταπεισθῆναι· ἓν μόνον οἶδα μὴ σωφρονοῦσα, τὸν ἐξ ἀρχῆς ἐπὶ σοὶ πόθον· ἀλλὰ καὶ τοῦτον ἔννομον· οὐ γὰρ ὡς ἐραστῇ πειθομένη ἀλλ᾽ ὡς ἀνδρὶ συνθεμένη τότε πρῶτον ἐμαυτὴν ἐπέδωκα καὶ εἰς δεῦρο διετέλεσα καθαρὰν ἐμαυτὴν καὶ ἀπὸ σῆς ὁμιλίας φυλάττουσα, πολλάκις μὲν ἐπιχειροῦντα διωσαμένη, τὸν δὲ ἐξ ἀρχῆς ἡμῖν συγκείμενόν τε καὶ ἐνώμοτον ἐπὶ πᾶσι γάμον ἔνθεσμον εἴ πῃ γένοιτο περισκοποῦσα.

I do not deny that we are in a sorry plight, but no danger could be so great that I could be induced not to be virtuous. I know of only one thing in which I have not been virtuous: my original passion for you. But even that was lawful, for I first gave myself to you then not as a woman consenting to her lover, but as a wife pledging herself to her husband, and to this day I have continued to keep myself pure, even from intercourse with you, many times repelling your advances, safeguarding the union which we pledged at the outset and swore to honour whatever befell, in the hope that one day it will be legally solemnized.

1.25.4[167]

Although this speech from Chariclea might strike the reader as a perfect encapsulation of *her* position vis-à-vis *sōphrosunē*, it is also strongly suggestive of Theagenes' position, but only, once again, from Chariclea's perspective. While it could be argued, therefore, that the speech tells us more about Chariclea's obsession with sexual purity and her prioritizing of marriage over physical union, a view does emerge of Theagenes here, albeit a blinkered one. From this speech and from the one at 1.8 mentioned above, the reader perceives the hero's sexual abstinence as caused primarily by Chariclea's insistence upon it, which means that he does not possess *sōphrosunē*, if we understand the virtue to be something beyond a display of abstinence, as something involving an intrinsic commitment to a moderation of desire. The oaths that are mentioned here are not sworn until much later in the *récit* (4.18), and their role is significant, as will be discussed. Here, it is enough to note that the couple are pledged to one another in readiness for marriage, but they have agreed to no carnal contact before their wedding. The focalization through Chariclea, and the motivation behind her speech, which stems from a need to reassure an anxious Theagenes, both imply that our initial view of Theagenes and of his position regarding *sōphrosunē* is not clear. However, we can tentatively gauge a partial view and, even at this early point in the novel, it is implied that his stance is strongly influenced by his desire for and dependence on the *sōphrōn* and wily Chariclea.

A further important consideration is the fact that Chariclea claims that she has rejected Theagenes' advances many times previously. This statement is problematic, not just because there is only one narrated occasion when Chariclea has to remind Theagenes of his oath to respect her *sōphrosunē*, namely at 5.4, but also because it does not sit easily with the rest of what she says at 1.25. While it can be read as an indication of the determined nature of Chariclea's restraint, it remains significant for our reading of Theagenes' behaviour, or at least his behaviour as viewed and represented by Chariclea. As we do not see many sexual advances on Theagenes' part in the novel, it is either the case that Chariclea, because of her obsessive preoccupation with chastity/virginity, is exaggerating the necessity for resistance to such advances, or it suggests that the primary narrator and the secondary narrator, Calasiris (who narrates from 2.21 through to 5.1, and again from 5.17 through to the end of Book 5) limit our access to Theagenes' behaviour to a considerable degree.

1.5.2 Theagenes' restraint

At 3.17, Calasiris reports Theagenes' claim that he has never found sex and women appealing before seeing Chariclea. This claim, like much of Theagenes' speech in both the primary and secondary narratives, is reported indirectly:

Ὁμιλίας γὰρ ἔτι γυναικὸς ἀπείρατος εἶναι διετείνετο πολλὰ διομνύμενος· ἀεὶ γὰρ διαπτύσαι πάσας καὶ γάμον αὐτὸν καὶ ἔρωτας εἴ τινος ἀκούσειεν, ἕως τὸ Χαρικλείας αὐτὸν διήλεγξε κάλλος ὅτι μὴ φύσει καρτερικὸς ἦν ἀλλ' ἀξιεράστου γυναικὸς εἰς τὴν παρελθοῦσαν ἀθέατος.

He maintained, swearing many oaths, that he was still without experience of intercourse with a woman, for he had always spat upon them all and marriage itself and amours, if ever anyone mentioned them to him, until Chariclea's beauty had proved that he was not naturally immune but until yesterday had never set eyes on a woman worth loving.

3.17.4

While this indirect speech on the surface implies that Theagenes is similar to Xenophon of Ephesus' Habrocomes in his resistance to *erōs*, this is not necessarily true. On closer reading and bearing in mind the indirect reporting of this claim, it seems that Theagenes' rejection of women and sex is not quite on a par with Habrocomes', whose rejection of love stems from a vain impiety rather than contempt for (literally 'spitting upon') women.[168] Therefore, Theagenes displays a strain of misogyny that is not present in Habrocomes' attitude.

His apparent misogyny sets Theagenes apart from the generic norm and does not lend itself easily as proof that he has been *sōphrōn* in the past, despite De Temmerman's argument that this speech is evidence of his *sōphrosunē*.[169] If we render *sōphrosunē* as merely 'chastity' then a non-erotic lifestyle as depicted here does justify De Temmerman's argument. However, *sōphrosunē* implies a mindset that motivates chastity, a self-restraint that, by implication, must react to feelings of desire: Theagenes has not experienced such feelings, according to his speech here, until he met Chariclea. There is also a tacit recognition in this speech that his previous attitude was not indicative of a nature which was able to display enduring resistance to sex (μὴ φύσει καρτερικὸς ἦν). Calasiris is ensuring that his narratee recognizes the 'game-changing' nature of Chariclea, and the indirect speech suggests that the narrator has a high level of control over how he represents Theagenes' speech. This indirect representation complicates our view of Theagenes. It is tempting to assert that this statement is indicative of character development: Theagenes' world-view is altered by his encounter with Chariclea. Misogyny is cast out by desire. Whereas his previous stance did not necessitate the possession of *sōphrosunē*, now he will be tested in this respect. However, the narrative levels and Calasiris' desire to tell a good story mean that we cannot take this passage at face-value and we must be cautious in interpreting this as a genuine representation of the young man's words. Here, we see Theagenes darkly: he is obscured by the manipulative Calasiris who does not represent his speech directly. The reader can therefore ask: is this really how Theagenes saw the situation, or is this speech part of Calasiris' 'spin', which aims at maximizing the erotic power of Chariclea at all times? Perceiving a 'true' picture of Theagenes is not easy in this text, and this passage, while offering some tempting suggestions about his non-erotic history and the potential importance of *sōphrosunē* now that he is in love, remains frustrating in the way in which it is part of Calasiris' narrative strategy.

A similar situation regarding Calasiris' manipulation of Theagenes' view occurs at 4.18. Theagenes' plea to Calasiris, which precedes the representation of Chariclea's anxiety over being left alone with him, is indicative of his view of the nature of his and Chariclea's relationship:

… σῷζε τύχης λοιπὸν ἀγώγιμα σώματα καὶ σωφρονοῦντος ἔρωτος αἰχμάλωτα
…

… Save us, who are now Fortune's disposable chattels, the captives of a chaste love …

4.18.2

While Theagenes recognizes, and seems to emphasize, the *sōphrōn* nature of his and Chariclea's love, there is in this speech the suggestion that this love is not particularly pleasant at this point. His desperation and his view of the couple as victims of Fortune and prisoners of their love indicate that although he is able to be *sōphrōn*, he is not finding it easy. This plea to Calasiris serves the dual purpose of highlighting that Theagenes recognizes the importance of *sōphrosunē*, and of illustrating that he adheres because he must: he will maintain this self-restraint although he feels imprisoned by it. Chariclea perhaps perceives his frustration, thus making more understandable her plea for the oath, which follows at 4.18.4–5.

When reacting to Chariclea's insistence that he swear an oath promising not to have sex with her until they are married, Theagenes remonstrates with this unfair judgement on his character. However, he expresses this indirectly, once more through Calasiris' filter. A fuller analysis of Chariclea's speech will be provided later in this chapter:[170] for now, the lack of symmetry in how the protagonists' words are represented is an important factor. Whereas Calasiris represents Chariclea's pleas in full and directly, he represents Theagenes' reaction indirectly:

… ἐπώμνυεν ὁ Θεαγένης, ἀδικεῖσθαι μὲν φάσκων εἰ προλήψει τοῦ ὅρκου τὸ πιστὸν τοῦ τρόπου προϋποτέμνεται, οὐ γὰρ ἔχειν ἐπιδείξειν προαίρεσιν φόβῳ τοῦ κρείττονος κατηναγκάσθαι νομιζόμενος·

... Theagenes swore his oath ... protesting that he was being treated unfairly if by an anticipatory oath the trustworthiness of his character was undercut in advance for he would not be able to display a moral choice, since he would be supposed to be compelled by fear of the Greater Power.

4.18.6

Theagenes' indirect speech reflects Chariclea's vocabulary (ἀδικεῖσθαι (4.18.6) = ἀδικίας (4.18.4); πιστὸν (4.18.6) = ἄπιστον (4.18.4)). While it is plausible that Theagenes responded to Chariclea's words by using equivalent terminology, the use of indirect speech implies that this is Calasiris' rhetoric for the sake of narrative flow rather than a genuine representation of Theagenes' anger in defence of his *sōphrosunē*. Although it is perfectly plausible for Theagenes to react to Chariclea's mistrust in this way, Calasiris' admiration of Chariclea's speech (4.18.6), and the way in which Theagenes immediately complies despite his complaint, both suggest that Calasiris is keen to emphasize Chariclea's *sōphrosunē* and her pragmatism in maintaining it. Therefore, the episode at 4.18 does not stand as an honest representation by Calasiris of an apparent disagreement between the lovers.

By reading between the lines in these passages it is possible to gauge a clearer picture of the sexual dynamics and how Theagenes adheres to *sōphrosunē*, despite the fear or lack of trust from Chariclea and despite her guardian Calasiris' implicit prioritizing of her volition and prowess. One other point that emerges is that Theagenes, in contrast to Chariclea, seems to want to prove his love for Chariclea by agreeing to her terms, and this is his priority, rather than the need to prove his *sōphrōn* nature without being under duress. While consistently Chariclea proves that she must be *sōphrōn* even in regard to Theagenes, which seems to place her adherence to the virtue over her desire for him, there is the implicit suggestion in much of the representation of Theagenes that, for him, Chariclea is worth being *sōphrōn* for: the *sōphrosunē* follows the erotic desire, rather than the erotic desire becoming subordinate to an underlying *sōphrosunē*.

The next passage which demonstrates Theagenes' restraint in action comes at 5.4.[171] The couple find themselves alone together for the first time in a cave. Following much cuddling and kissing, Theagenes' arousal is cooled by Chariclea's reminder of his oaths:

... ἡ γὰρ Χαρίκλεια τὸν Θεαγένην εἴ τι παρακινοῦντα αἴσθοιτο καὶ ἀνδριζόμενον ὑπομνήσει τῶν ὅρκων ἀνέστελλεν, ὁ δὲ οὐ χαλεπῶς ἐπανήγετο καὶ σωφρονεῖν ῥᾳδίως ἠνείχετο ἔρωτος μὲν ἐλάττων ἡδονῆς δὲ κρείττων γινόμενος.

For if ever Chariclea found Theagenes becoming too passionate and playing the man, she would subdue him with a reminder of his oaths, and he would draw back without resentment and happily bear to be self-controlled, being weaker than love but stronger than pleasure.

5.4.5

The use of the verb ἀνδρίζομαι is significant here and, it seems, can only mean one thing in this context.[172] While elsewhere in Heliodorus the verb is used to express courage (2.11.3; 5.32.5), it occurs in only one other of the extant novels, Achilles Tatius' *Leucippe and Clitophon*, at 2.10.1 and 4.1.2, both times alluding to the assertion of male sexuality. Here, as the couple are intimate for the first time and Chariclea checks Theagenes by reminding him of his oaths, he is clearly physically aroused. The narrator is quick to assert that this is soon dealt with, and that Theagenes easily relents, moderating his behaviour (σωφρονεῖν) and that he then draws back (ἐπανήγετο). While ostensibly this illustrates Theagenes' self-restraint, there is the obvious implication that he is unable to remain as cool and collected as his beloved Chariclea. The male perspective is fairly clear: Chariclea's individual actions are verbal rather than physical. While she indulges in the same kisses and embraces there is no depiction of her arousal, which is indicative perhaps of her greater self-control, but could also be read as significant for the novel's gender politics wherein the expression of overt female sexual impetus is limited to antagonistic women such as Arsace and Demaenete.[101]

There is also potential intertextuality with the instances of the verb in Achilles Tatius, which are closer in semantics to the usage at Heliodorus 5.4.5 than are the other instances in the *Aethiopica*. The implications of this are that the reader is encouraged to recall Clitophon's opportunistic sexual advances, particularly at 4.1.2, where his actions are clearly made with one thing in mind. Leucippe's new-found maidenly restraint (she has had a dream involving Artemis) is expressed in direct speech, which is unusual in Clitophon's narrative. This draws attention to the import of her words and their results. Further, if we are to recall the passage when reading the scene in Heliodorus, our recollection of the emphasized instance of direct speech on Leucippe's part draws our attention to the lack of direct speech here. It seems that the primary narrator at 5.4 is keen to be discreet in terms of conveying this intimate episode: neither Theagenes nor Chariclea speak directly and this has the effect of distancing the reader from the scene to a certain extent. The allusion to Achilles Tatius also raises questions regarding Theagenes' role here and whether he is a 'better' example of a male protagonist than Clitophon is. Both male lovers are checked by their girlfriends, but Theagenes' compliance is couched in the language of restraint, whereas

Clitophon submits only from fear brought about by divine intervention via Leucippe's and his own dreams (the veracity of which is discussed above).[173] There is also the possibility that we are meant to consider how different the two protagonists really are. Is Theagenes only self-controlled because Chariclea was clever enough to lay down the parameters on the outset of their journey? Further, if he was narrating his own adventures, would the narrative take on a more 'Clitophontic' style? The nature of Theagenes' *sōphrosunē* can thus be seen to be somewhat complicated, especially when considering the various implications of the use of ἀνδρίζομαι, and, once again, given the lack of direct speech from the protagonist.

Another place where we witness Theagenes' restraint in action is at 7.25: the situation in Memphis has taken a turn for the worse for Theagenes and Chariclea. Theagenes is facing enslavement by Arsace should he not submit to her lust, and Chariclea has been promised in marriage to Cybele's son, Achaemenes. Chariclea suggests that by conceding to Arsace's wishes, Theagenes might save Chariclea from an abhorrent marriage. Theagenes' response is clear, and marks a turning point in his representation by the primary narrator: until now Theagenes has been consistent in resisting Arsace, but he has not used any guile to do so, just honest refusal.[174] His reply to Chariclea, which takes the form of a prayer, reveals the principal motivation behind his resistance, before he tells her that he now has an idea:

> Εὐφήμησον' ἔφη· 'μὴ γὰρ οὕτως ἡ δαίμονος τοῦ ἡμετέρου βαρύτης ἰσχύσειεν ὥστε με τὸν Χαρικλείας ἀπείρατον ἄλλης ὁμιλία παρανόμως μιανθῆναι. Ἀλλά τι δραστήριον ἐπινενοηκέναι μοι δοκῶ· εὑρέτις ἄρα ἐπιλογισμῶν ἡ ἀνάγκη.

> You must not speak like that!' he answered. 'May the god who has us in his power never be so cruel that I, who have never known Chariclea, am compelled to defile myself in illicit intimacy with another woman! But I think I have an idea that may work. Necessity is the mother of invention!

> 7.25.7

This speech, while clearly expressing his devotion to Chariclea, whom he has not yet 'known' (ἀπείρατον), also recalls the indirect speech narrated by Calasiris at 3.17.3–4 (discussed above), where Theagenes' lack of interest in sex prior to meeting Chariclea was emphasized. The language is significant here, clearly demonstrating a view of sex with anyone other than Chariclea, as illicit (παρανόμως), and polluted or stained (μιανθῆναι). A similar tone emerges to that used by Calasiris at 3.17.4 to suggest a distaste for women and sex. At 3.17, the use of διαπτύσαι has been mentioned above, and there is a clear fixation on severe distaste for sex. At 7.25, the distaste is for sex with women other than Chariclea: this suggests that Theagenes' resistance to sexual advances is something which comes from his love for Chariclea. However, there is also the implication that Arsace would never succeed in seducing Theagenes, whether Chariclea was present or not. His lack of experience (at 3.17.4: ἀπείρατος; at 7.25.7: ἀπείρατον), combined with his contempt, make Theagenes appear *sōphrōn* in both passages. However, I maintain, in line with my comments on 3.17, that he only demonstrates true *sōphrosunē* in relation to Chariclea, the only woman in whom he is interested.

Theagenes' resistance to the lust of Arsace is twice couched in terms relating to *sōphrosunē*, when he is being tortured for that very resistance, first alone (8,6,4), then with Chariclea (8,9,22). Heliodorus' omission of direct speech might be explained by a desire to limit the reader's access to the emotional impact of violence on the victim, with the aim of retaining their dignity and apparent strength (cf. Xen. Eph. 2,6,2–2,7,1; Ach. Tat. 6,21–22). Again, the role of *sōphrosunē* is central to Theagenes' lack of submission to Arsace despite his physical sufferings and this is made explicit in the words of the primary narrator at 8,6,4: '... τὸ μὲν σῶμα καταπονούμενος τὴν δὲ ψυχὴν ἐπὶ σωφροσύνῃ ῥωννύμενος ...' ('... though he was exhausted in body, his spirit was strong in chastity ...' (my translation)). However, once more we are faced with distancing by the primary narrator, which frustrates efforts to see clearly how Theagenes expresses this restraint. The primary narrator is determined to imbue Theagenes' *sōphrosunē* with his devotion to Chariclea (her name is repeated as Theagenes is said to regard it as a kindness from Fortune that he can display his devotion to his beloved, and he is said to call her his life, his light, his soul). While the consistent emphasis on Theagenes' relationship with Chariclea is an essential thread running through the novel, the fact that this emphasis often comes indirectly from Theagenes raises doubt: should the reader trust a narrator who veils his hero's speech in this way? Is this indicative of a narrator who prioritizes the representation of Chariclea's *sōphrosunē* over Theagenes'? Further, if Theagenes' chastity is only represented in relation to his heartfelt regard for Chariclea, is it then reduced in value as a virtue? Surely, if one's *sōphrosunē* is tied so directly to one other person, it is lessened in its validity.

1.5.3 Theagenes' doubt

There are two occasions where Theagenes seems to express some doubt about the value of the *sōphrosunē* which Chariclea prizes so highly. At 2.4, when he thinks Chariclea dead, he seems to question whether her *sōphrosunē* was worth retaining if this is the cost; at 10.9, a desperate Theagenes questions whether *sōphrosunē* was the right path for the two of them, now that they face sacrifice as a direct result of their virginity being proven. Both of these occasions involve direct speech from Theagenes, and both occur in the primary narrative, as opposed to Calasiris'.

Theagenes' lament over the apparently dead Chariclea involves the following statement:

> ... δῆλον μὲν ὡς σωφροσύνης ἀντεχομένη καὶ ἐμοὶ δῆθεν ἑαυτὴν φυλάττουσα· κεῖται δ᾿οὖν ὅμως ἡ δυστυχής, οὐδὲν μὲν αὐτὴ τῆς ὥρας ἀποναμένη, εἰς οὐδὲν δὲ ὄφελος ἐμοὶ γενομένη.

> ... [my dearest has fallen victim to an enemy's hand] obviously defending her chastity and keeping herself for me. For me! Nonetheless, she is dead, poor girl, having had no joy of her beauty herself, and having been of no benefit to me.

> 2.4.2

The logic of Theagenes is not wholly sound. The woman he supposes to be Chariclea lies dead, and he assumes it is because she was defending her chastity. Why does he not consider other options? Violence could be induced by causes other than sexual rejection: for example, the reader is aware that Thyamis killed 'Chariclea', not because she was defending her chastity, but his motivation was more complex, involving jealousy and fear that he would lose her to another. A more obvious motive for her killer might be fear at being surprised at the entrance to a cave. Theagenes' reaction is understandable given his beloved's constant emphasis on the virtue, but there is no real rationale behind the assumption. This could be explained by his grief, and his need to make sense of the situation. However, I think there is more to it than that: his subsequent statement about the fact that she was 'keeping herself' for him speaks volumes about the nature of his viewpoint. He clearly views Chariclea in close relation to himself: he cannot envisage a death for her in which he was not on her mind. Her supposed defence of her *sōphrosunē* then, is also part of Theagenes' definition of Chariclea as preoccupied by love of him. This perception is not mistaken: she consistently demonstrates preoccupation with him and with *sōphrosunē*. The discomfiting side of this speech is its self-indulgence, which is borne out again in his repetition of *emoi*, when suggesting that her death means she was not, and now will never be, of benefit to him. The implication of this is fairly clear: Theagenes expresses doubt over Chariclea's choice to defend her *sōphrosunē* because he will now never get to express his love for her sexually. The lost opportunity to enjoy her beauty is detrimental to her too, but the focalization through Theagenes and the emphasis on his loss rather than on hers (and she is the one lying dead!), suggests a self-interested grief. Theagenes is ready to join Chariclea in death (2.4.4), and this readiness is a generic necessity, but in the first section of his speech it is clear that he grieves primarily for his own lost erotic fulfilment, and he doubts the value of *sōphrosunē* if this is the result.

At 10.9.1–2, Theagenes challenges Chariclea to reveal her identity, which he believes (mistakenly, as it turns out) will save them from certain death as the virginal sacrificial victims of the Ethiopians. A part of his plea to his beloved is as follows:

> Καλὰ . . . τἀπίχειρα παρ᾽ Αἰθίοψι τῶν καθαρῶς βιούντων· θυσίαι καὶ σφαγαὶ τὰ ἔπαθλα τῶν σωφρονούντων . . .
>
> A life of purity earns a fine wage with the Ethiopians: sacrifice and slaughter are chastity's rewards!
>
> 10.9.1

Morgan notes that this sentence echoes the words of the oracle at 2.35.5, and thus Theagenes' sarcasm unsettles the naïve reader with a seed of doubt over the oracle's veracity.[175] The sarcastic comment can be read not just as doubt on Theagenes' part about the value of *sōphrosunē*, but also as an implicit criticism of the barbaric customs of the Ethiopians, and it is notable that, either way, there is criticism of factors closely related to Chariclea: her life-choices, or her forebears. Theagenes' pragmatic understanding of the situation contrasts with Chariclea's confidence in her destiny which seems based on a less than rational self-belief (10.9.3). It is clear, then, that Theagenes does not possess the same unquestioning belief in *sōphrosunē* as Chariclea. His adherence to the virtue is never in doubt, but he has doubt about its ultimate worth unless it is rewarded. While at 2.4, there is a self-interested tone, and this is not completely absent at 10.9, Theagenes' questioning of Chariclea's most deeply held virtue implies a pragmatic and not unintelligent approach to erotic temperance: for him the virtue is not sacred. Chariclea's viewpoint seems to be validated by the text, but Theagenes' nuanced perspective and representation are significant for a holistic reading of this central concept of *sōphrosunē*.

1.5.4 Calasiris and Thyamis

At 2.25, Calasiris is beginning his narrative-proper, and he launches into an explanation for his presence in Delphi, where he met Charicles and, subsequently,

Chariclea. The content of this chapter involves the Egyptian high-priest being tempted by a courtesan, Rhodopis, whose beauty is said to be second only to Chariclea's. Before analysing this episode in detail, it is worth mentioning at this point that Calasiris never refers to himself in terms of *sōphrosunē*, nor does anyone else, including the primary narrator, refer to him in this way. Perhaps his age and position make the virtue irrelevant: the reader is not expecting him to have to resist amorous adventures. It is significant, then, that shortly after he is introduced into the novel, he narrates this encounter with Rhodopis and how he had to resist temptation. It is even more significant that in his eagerness to avoid sexual transgression and the pollution of the god's temples (and, incidentally, he is avoiding the sight of his sons' battling each other), Calasiris leaves Memphis and eventually comes to Delphi, where his role as the prime engineer of Chariclea's journey comes to fruition.[176] This scene is clearly important, and I will explore how Calasiris' self-control is represented here.

Following encounters with Rhodopis who regularly visits the Temple of Isis where Calasiris is priest, he narrates, although ashamed (αἰσχύνομαι 2.25.2), how the self-control he had always practised is threatened by this woman's charms:

> ... ἐνίκα τὴν διὰ βίου μοι μελετηθεῖσαν ἐγκράτειαν, ἐπὶ πολύ τε τοῖς σώματος ὀφθαλμοῖς τοὺς ψυχῆς ἀντιστήσας ἀπῆλθον τὸ τελευταῖον ἡττηθεὶς καὶ πάθος ἐρωτικὸν ἐπιφορτισάμενος.

> ... she defeated the self-control practised throughout my life. Though for a long time I pitted the eyes of the soul against those of the body, in the end I left the field worsted and bearing a heavy weight of sexual passion.
>
> 2.25.2

Here, then, Calasiris alerts Cnemon to the nature of this challenge to his *enkrateia*, but he also ensures that he persuades Cnemon of his life-long practice of that *enkrateia*. The physical nature of his erotic desire is encapsulated by the struggle between 'the eyes of the soul' and 'those of the body', and the ultimate victory of the flesh is implied when he is overcome (ἐπιφορτισάμενος) by his πάθος ἐρωτικὸν. Focalization is important here: there is no real indication of how Rhodopis attempts to seduce Calasiris, and it is not even clear from his account if this is what she does. Her regular attendance at the temple (2.25.2) does not prove that she desires Calasiris. He represents her as sexually voracious at 2.25.1:

> ... κακῇ μοίρᾳ τῶν ἐγνωκότων ὁρμηθὲν ... πᾶσι δ᾽ ἀφροσισίοις θηράτροις ἐξησκημένη· οὐ γὰρ ἦν ἐντυχόντα μὴ ἡλωκέναι, οὕτως ἄφυκτόν τινα καὶ ἀπρόσμαχον ἑταιρίας σαγήνην ἐκ τῶν ὀφθαλμῶν ἐπεσύρετο ...

... she brought evil to all she met ... thoroughly practised with all instruments of the sexual hunt. It was impossible to encounter her and not be ensnared, so inescapable and irresistible was the net of harlotry that she trailed from her eyes.

This does not mean that she necessarily used her skills against Calasiris. This episode seems to be mirrored by one which occurs at 7.2, when Arsace attends the temple where Thyamis is priest (in Memphis following Calasiris' departure), with the intention of seducing him. Here is Thyamis' (lack of) response:

Καὶ ταῦτα ὁ μὲν Θύαμις οὐδὲ κατὰ μικρὸν προσίετο, φύσει τε καὶ ἐκ παίδων εὖ πεφυκὼς τὰ εἰς σωφροσύνην ...'

Thyamis did not respond to this in the slightest, for by nature and from his earliest years he was congenitally inclined to the path of virtue ...

7.2.3

The parallels are particularly significant when considering the two characters' reactions: while Calasiris refers to his long-practised *enkrateia*, he failed to enact it during the events narrated at 2.25, and he perceives Rhodopis' visits to the temple as a sexual pursuit, which is a subjective assumption. In contrast, Thyamis' upbringing and his nature both ensure that he is too *sōphrōn* to respond to the lewd signals Arsace gives on her frequent visits to the temple. The fact that the two are father and son implies a degree of irony: it seems that Calasiris was unable to display the *sōphrosunē* which he encouraged in his son. While Thyamis' upbringing (which Calasiris must be at least partially responsible for) has endowed him with qualities which ensured that he did not fall victim to Arsace's lust, his father was unable to overcome desire for Rhodopis, whose intentions towards him are not clearly demarcated even in Calasiris' own representation of these events.

The Platonic overtones of the comments about the eyes of the soul at 2.25 are developed further a little later in the passage, when the struggle between desire and reason is depicted in terms which clearly echo those present in the *Republic*:

... δικαστὴν ἐμαυτῷ τὸν λογισμὸν ἀναδείξας, φυγῇ κολάζω τὴν ἐπιθυμίαν ...

...I referred my case to the court of reason ... exile was the sentence I pronounced on my concupiscence ...

2.25.4

Repath has noted Heliodorus' use of Platonic language here, and makes the suggestion that although Calasiris is able to recognize and flee from his illicit desire, and his struggle is couched in philosophically loaded terms, he does not succeed in conquering his passion by will-power alone, which draws a negative comparison with Chariclea's consistently self-controlled sexual behaviour.[177] The emotional effect of the use of such language is clear: this is a difficult and painful struggle which Calasiris freely admits is too much for him. His limitations regarding self-control are not presented in terms of *sōphrosunē*, but instead in terms of *enkrateia*, which Heliodorus then bolsters by using the Platonic terminology of passion and reason. Calasiris' perspective cannot entail knowledge of Plato (he exists in a fiction set before the philosopher), but the primary narrator clearly wishes to embellish this passage with his philosophical terminology. *Sōphrosunē*'s omission supports Repath's recognition of the divergence between Calasiris' reaction to desire and that of the protagonists, in that Calasiris does not deserve to claim that he possessed *sōphrosunē* because his resort to fleeing the sight of the object of his desires demonstrates the lack of this virtue. While his *enkrateia* is overcome, *sōphrosunē* was perhaps never present. Terminology relating to the lower regions of the soul (appetitive and spirited) are also used of Arsace (7.4.2: θυμοῦ – against Petosiris; ἐπιθυμίαν – for Theagenes and Thyamis) and Oroondates (8.2.3 θυμοῦ καὶ ἐπιθυμίας on hearing about Arsace's deception and Chariclea's beauty) who, as Persians, seem to lack the *logistikon*. Calasiris' ethnicity is also a factor which is likely be one of the reasons why he does not seem to be *sōphrōn*, although Thyamis' apparent possession of the virtue counts against this theory.

1.5.5 Chariclea's zealous *sōphrosunē*

At the very beginning of the novel, we see a divinely beautiful girl and an injured and extremely attractive young man through the eyes of the bandits who discover them.[178] Soon after this, the unknown girl speaks, and, before we know her name, we know that she suggests the defence of *sōphrosunē* as one of the reasons for the slaughter of those around her (1.3.1).

> … ὅσοι δὲ πρὸς ἡμῶν, ἀμύνης νόμῳ καὶ ἐδικίας τῆς εἰς σωφροσύνην ὕβρεως πεπόνθατε …

> … but those killed by us have suffered by the law of self-defence and of retribution for outrage against chastity.

1.3.1

The reader becomes conscious of the centrality of *sōphrosunē* even prior to his knowledge of who this girl is and how she will fit into this novel. While her stunning beauty could give away the fact that she is the female protagonist to any experienced reader of the genre,[179] we must now allow the narrative to lead us to the truth about exactly who she is and what has happened to her. Her opening statement is paradigmatic as the first of numerous references to this virtue in relation to Chariclea. It is analeptic of this girl's experience and of the *histoire*. The external analepsis is also an internal prolepsis: this statement will only be explained by events narrated by Calasiris at the end of the fifth book of this novel. The complicated narrative structure ensures that immediately upon reading the speech at 1.3.1, the reader is potentially hooked: fascinated by this girl with divine beauty, her handsome companion, and her apparent defence of *sōphrosunē*.

While the defence of her *sōphrosunē* referred to above functions as a form of self-defence, it soon becomes clear that there is more zeal involved in Chariclea's possession of this virtue. Chariclea, whom the narrator has not yet named, laments to Apollo at 1.8.3, and this is the first occasion on which she expresses the depth of her commitment to *sōphrosunē*:

> Καὶ ποῖ ταῦτα στήσεις; Εἰ μὲν εἰς θάνατον ἀνύβριστον, ἡδὺ τὸ τέλος, εἰ δὲ με γνώσεταί τις αἰσχρῶς, ἣν μηδέπω μηδὲ Θεαγένης, ἐγὼ μὲν ἀγχόνῃ προλήψομαι τὴν ὕβριν, καθαρὰν ἐμαυτὴν ὥσπερ φυλάττω καὶ μέχρι θανάτου φυλάξασα καὶ καλὸν ἐντάφιον τὴν σωφροσύνην ἀπενεγκαμένη·

> Where will you end this? If it is in an inviolate death, then my end will be sweet. But if someone is to know me shamefully – whom even Theagenes has not yet known – then I shall forestall the outrage with a rope, preserving myself as pure as I now preserve myself, even unto death, and winning a fine shroud in my chastity.

She and Theagenes have been taken captive by the bandits, and she bemoans her lot in a similar vein to other novelistic heroines, such as Callirhoe and Anthia.[180] While this kind of lamentation is familiar to the reader of novels, this is not straightforward generic conformity, because implicit in examples from Chariton, Xenophon of Ephesus and Achilles Tatius is the reader's recognition of the events lamented which have already been narrated in the *récit*. This is not the case here: this is the first we have heard of these experiences. The passage thus allows the reader some insight into the immediate past experiences of this mysterious couple. I have referred already to the implications of this speech for our view of Theagenes,[181] but the implications for Chariclea's characterization are clear: she is determined to die with her *sōphrosunē* preserved rather than suffer any sexual *hubris*, which demonstrates a strong commitment to the virtue, which is expressed as something she exercises even in relation to Theagenes. The wish not to be raped or coerced into sex by threats does not mark the girl out as unusually preoccupied with *sōphrosunē*, but her expressed intention to kill herself to avoid such violation, and her view of *sōphrosunē* as a 'fine shroud' does. Threats of suicide are not unusual in the genre, but they are usually made by both heroes and heroines in relation to their forced separation from their beloveds. The overt emphasis on *sōphrosunē* in this girl's speech firmly places the virtue at the heart of her self-representation.[182] It is significant that Theagenes, who subsequently warns her not to admonish Apollo in this way (1.8.4), is the only one present to hear this speech (the guard, who turns out to be Cnemon, is there, but asleep), with its clear communication of her ethical stance and her emotional predicament.[183] Chariclea perhaps intends, in the midst of her fervour, to remind Theagenes that should he make any sexual advances, she will reject them, which would fit well with her subsequent behaviour depicted at 5.4, temporally close to the events depicted at 1.8.3.

It is not until well into the second book that we begin to perceive Chariclea's motivation. Calasiris is narrating his adventures to Cnemon and there is partial explanation at 2.33.4–5, when Charicles tells Calasiris about how his adopted daughter Chariclea values her virginity with a religious zeal:

> ... ἀπηγόρευται γὰρ αὐτῇ γάμος καὶ παρθενεύειν τὸν πάντα βίον διατείνεται καὶ τῇ Ἀρτέμιδι ζάκορον ἑαυτὴν ἐπιδοῦσα θήραις τὰ πολλὰ σχολάζει καὶ ἀσκεῖ τοξείαν ... ἐπανατείνεται ἐκθειάζουσα μὲν παρθενίαν καὶ ἐγγὺς ἀθανάτων ἀποφαίνουσα, ἄχραντον καὶ ἀκήρατον καὶ ἀδιάφθορον ὀνομάζουσα, Ἔρωτα δὲ καὶ Ἀφροδίτην καὶ πάντα γαμήλιον θίασον ἀποσκορακίζουσα ...

> ... she has renounced marriage and is determined to stay a virgin all her life; she has dedicated herself as a sacred servant to Artemis, spends most of her time in the hunt and practises archery ... deifying virginity and proclaiming it close to the immortals, giving it the titles of unstained, untainted, uncorrupted, and cursing to damnation Erōs and Aphrodite and the whole nuptial company.

While this explains a commitment to virginity, it is not expressed in terms relating to *sōphrosunē*. At this point, as Charicles understands it, Chariclea sees virginity as sacrosanct and rejects marriage and everything related to it. This stands in contrast to her apparent acceptance of the idea of marriage at 1.25, which indicates that a change of heart is to come and the reader can surmise that this change is brought about by Theagenes' appearance in her life.

The absence of terms relating to *sōphrosunē* in the passage quoted above must first be considered in terms of focalization. These words are Charicles', related by the primary narrator via Calasiris, and this considerable distancing from

Chariclea's own assertions should alert the reader to the motivations of the three filters through which the girl's views are conveyed. Charicles is motivated by a need to persuade Calasiris to help him overcome Chariclea's marital resistance with Egyptian spells. He wants her to marry his 'pleasant' (ἀστείῳ) nephew (2.33.4), and presumably produce heirs and ensure a secure future for himself. Therefore, he presents Chariclea's commitment to virginity as being outside normality, and as something which she has made abnormally precious.[184] *Sōphrosunē* is not part of his representation because it would imply that the girl is virtuous rather than fanatical. Calasiris and the primary narrator may be keen to convey that Chariclea's view of virginity is not grounded in a *sōphrōn* approach to life but is based on a lack of experience of love and a consequent disregard for its meaning and benefits. Therefore, before she understands why sex is tempting, and desire is hard to resist, has her adherence to virginity anything to do with *sōphrosunē*? Is Chariclea's abstinence in fact like that of Hippolytus or Habrocomes, in that she bases it on a fundamental misapprehension about what constitutes a virtuous lifestyle?[185] Hippolytus' mistake is in his dismissal of Aphrodite,[186] and Habrocomes brings about his misfortunes due to a similar impiety, but regarding Erōs, rather than Aphrodite.[187] In Charicles' description of Chariclea's reverence for virginity, it seems that she makes a similar misjudgement in that she rejects Erōs and Aphrodite, and the reader might expect some form of erotic revenge, along the lines of that found in both the *Hippolytus* and the *Ephesiaca*. However, if Erōs wreaks revenge on Chariclea for this early anti-erotic stance by causing her intense desire for Theagenes, then Calasiris, despite implying his knowledge of divine intentions elsewhere,[188] does not make this explicit in his narrative, although he does refer to Erōs as the most powerful of the gods at 4.10.5.[189]

The thematic connection to the *Hippolytus* is emphasized by Heliodorus' use of the term ἀκήρατος to describe Chariclea's view of virginity. Ἀκήρατος is a key word in Hippolytus' speech in honour of Artemis (73–87: the term is used twice, at 73 and 76), and is also used by Theseus as he chides Hippolytus for his claim to be *sōphrōn* (at 949). Chariclea, according to Charicles, did not mention *sōphrosunē* or *aidōs* in relation to her praise of the *parthenia* which she calls ἀκήρατος. I have already mentioned the factor of focalization in this indirect speech, which may explain the absence of terminology directly related to *sōphrosunē*. However, this could also be explained by Heliodorus' awareness that his readers will recall the similar rejection of marriage and sex by Euripides' Hippolytus along with his devotion to Artemis, and then pick up on the allusive use of ἀκήρατος. Given the way in which it is loaded with ethical import in the tragedy, the necessity to spell out the role of *aidōs* and *sōphrosunē* in relation to Chariclea's approach to life, or how she views that approach, becomes less important: the allusive use of this term acts in place of any explicit emphasis on *sōphrosunē* or *aidōs*.

Heliodorus' method of distancing the reader from a clear view of Chariclea at 2.33 further aligns this passage with Euripides' *Hippolytus*, where the audience receive their first view of Hippolytus from Aphrodite in the Prologue. Both Aphrodite and Charicles present a view of Hippolytus and Chariclea which is affected by their respective motivations. In Aphrodite's case she has been insulted by Hippolytus' overt disrespect and states how she must take vengeance. On a far more bathetic level, Charicles is affronted by Chariclea's disregard for marriage: this endangers his plans for her future and his own familial security, and he is determined to make Calasiris help him. The similar distancing techniques, and the invited contrasts between these representations imbue the passage at 2.33 with a layer of irony: the tragic potentialities which are invoked can never be realized in this genre, and Chariclea's *sōphrosunē* will allow her to love, and to be happy to do so, an experience which is, of course, denied Hippolytus.

At 4.10.2–3, Chariclea still resists expressing how she feels truthfully to Calasiris, who has revealed that he has the power to know everything anyway. Here, Chariclea's excuses for not admitting the cause of her illness involve shame, and this is linked to her view of virginity as sacred:

... ἔασὸν με **σιωπῶσαν** δυστυχεῖν, αὐτὸς ὡς βούλει γνωρίσας τὴν **νόσον**, καὶ τὴν γοῦν **αἰσχύνειν** κερδαίνειν, **κρύπτουσαν** ἃ καὶ πάσχειν **αἰσχρὸν** καὶ ἐκλαλεῖν **αἰσχρότερον**. Ὡς ἐμέ γε λυπεῖ μὲν καὶ ἡ **νόσος** ἀκμάζουσα, πλέον δὲ τὸ μὴ κρατῆσαι τῆς **νόσου** τὴν ἀρχὴν ἀλλ᾽ ἡττηθῆναι πάθους ἀπειρημένου μὲν ἐμοὶ τὸν πρὸ τούτου πάντα χρόνον λυμαινομένου δὲ καὶ μέχρις ἀκοῆς τὸ παρθενίας ὄνομα σεμνότατον.

... allow me to endure my misfortune in silence, and at least spare myself disgrace, by keeping secret things which it is shameful to suffer but more shameful to divulge. How I am vexed by the sickness which is at its height, but even more by not having overcome the sickness at the outset, but having succumbed to a passion which had been renounced by me throughout all time previous to this, and the merest mention of which insults the most august name of virginity.

4.10.2–3

This is a significant speech, demonstrating Chariclea's continuing wish to present herself as committed to virginity, even though her central emotional resistance is now overthrown by desire. Calasiris ensures that his narrative has cogency: the content of the speech picks up on Charicles' picture of Chariclea at 2.33. The sentiments expressed here lie behind Chariclea's extreme ill-health, and explain her continuing fervour in regard to her views on sexual desire, which are present in the primary narrative too. While her early commitment to virginity is conveyed differently from her later *sōphrosunē*, there is a common strain of inflexibility underlying both approaches.

Here, at 4.10, she sees her inward desire as shameful, the expression of which would be more shameful still. She feels shame although she is not aware that anyone else knows what shames her, but she knows that making someone aware of it would lead to further shame. Two levels of shame are evoked: that caused by the judgement of the self and that caused by the judgement of the other. Further, it is not just that another's knowledge would add to her shame, it is that her voicing of her predicament would make her affliction worse: she would feel more culpable if she admitted how she feels.

The emotional tone and terminology which is used in this speech of Chariclea's is strongly evocative of that used by Phaedra in her famous speech at *Hippolytus*, 373–430: Phaedra's entire speech focuses on sexual virtue, reputation and female transgression of both, but it is particularly the section on how she viewed her choices in her predicament (391–405) which is important here. There is very similar emphasis on shame, silence and the efforts to hide lovesickness, with verbal parallels: (note the terms which I have highlighted in the passage from Heliodorus above) κρύπτω and νόσος at 393; νόσος is repeated by Phaedra at 405; σιγᾶν at 393; αἰσχρά occurs at 404. The central purpose of Phaedra's speech is to tell of her resolve to die and its unimpeachable logic: her decision forms the ethical highpoint of her self-knowledge. Her fear of having witnesses for her shameful deeds and her awareness of the infamous nature of the deed and the sickness (for which we can read desire for sex with Hippolytus) are indicative of her prioritizing of reputation. However, this is no vain concentration on how one appears to others: the effect on those close to the guilty perpetrator of these αἰσχρά is most important to her, as expressed in the final portion of this speech (419–430).[190] It is Phaedra's failure to carry through this decision that allows the tragedy its awful denouement. As Kovacs recognizes, Phaedra's *aidōs* is what governs this decision, and it is also what makes her suffer following her madness (244) and submit to the supplication of the nurse (335), both of which allow Aphrodite's revenge its full scope.[191] Chariclea's *aidōs* also governed her speech, as the repeated use of terms with the αἰσχ- root show. The reader of Heliodorus, recognizing the parallels in the emotions and perspectives of these two characters, is aware of the subsequent divergence of these parallels. A significant intention of Heliodorus' use of Phaedra's sentiment in this speech from Chariclea is subtly to subvert the heroine's anxiety: the reader's superior awareness of Chariclea's future relationship with Theagenes (as narrated in Book 1) comes into play here. In addition, Heliodorus allows Chariclea's speech this common ground with Phaedra's not in order to condemn Chariclea to the same level of self-punishment that the Euripidean heroine indulges in and inflicts upon herself, but in order to demonstrate that a truly *sōphrōn* soul needs guidance when afflicted by *erōs*. As with the earlier evocation of Hippolytus in Chariclea's attitude towards marriage, this allusion to Phaedra highlights the generic differences in terms of how desire is represented and in terms of how it is resolved, while adding depth to Chariclea's commitment to *sōphrosunē*.[192]

This psychological situation is exacerbated by Chariclea's belief in the sanctity of virginity. She indicates that before now she has not experienced this passion, which emphasizes her lack of experience and therefore understanding of the desire she now feels. Finally, her mention of the 'most august name of virginity' provides the climax to her speech and it is this closing statement which marks the end of this phase of her life: following Calasiris' response and the revelations to come about her origins, Chariclea's zealous religious perspective will alter, with *sōphrosunē* becoming overt and displacing virginity in the psyche of this girl, allowing the prospect of marriage to the one she desires to become part of her *raison d'être*. However, it also remains the case that Chariclea's enthusiasm in preserving her sexual virtue loses none of its vehemence in the remainder of this novel.

Two occasions at which Chariclea diplays the vehemence discussed above occur at 8.9.13, when Chariclea is sentenced to burn but the flames resist her, and at 10.9.3, when, again facing death, she leaps on the virginity-testing gridiron which should seal her fate, but, as she well knows, will not.[193] Some of this imagery seems to echo early Christian texts, as I will discuss. At 8.9.13, Chariclea has been sentenced to death by a furiously jealous Arsace on a trumped-up murder charge. She eagerly confesses to the charges laid against her and invents more in order to guarantee her death, rather than endure further agonies sent by fate (8.9.12). She is to be burned at the stake and now, in full view of the assembled populace of Memphis, the flames refuse to burn her.[194] She moves towards the fire, but to no avail. There is repeated use of light imagery in this scene (ἐπιφαιδρυνομένην, and two rare terms: περιαυγάζεσθαι, περιαυγάσματος), indicating that Chariclea's beauty is illuminated by the flames. The final image the reader is given concerning this miraculous development is as follows:

... οἷον ἐν πυρίνῳ θαλάμῳ νυμφευομένην.

... like a bride in a chamber of flame.

8.9.13

This phrase seems strange in this context: why is Chariclea 'like a bride', as she stands in this 'chamber of flame'? This could work as an analepsis of the earlier death by fire of Charicles' natural daughter on her wedding night (2.29.4: ... πυρὸς τοῖς θαλάμοις ἐμπεσόντος ...), contrasting the two daughters of Charicles while suggesting an ironic connection: the fire killed the married daughter, but the unmarried daughter escapes death and looks like a bride, which she will later become. This image, then, looks both back to Charicles' daughter's death, which was narrated, and forward to Charicles' other daughter's marriage, which is not narrated. The horrific but plausible fate of the first daughter is contrasted with the glorious but implausible fate of the second, but both involve marriage.

There was another occasion when Chariclea seemed to be in a bridal chamber: Pelorus sees her in her finery on the ship at 5.31.2 (... σχῆμα παστάδος ἀπομιμούμενα ...),[195] and it is notable that both occasions involve light imagery, depicted with almost identical terminology (5.31.2: καταυγάζουσαν ... τἆλλα περὶ αὐτὴν φαιδρυνόμενα; 8.9.13: περιαυγάζεσθαι ... ἐπιφαιδρυνομένην ... περιαυγάσματος). Each instance is deceptive: Chariclea is not actually in a bridal chamber, and is not actually a bride. The first, at 5.31, is designed to deceive Pelorus into enacting mutiny so that he can marry Chariclea, and the second displays Chariclea's beauty as a bride seemingly to encourage onlookers to perceive her true destiny. While Chariclea's *sōphrosunē* is not mentioned here, it is present by association: her implied marriage is the *telos* of her *sōphrōn* life.

The way in which the fire resists burning her recalls a similar event in the *Acts of Paul and Thecla* (Chapter 22), when Thecla is condemned to be burnt and a storm is sent from heaven and extinguishes the flames.[196] Just prior to this event, when Thecla is brought to trial, her mother demands that she be burnt as one 'that is no bride': Thecla is to be executed because of her transgression of her betrothal to Thamyris.[197] If Heliodorus is intending his reader to recall this episode then the reference to Chariclea as a bride could be an indication of the essential difference between these two virgins: one is never to marry and will dedicate her life to Christ; the other will marry, but only after enduring trials which re-emphasize her *sōphrosunē*. Chariclea has already suggested that the promise of marriage and the way in which she pledges herself to Theagenes allow her to be *sōphrōn* even while in love (1.25), and here, in the midst of a miracle, the narrator presents her as that *sōphrōn* bride. While Heliodorus presents us with an event which seems Christian in tone, the contrast between the two genres is brought out by this use of allusion.[198]

At 10.9.3, Chariclea is again depicted by the use of light imagery (... ἀκτῖσι κατάπαστον ... (... embroidered with rays ...); ... τῷ ... κάλλει τότε πλέον ἐκλάμποντι καταστράπτουσα ... (... blazing with then more dazzling beauty ...)) which evokes the earlier execution scene. This is, of course, apt. Chariclea is to be sacrificed if proved virginal: for the second time she is to die, but this time there is no charge laid against her: rather, her very innocence condemns her. She has an unerring confidence that her destiny will be fulfilled and she fearlessly leaps onto the gridiron that will prove her chaste. Now, rather than looking like a bride, her radiant appearance makes her seem like an image of a goddess:

> ... καὶ πρὸς τοῦ σχήματος τῆς στολῆς ἀγάλματι θεοῦ πλέον ἢ θνητῇ γυναικὶ προσεικαζομένη ...

> ... in her magnificent robe she seemed more like an image of a goddess than a mortal woman ...

10.9.3

De Temmerman suggests that Chariclea's apparel brings to mind her 'Artemisian chastity' and 'Apollonian resourcefulness',[199] by recalling the earlier points at which she dressed in this Delphic robe (1.1; 5.29). The confidence with which she displays her beauty and *sōphrosunē* is, therefore, supported by the confidence she now has in her ability to manipulate situations to her own advantage. Also, in contrast to Theagenes' doubt of the worth of *sōphrosunē*,[200] Chariclea's bold display is indicative of the extent to which she defines herself as *sōphrōn*. The narrator's comment about the crowd's amazement that such a beautiful woman can also be pure of sexual taint is followed by this statement:

> ... ἔχειν ἐνεδείκνυτο σωφροσύνη πλέον ἢ τῇ ὥρᾳ κοσμούμενον ...

> ... visible proof had been furnished that ... the greatest ornament to her beauty was chastity ...

10.9.4

Here, *sōphrosunē* is seen to embellish Chariclea's attractions, but the crowd's focalization seems to belie Chariclea's intent. By equating *sōphrosunē* with a cosmetic decoration, the narrator fails to emphasize that, for Chariclea, this virtue is central to who she is: she displays it proudly not to add to her allure, but to underscore its primacy as a factor which should aid her identification. Her mother is watching: the very woman who entreated her daughter to value *sōphrosunē* above all else (4.8.7).[201] Chariclea's zeal at this point, then, is evidently exercised with a view to bringing about the final recognition which should save her and Theagenes. While the situation is not resolved by her actions here, it is still the case that Chariclea's attention-seeking is not founded on vanity, but instead is representative of her deeply held conviction that *sōphrosunē* will be rewarded in Ethiopia, not with death, as Theagenes supposes,[202] but with the longed for *telos* involving homecoming and, finally, marriage to her beloved Theagenes.

Finally in this section, I will turn to look at how Chariclea's version of events is veiled by the narrator at 10.33.4,[203] something which again draws attention to how closely guarded Chariclea's *sōphrosunē* is. Book 10 is prolonged by the confusion caused by Chariclea's virginity and by her claim that she has a husband in the equally chaste Theagenes. When Chariclea perceives that the only way to resolve this confusion is to speak truthfully to her mother, it is said that:

... πρὸς τὰ καιριώτερα τῶν διηγημάτων ὥρμησεν ...

... she proceeded straight to the heart of her tale ...

10.33.4

This secret interchange between daughter and mother is not revealed to the reader, but it is effective. Presumably, Chariclea reports the events which have already been narrated, which partially explains why it need not be repeated. However, 'the heart of her tale' surely involves the way in which she has been consistently *sōphrōn*, yet has promised herself to Theagenes. I suggest that the problem of her virginity and her relationship with Theagenes is resolved by an understanding of this *sōphrōn* commitment. The prolonged nature of Book 10 alerts the reader to the fact that although Chariclea displays her *sōphrosunē* at 10.9.3 with the apparent belief in its power to resolve the situation, this is not how the circumstances are brought to a conclusion: much more in the way of explanation is required by the Ethiopians. This indicates how the complexity of Chariclea's life must be gradually revealed. As readers, we have come to accept several 'impossible' facts about this girl. She is white, but born of black parents. That has been explained by Sisimithres, and Hydaspes now accepts this. She is committed to a man, yet is not married and has not had sex with him. Only she can properly explain this, but the reader is not given access to this very personal explanation. Chariclea has been too modest, too *sōphrōn*, to express how she loves Theagenes like a husband, yet has no sexual history with him. Now she is forced to speak, but, as she said to Calasiris at 4.10.2–3, to speak of how she has been engulfed by passion is to make it more shameful. If she has changed her mind on this (which could be surmised from her willingness to speak to her mother), the narrator at 10.33.4 still allows her words to be obscured in order that her most deeply felt emotions, her love for Theagenes and the *sōphrōn* way in which she has controlled that desire, remain hers to express away from the crowd, and away from the reader. However, in contrast to Ormand's claims regarding the ambiguity of Chariclea's virginity from the perspective of the reader,[204] I suggest that although we are not party to Chariclea's explanation to her mother, we are witnesses of Chariclea's exceptional ability to retain her *sōphrosunē* throughout this complex narrative, and this should leave us in no doubt about her *sōphrōn* and, therefore, virginal status.

1.5.6 Chariclea: defending *sōphrosunē* with manipulation

In this section, I will discuss how Chariclea can be seen to manipulate situations for the purpose of defending her *sōphrosunē*. The previous section established the zeal with which she displays the virtue and the way in which it is the crucial part of her psychological characterization: here it will become clear that she must deceive or, at least, mislead in order to preserve this much-valued *sōphrosunē*.

Chariclea's manipulation of those around her is evident at 4.18,[205] where she successfully convinces her guardian to make Theagenes promise to respect her virginity.[206] Here is her speech to Calasiris:

Ὦ πάτερ, ἀδικίας … ἀρχὴ τοῦτο μᾶλλον δὲ προδοσίας, εἰ μόνην οἰχήσῃ με καταλιπών, Θεαγένει τὰ καθ᾽ ἡμᾶς ἐπιτρέψας, οὐδὲ ἐννοήσεις ὡς ἄπιστον εἰς φυλακὴν ἐραστὴς εἰ γένοιτο τῶν ἐρωτικῶν ἐγκρατὴς καὶ οὐχ ἥκιστα τῶν καταιδέσαι δυναμένων μονούμενος. Ἀναφλέγεται γάρ, ὡς οἶμαι, πλέον ὅταν ἄνευ προμάχου βλέπῃ τὸ ποθούμενον προκείμενον, ὥστε οὐ πρότερόν σε μεθίημι πρὶν δή μοι τῶν τε παρόντων ἕνεκα καὶ ἔτι μᾶλλον τῶν μελλόντων ὅρκῳ πρὸς Θεαγένην τὸ ἀσφαλὲς ἐμπεδωθείη ὡς οὔτε ὁμιλήσει τὰ Ἀφροδίτης πρότερον ἢ γένος τε καὶ οἶκον τὸν ἡμέτερον ἀπολαβεῖν ἤ, εἴπερ τοῦτο κωλύει δαίμων, ἀλλ᾽ οὖν γε πάντως βουλομένην γυναῖκα ποιεῖσθαι ἢ μηδαμῶς.

Father … this will be the beginning of iniquity, or rather of betrayal, if you go off leaving me alone, entrusting my safety to Theagenes and do not reflect that a lover is something not to be trusted for protection if he gains possession of the object of his love, particularly when he is isolated from those who can put him to shame. He blazes more with passion, I think, when he sees the object of his desire offered up to him without a defender, so I am not letting you go until, both for the present and even more so for the future, my safety is assured against Theagenes with an oath that either he will not have the intercourse of Aphrodite with me until I regain my race and home, or, if a *daimōn* is preventing this, he will make me his wife with my full consent or not at all.

4.18.4–5

This speech does not contain any direct reference to why she suspects Theagenes is likely to make advances which would compromise her *sōphrosunē*. Rather, she resorts to generalizations about lovers and the way in which they react to being alone with the object of their desires. This suggests that Chariclea has perhaps learnt of the theory of such behaviour while among learned men in Delphi (2.33), but it is also perhaps indicative of her own emotions: she could be finding the thought of being alone with Theagenes frightening because of her own desire, and she now assumes that he must feel the same, and she does not think that he is committed to *sōphrosunē* to the extent that she is.[207] Her view of male desire is couched in terms referring to *enkrateia* and *aidōs*. By using the term *enkratēs* in this context, there is some irony: the self-mastery implied by the term is conspicuously absent in this generalized lover. *Aidōs* has its gravitas somewhat reduced here too: it is represented in the use of the term καταιδέσαι as something which is only necessary when witnessed by others. Again, as she continues, Chariclea presents a sentitious image of the male lover which has little relation to Theagenes as he is represented in this text. Here, the lover is aroused by his beloved being vulnerable and undefended, implying an almost animalistic desire. It is clear that Chariclea uses this sentitious picture of the male lover because this is likely to persuade Calasiris that she is in danger. She does not know whether Theagenes is like this or not, and she is taking no chances. She expresses the potential danger to her virtue in the strongest terms. This is a speech self-consciously engineered to persuade, so is not necessarily representative of Chariclea's true suspicions regarding Theagenes, but we can still accept that she is by nature suspicious of male ardour.

Chariclea continues by telling Calasiris exactly what she wants: she has used emotive language to persuade him of the need for action, and now she outlines her demands. Calasiris then tells Cnemon that he marvelled at this speech (4.18.6), which alerts the reader to the different narrative levels at work. Is this rhetorical ability really Chariclea's? Calasiris uses sentitious speech elsewhere in order to persuade (e.g. 3.7–8, to Charicles), so we could be seeing his colouring of Chariclea's words here, to maximize the impact.[208] He could be admiring his own narrative ability. The primary narrator is also capable of lapsing into generalizations (e.g. 8.5.1), so Chariclea's words can be seen to be coming through a hierarchy of narration, and it is not a simple matter to assert precisely who is responsible for them. However, Chariclea's rhetorical ability is represented so often in both Calasiris' narrative and the primary narrative, that her performance of such a speech in order to protect her *sōphrosunē* is not impossible. While Calasiris' ability to recreate speeches word for word can be called into question, it is perhaps not altogether implausible that he recalls the gist of the speech she made and now ensures that it sounds as persuasive as he found it at the time, rather than completely reinventing it. Chariclea once more demonstrates, albeit through two levels of narration, that she is able to use language creatively in order to protect her from a situation which is potentially threatening to her *sōphrosunē*. She also seems to prioritize this need for protection over her love and respect for Theagenes: the collateral damage of her manipulative speech (as seen in Theagenes' reaction; also, see 2.25, with discussion at section 1.5.1 above) does not seem to be a factor which Chariclea considers.

Another significant passage for this discussion regarding Chariclea's manipulative defence of her *sōphrosunē* is at 7.25, when she suggests that Theagenes might submit to Arsace's wishes in order to prevent her (Chariclea's) marriage to Achaemenes.[209] To be clear, here are her words, in response to Theagenes, who asks what plan can prevent their unions with Arsace and Achaemenes:

> Μίαν . . . κατανεύσας τὴν ἑτέραν, τὴν κατ᾽ ἐμὲ διακωλύσεις.

> One only . . . By consenting to the one you will be able to prevent mine.

7.25.6

This is a comment born of desperation, but it seems clear where Chariclea's priorities lie: she would rather allow Theagenes to degrade himself with Arsace than allow her own *sōphrosunē* to be endangered. However, considering the events which follow, this comment could be indicative of even greater manipulation on Chariclea's part. Theagenes is spurred into action by this display of defeatism in his beloved's speech. He now gains Arsace's promise to release Chariclea from her betrothal to Achaemenes by revealing the true nature of the protagonists' relationship, and by promising to submit to Arsace's wishes in the future (7.26). Does Chariclea perceive the need to shock Theagenes into action? He actually does as she suggests, but his submission to Arsace is a deception (which indicates that perhaps this is what Chariclea was aiming at): he is playing for time, and Chariclea's suggestion has, albeit indirectly, brought about a temporary respite for the pair. There are two different levels of manipulation on Chariclea's part here: on the surface she seems ready to allow Theagenes to suffer indignity on her behalf, but beneath this statement lies the intention to make her beloved act with duplicity in order to save both of them from results which would undermine their relationship and their *sōphrosunē*.

I will now consider how Thisbe can be read as an antitype to Chariclea, and how her disregard for sexual morality throws Chariclea's *sōphrosunē* into sharp relief, while their mutual intelligence suggests some further implications for how we may view Chariclea's manipulative tendencies. Morgan makes a clear and convincing argument regarding how Heliodorus invites the direct comparison between the two characters,[210] and I will not reproduce this here. It is enough to suggest the following scenes as evidence that readers should see the two women in parallel: events at 2.5, where it is discovered that the corpse thought to be Chariclea's is actually Thisbe's; the narrator's revelation at 5.4 that the woman who Cnemon thinks is Thisbe (or, at least, her ghost) is Chariclea; and the incident at 5.8, where Chariclea's willing participation in Nausicles' ruse involves her pretending to be Thisbe.

One element of characterization shared by Chariclea and Thisbe is their cleverness, although Thisbe's clearly does not succeed as Chariclea's does: she ends up dead. Thisbe's manipulative intelligence is particularly demonstrated in the episode related through four levels of narration, when the story she has told is conveyed by Charias to Cnemon, who then tells Chariclea and Theagenes, and which is, of course, narrated by the primary narrator. At 1.15, Thisbe perceives Demaenete's resentment towards her and so, in a pre-emptive strike, offers to 'help' her mistress, who is still suffering on account of her unrequited desire for the now-exiled Cnemon. Thisbe's plan is revealed as it happens, so that her ingenious plotting gradually becomes clear (1.15–1.17). The resulting death of Demaenete is already known to Cnemon, to his narratees, and to the reader, so the aim of this method of revealing Thisbe's designs seems to be to create tension, not about the outcome, but about the process, and it also highlights the machinations of this slave-girl. While Chariclea's intelligence is often used to protect her *sōphrosunē*, as we have seen, Thisbe's intentions in using manipulative means are purely self-serving: hers is a world where slaves must outwit their masters to survive, and she intends to do just that. While self-preservation is at the root of both women's displays of intelligence, Chariclea is often seen to prefer death to losing her *sōphrosunē*, in contrast to Thisbe's opportunistic sexual activity which often forms a part of her plotting or, pragmatically, her trade (1.11.3; 2.8.4). The contrast between these two representations of female intelligence, the one firmly based on a *sōphrōn* approach to life, the other founded on pragmatic self-preservation, implies that the reader is invited to consider not only how disparate these two characters are, but also how cleverness is not enough to preserve 'bad' characters, such as Thisbe. Their respective ends are justified in terms of the novel's morality. Thisbe must die as she has a flagrant disregard for sexual, and indeed, any other kind of propriety, and her plans bring about destructive consequences. Chariclea must be vindicated because she is *sōphrōn* and she loves one man with the aim of marrying him, and because she uses her intelligence and wisdom for 'good' purposes. By displaying Thisbe in this way, Heliodorus' alternative representation of female intelligence when used *without sōphrosunē* serves as a strong indication of how Chariclea's intelligence serves her *sōphrosunē*.

1.5.7 Chariclea: a *Phaedran* lover?

There are several places in Heliodorus' text where Platonic ideas are evoked, particularly with reference to the soul.[211] In this section, I will consider the role of Platonic allusion in the representation of Chariclea, where this affects our view of her *sōphrosunē*. At 4.4.4, Calasiris describes how Chariclea is defeated by her passion for Theagenes when she watches him win the foot race against Ormenus. Chariclea is waiting at the end of the track to award the winner the prize, and Theagenes collapses into her arms on achieving his victory (4.4.2). Chariclea's desire is re-awakened by this experience and Calasiris' description contains the following sententious statement:

> … Ἡ γὰρ τῶν ἐρωτικῶν ἀντίβλεψις ὑπόμνησις τοῦ πάσχοντος γίνεται καὶ ἀναφλέγαι τὴν διάνοιαν ἡ θέα καθάπερ ὕλη πυρὶ γινομένη.

> …For the mutual gaze of lovers is a reminder to the one suffering, and the sight inflames the thoughts, like fuel to a fire.

4.4.4

This passage seems to pick up on ideas from the *Phaedrus*:

> … ταὐτὸν δὴ πέπονθεν ἡ τοῦ πτεροφυεῖν ἀρχομένου ψυχή· ζεῖ τε καὶ ἀγανακτεῖ καὶ γαργαλίζεται φύουσα τὰ πτερά. ὅταν μὲν οὖν βλέπουσα πρὸς τὸ τοῦ παιδὸς κάλλος, ἐκεῖθεν μέρη ἐπιόντα καὶ ῥέοντ'—ἃ δὴ διὰ ταῦτα ἵμερος καλεῖται— δεχομένη [τὸν ἵμερον] ἄρδηταί τε καὶ θερμαίνηται, λωφᾷ τε τῆς ὀδύνης καὶ γέγηθεν·

> …such is the state affecting the soul of the man who is beginning to sprout wings – it throbs and aches and tickles as it grows its feathers. So when it gazes at the boy's beauty, and is nourished and warmed by receiving particles (μέρη)

which come to it in a flood (ῥέοντ᾽) from there – hence, of course, the name we give them, 'desire' (ἵμερος) – it experiences relief from its anguish and is filled with joy.

251c3–d1: trans. Rowe 1986

Socrates' theory about the way in which beauty coming through the eyes[212] directly nourishes the soul and precipitates the growth of its wings is important for an informed reading of Heliodorus' text. In Heliodorus, this passage at 4.4.4 is preceded by the race, as I have mentioned, and, prior to this (4.2.3), Theagenes, when dismissing Calasiris' objections to him running in the race, suggests that the sight of Chariclea can give him wings (πτερῶσαι δύναται) and that Erōs is represented as winged by painters (τὸν Ἔρωτα πτεροῦσιν οἱ γράφοντες). A little further on, Chariclea is described when watching Theagenes running, and Calasiris suggests that it seemed to him that Chariclea's soul were raised up beside Theagenes, and she shared in his passion for the race (τῆς ψυχῆς τῷ Θεαγένει συνεξαιρμένης καὶ τὸν δρόμον συμπροθυμουμένης: 4.3.3). Together with the allusion to Phaedran ideas at 4.4.4, I think that there is significant playful engagement with aspects of Socrates' second speech in the *Phaedrus*: this section of the text implies that for Chariclea, the process of desire raises her soul and the sight of Theagenes' eyes nourishes her desire.

Chariclea's *sōphrosunē* or, at least, her commitment to virginity, is challenged by the sight of Theagenes, and the sententious passage at 4.4.4 makes this clear. Also, the nourishing of the soul which is implied by the references to wings and souls at 4.2.3 and 4.3.3 suggests that for Chariclea, viewing her beloved is as powerful an erotic experience as that depicted in the *Phaedrus* in the passage quoted above. It is important to note that at this point in the narrative, Chariclea is still responding to the onset of desire, in a similar way to the lover in Socrates' speech, and the real test for her *sōphrosunē* is in how she proceeds from now on. Desire is being presented at this juncture, particularly with the Platonic overtones, as something which has the potential to give wings to the soul. While the *telos* of desire in the *Aethiopica* is, we assume, radically different from that evoked in the *Phaedrus* (married love involving implied consummation, rather than a love aimed at philosophizing and the denial of sexual consummation), it remains likely that Heliodorus invites consideration of the process of desire in the light of Platonic theory as represented in the *Phaedrus*. The implications for Chariclea's *sōphrosunē* are twofold: first, it is implied that she must learn how to withstand physical temptation, despite the power of erotic desire which besets her, just as this is encouraged by Socrates' second speech; second, and the reader can acknowledge this on a second reading, she will come to show an inherent tendency to behave with *sōphrosunē*, and while the desire which she experiences will come to have marriage as its aim, there are parallels between her approach to love and that advocated in the *Phaedrus*.

There remains a hint of doubt regarding what does actually follow the wedding of Chariclea and Theagenes. Much has been made of how conclusive Heliodorus' ending really is,[213] and another element complicates matters further. There are ten instances in Heliodorus' text where there appear to be puns on the name of the *Phaedrus*.[214] The final one occurs in the very last sentence of the novel (apart from the auctorial signature), and could hint at doubt over what follows:

> ... τῶν ἐπὶ τῷ γάμῳ μυστικωτέρων κατὰ τὸ ἄστυ φαιδρότερον τελεσθησομένων.

> ... the more mystic parts of the wedding ritual were to be performed with greater magnificence.

10.41.3

It is plausible that, as the translation conveys (it is not easy to translate in a way which successfully retains the potential ambiguity of the term, φαιδρότερον), the use of this term could be unambiguously indicating the magnificent nature of the marriage rites which follow. However, given Morgan and Repath's observations, and given the wider engagement with Plato's *Phaedrus* as discussed above, is Heliodorus indicating how marriage can be *Phaedran* when it involves such a *sōphrōn* wife as Chariclea? Marital sex, if we assume that this follows the wedding, will not, it seems, disrupt the *sōphrosunē* of Chariclea, and Heliodoran love matches Platonic love in its capacity to include regard for *sōphrosunē*.

*

Heliodorus' representation of *sōphrosunē* is similar to that of the earlier Greek-novel authors in its semantic range, which covers sexual restraint and the motivation behind chastity, and only very occasionally implies a more general self-control.[215] However, in his characterization of his protagonists, Heliodorus presents his readers with a hero who is subordinate to the heroine, in terms of how central he is to the plot, in terms of the amount of direct speech he is given, and in terms of how committed he is to maintaining *sōphrosunē* in his relationship with the heroine. In this section, I discussed the ways in which Theagenes is subtly and, in places, opaquely characterized in relation to his *sōphrosunē*, with the result that it is very difficult to gauge exactly what Theagenes feels and thinks about the virtue. He never defines his own behaviour by use of σωφρ- root terms, suggesting, in contrast to Chariclea, that he does not view his own thoughts or actions in this light. What does emerge from close reading is that Theagenes, in contrast to Chariclea, is represented as primarily committed to Chariclea, and that his *sōphrosunē* is secondary to his desire for his beloved. In places, he seems to challenge Chariclea's unquestioning adherence to practising *sōphrosunē*, namely when it seems to threaten their survival, which demonstrates a pragmatism that stands in opposition to Chariclea's attitude. For the other male characters within this text, *sōphrosunē* is not a prominent feature of their characterization, either explicitly or implicitly, but in the cases of Calasiris and Thyamis, the concepts of *enkrateia* and *sōphrosunē* have a significant role to play. Their respective possession of sexual self-control is couched in different terms, and this contrast in representation is important: for Calasiris, his *enkrateia* is challenged by his feelings of desire for the courtesan, Rhodopis; for Thyamis, his inherent *sōphrosunē* means that he is not susceptible to the allure of the lustful Arsace. In the discussion concerning Chariclea, the intensity which lies behind her *sōphrosunē*, which developed from an early religious commitment to virginity, and the various manipulative methods she employs to preserve it both illustrate how the virtue is not only central to her characterization, but *sōphrosunē* is also used to give her an ethical stance which goes beyond that of other protagonists in the genre. Thisbe, as Chariclea's opposite, is perhaps just as clever as the heroine, but this is not enough to ensure her survival: female intelligence is subordinate to *sōphrosunē* and it is only the combination of the two which allows their possessor to flourish. Chariclea's *sōphrosunē* is crucial to her characterization to the extent that the reader is given hints involving Platonic echoes which suggest she will always be *sōphrōn*: marriage will not change her in that respect.

2

Readerly *Sōphrosunē*: Reader as Voyeur

Readerly *sōphrosunē* has the potential to act as a tempering force on voyeuristic reactions to certain scenes in the texts: as the protagonists are often exposed to viewers within the text, who can have lustful or *sōphrōn* reactions, they are also exposed to the reader, whose reaction can involve *sōphrosunē* to varying degrees depending on the tone and nature of the narrative at these junctures. This chapter will be concerned with the extent to which readerly *sōphrosunē* tempers voyeurism,[1] a response which plays a major role in the reading process, particularly in those sections of the texts which put the protagonists and their beauty and sexual desirability on display. I will discuss this aspect in the novels of Chariton, Longus, Achilles Tatius and Heliodorus in the first four sections of this chapter, before considering the alignment of heroines with texts in those four novels in section 2.5.

2.1 Voyeurism in Chariton's *Callirhoe*

There are places in Chariton's *Callirhoe* where the reader has a certain amount of access to very private scenes involving major characters. What concerns me at this point is how the reader becomes a voyeur of specifically erotically charged moments, and how this is tempered, if at all, by *sōphrosunē*. A crucial passage comes at 2.2.2–3: Callirhoe, who is shy about revealing her body, reluctantly takes a bath, attended by the serving women of Dionysius' household. This description of Callirhoe's naked beauty focuses on her skin and flesh, how they look and feel to the maidservants:

… καὶ μᾶλλον ἀποδυσαμένης κατεπλάγησαν· ὥστε ἐνδεδυμένης αὐτῆς θαυμάζουσαι τὸ πρόσωπον ὡς θεῖον, <ἀ>πρόσωπον ἔδοξαν <τἄνδον> ἰδοῦσαι·[2] ὁ χρὼς γὰρ λευκὸς ἔστιλψεν εὐθύς μαρμαρυγῇ τινι ὅμοιον ἀπολάμπων· τρυφερὰ δὲ σάρξ, ὥστε δεδοικέναι μὴ καὶ ἡ τῶν δακτύλων ἐπαφὴ μέγα τραῦμα ποιήσῃ.[3]

... and they were struck with amazement all the more when she was undressed: as while she was dressed they marvelled at her face as though it were divine, but seeing what was hidden they thought she had no face; for her skin shone white, gleaming just like a sparkling surface, and her flesh was delicate, so that one was afraid lest even the the touch of one's fingers make a great wound.

The focalization through female servants seems to provide an instance where Callirhoe's beauty is not necessarily directly linked to her sexual attraction.[4] However, there is still the suggestion of objectification in the viewing of her form, aided by the forgetting of her face. Further, while the focalization seems to allow non-sexualized, and perhaps, a religiously informed admiration (when she is dressed they marvel at her face as if it is divine, and her body sparkles like a marble statue), this easily tips into titillation for the reader.[5] This is underlined by the potential wound on her skin, implying sexual wounding.

The text has been reconstructed based on similar phrasing in Plato's *Charmides* (154d), and this is very significant for this discussion, given the centrality of *sōphrosunē* in the Platonic dialogue, and the voyeuristic perspective of those looking at Charmides. This instance of voyeurism is potentially enhanced for the reader by the Platonic intertext (and I acknowledge that this argument is dangerous, based as it is on textual reconstruction), and a different and more sexually charged reading becomes viable. Here is the relevant passage in the *Charmides*:

Χαιρεφῶν καλέσας με, 'τί σοι φαίνεται ὁ νεανίσκος', ἔφη, 'ὦ Σώκρατες; οὐκ εὐπρόσωπος;' 'ὑπερφυῶς', ἦν δ' ἐγώ. 'οὗτος μέντοι', ἔφη, 'εἰ ἐθέλοι ἀποδῦναι, δόξει σοι ἀπρόσωπος εἶναι; οὕτως τὸ εἶδος πάγκαλός ἐστιν.'

Chaerephon called to me, 'How does the youth appear to you, Socrates?', he said, 'Is that not a fine face?' 'Exceedingly so', I replied. 'Yet, if he would agree to undress', he said, 'you would think he had no face, such is the perfect beauty of his form.'

154d

If Chariton had this passage in mind when describing Callirhoe in the bath, the consequences are significant: the maids' viewing of Callirhoe's beauty is eroticised further by this allusion to older men clearly finding the beautiful Charmides sexually arousing. Chaerephon's comment about Charmides' unseen beauty proves proleptic when Socrates glimpses the boy's body beneath his cloak and is inflamed (ἐφλεγόμην) with desire and is 'beside himself'[6] (οὐκέτ' ἐν ἐμαυτοῦ ἦν) (155d). Socrates' mastering of his passion demonstrates how he is in possession of *sōphrosunē*, which is about to be discussed in the subsequent dialogue, as Sprague notes.[7] Thus the viewing of a beautiful body, differentiated from facial beauty, causes a sexual reaction in Socrates, which he has to overcome with self-control. While the maidservants in *Callirhoe* are amazed rather than aroused by their view of the naked heroine, this intertext emphasizes that the reader may need to master himself just as Socrates does. The clear differentiation in scale of reaction between viewing the face or the body of someone beautiful is present in both texts, and surely Callirhoe, depicted as the most beautiful woman ever seen, is Charmides' equal as far as the power of nude beauty is concerned. Therefore, the reader needs to be as *sōphrōn* as Socrates in order to retain a balanced view of Callirhoe. The men who view Callirhoe in the text struggle to retain their self-control, and this is before they view her naked. The implications are serious for the reader who is susceptible to female beauty. Some readers will be like the maids – amazed, but not necessarily aroused. Others might well react like Socrates to his glimpse under Charmides' cloak: but whether they can then follow the Platonic example and regain self-restraint is very much dependent on the reader himself.

Towards the end of the narrative, Chaereas and Callirhoe have been reunited, and the narrator states, when the couple have retired (early) to the royal bedchamber on Aradus:

Τίς ἂν φράσῃ τὴν νύκτα ἐκείνην πόσων διηγημάτων μεστή, πόσων δὲ δακρύων ὁμοῦ καὶ φιλημάτων;

Who could depict that night filled with many stories, the many tears and and kisses just the same?

8.1.14

While this rhetorical question is designed self-consciously to draw attention to the inherent skill of the narrator,[8] it also invites the reader to imagine what happened on that night: tears, kisses and all. The narrative seems to avoid vulgarity by focusing on the narratorial recaps provided by the lovers for each other, before ending with an Odyssean quotation, which evokes the reunion of the hero and Penelope (8.1.14–17). There is once again, as with the bathing scene, the suggestion of a sexual frisson to the narrative. However, this is not fulfilled by what follows the question: the reader's voyeurism is not allowed to dominate. The narrator points her/him in the direction of voyeurism before correcting this by refocusing on the narrative. The reader is made aware that Chaereas and Callirhoe do not just have a conversation, but a veil is drawn over what follows their kisses. In this way, the narrator retains his *sōphrosunē* and this allows him to have sustained control over his narrative, and over the reader's voyeurism. By demonstrating his own ability to pull back from overt sexual suggestion, he also encourages *sōphrosunē* in his reader, but only after drawing back the curtain momentarily: *sōphrosunē* is only worth having if temptation is present. However, the very act of providing a suggestion of sexual frisson implies that the narrator allows the reader's imagination to be stirred: just as with the bathing scene discussed above, there are various readerly responses invited, and the scale of *sōphrosunē* depends on the individual reader.

Readerly voyeurism is a central concern at 6.4.5–6, where Erōs presents Artaxerxes and the reader with a sexy image of Callirhoe, aided by an allusion to an Odyssean simile comparing Nausicaa with Artemis. What concerns me in this section is the extent to which the allusion is intended for the implied reader, who, in recognizing it, should therefore understand how the allusion to Nausicaa affects this image of Callirhoe, and the extent to which this has an impact on the overall tone of the passage and, specifically, the reader's reaction to it.

This instance of voyeurism is different from the two described above in that there is no 'real' object of the voyeur here: what the reader 'sees' is an image put into Artaxerxes' imagination by Erōs. Indeed, at the beginning of his speech Erōs states:

... οἷον ἦν ἐνθάδε Καλλιρόην ἰδεῖν ...

... such a thing it would be to see Callirhoe here ...

Then, at the end of Erōs' description, we are given the King's reaction:

ταῦτα ἀναζωγραφῶν καὶ ἀναπλάττων ἐξεκαίετο σφόδρα.

Picturing and imagining these things he burned up fiercely.

Erōs' plan (to remind the King of the very thing which he is attempting to distract himself from) works. Voyeurism is at this point a natural reaction and readerly *sōphrosunē* will not necessarily be present in the immediate response to such a sexy scene. The reader might inadvertently find her/his desires aligning with Artaxerxes' as he imagines this version of Callirhoe, free of her constant *sōphrōn* assertions, and linked to a nubile Odyssean virgin. In addition, the fact that Erōs is once more described as φιλόνεικος/ φιλόνικος[9] suggests that, on a metaliterary level, the narrative force is continuing to seek disruption, just as the personified Love seeks to disrupt the emotions of Artaxerxes. This is particularly true if we read φιλόνεικος: if Erōs is 'strife-loving', rather than 'victory-loving' then his influence over events is differently perceived by the reader, with the consequence that his actions seem more vengeful towards his direct victim, Artaxerxes, but they might also appear to be demonstrative of his continuing desire to inflict turmoil on the text.

For the sake of balance, and in order to understand the different nuances at work in this passage, it is also worth considering that while the first-time reader should be subject to the above considerations, the *sōphrōn* reader, or a reader returning to the passage may well enter into a different appreciation of this episode. The reader is distanced from the image considerably: the narrator tells us what Erōs (who is within the King's mind) tells the King, who then imagines what has been suggested. The dual focalization allows the reader to experience the image from both perspectives: s/he understands Erōs' intention and Artaxerxes' reaction. The Odyssean quotation, surely intended to be recognized by the reader, even if not by the King, causes further distancing from the image. If this image of Callirhoe looks like Nausicaa who in turn looks like Artemis, then the multiplicity of imagery complicates the overall effect. The apparent availability inherent in the image, and strengthened by the allusion to Nausicaa, is also restricted by the allusion. Nausicaa, afterall, is only a **potential** wife for Odysseus: the potentiality is never realized. The reader, in recognizing this, can proleptically see that the King's suit will be unsuccessful, and, further, that Callirhoe's autonomy is not compromised. Erōs succeeds in deluding the King with this episode, but the reader is able to retain *sōphrosunē* through understanding the nuances brought about by the Odyssean allusion, and also because of the narrative distance from the imagery directed at the King. The alert reader is not necessarily reduced to a mere voyeur at this point. Rather, s/he appreciates the episode from a distance, observing the King's passion and its impetus with the superior knowledge that this is the closest Artaxerxes will come to obtaining his desire.

*

It is clear that while certain mores are suggested in Chariton's text, there is also a playfulness in how particular scenes are represented, meaning that the reader is not bound to follow a straight and narrow path through this narrative, and ensuring a multiplicity of reading experiences. Voyeurism is an important factor in these reading experiences, bringing a potency to those scenes with a sexual frisson to which the reader must react. While it is clear that, in places, the reader can succumb to the temptation to indulge in voyeurism, I suggest that readerly *sōphrosunē* has a central role in moderating this tendency. *Callirhoe* is a text which, to a certain extent, foregrounds the role of *sōphrosunē* for the reader as a reaction to opportunities for voyeurism, and this role becomes even more crucial, and more clearly expressed, in the novels of Longus and Achilles Tatius, which will be our next concern.

2.2 Programmatic *sōphrosunē* and readerly voyeurism

The narrator of Longus' Prologue describes the images he saw in a grove sacred to the Nymphs on the island of Lesbos while hunting. He then proceeds to give his reaction to the picture that explains his intention to respond to it creatively:

Ἰδόντα με καὶ θαυμάσαντα πόθος ἔσχεν ἀντιγράψαι τῇ γραφῇ, καὶ ἀναζητησάμενος ἐξηγητὴν τῆς εἰκόνος τέτταρας βίβλους ἐξεπονησάμην, ἀνάθημα μὲν Ἔρωτι καὶ Νύμφαις καὶ Πανί, κτῆμα δὲ τερπνὸν πᾶσιν ἀνθρώποις, ὃ καὶ νοσοῦντα ἰάσεται καὶ λυπούμενον παραμυθήσεται, τὸν ἐρασθέντα ἀναμνήσει, τὸν οὐκ ἐρασθέντα προπαιδεύσει. Πάντως γὰρ οὐδεὶς Ἔρωτα ἔφυγεν ἢ φεύξεται μέχρις ἂν κάλλος ᾖ καὶ ὀφθαλμοὶ βλέπωσιν. Ἡμῖν δὲ ὁ θεὸς παράσχοι σωφρονοῦσι τὰ τῶν ἄλλων γράφειν.

...looking and wondering, a longing seized me to write in response to the painting. Seeking out an interpreter of the picture, I have laboured hard to create four books, an offering to Erōs, the Nymphs and Pan, a delightful possession for all mankind, which will heal the sick and comfort the distressed, remind those who have been in love, and teach those who have not. Indeed, no one has ever escaped Love, nor ever shall, so long as there is beauty and eyes that see. For ourselves, may the god grant us to remain chaste in writing the things of others.

Pr. 3–4

The Prologue is widely discussed,[10] with the final sentence often drawing the interest of commentators. My first concern here is to consider the reason for the narrator/author's fear over remaining *sōphrōn*.[11] Why is this a priority for him? Second, and this is an aspect that remains unanalysed, why is it necessary to pray for *sōphrosunē* with hindsight: that is, *after* the books have been produced in response to the picture?

There is sustained emphasis on the erotic throughout the narrator's introduction of and description of the images in the grove: ἱστορίαν ἔρωτος ... τύχην ἐρωτικήν ... πάντα ἐρωτικά. The narrator states that a πόθος 'seized' him as he viewed the images in the grove, and this is what spurred him on to find an interpreter and produce the narrative which follows the Prologue. The language of desire is crucial in this passage and it is surely this πόθος with which the narrator responded to the painting which caused the prayer in the final lines.

The subsequent focus on how the coming narrative will be useful to the reader continues to emphasize the erotic: the books will be an offering to Erōs (and the Nymphs and Pan, but Erōs is placed first in the list for priority), and will 'remind those who have been in love, and teach those who have not' (τὸν ἐρασθέντα ἀναμνήσει, τὸν οὐκ ἐρασθέντα προπαιδεύσει). This erotic context implies that, just as Morgan observes, the *sōphrosunē* which the narrator views as endangered is related to sexual restraint.[12]

The narrator specifically states that it is in 'writing the things of others' that he prays to remain *sōphrōn*. Indeed, he is a tourist (hunting on Lesbos, but clearly also taking in the sights) who responded to a picture (depicting things which he needs an exegete to explicate) by turning the images into a narrative.[13] The 'things of others' are erotic adventures, and I suggest that there is a certain amount of voyeurism implied by this final sentence, which would further explain the narrator's prayer.

This voyeuristic aspect is a central concern in the subsequent narrative when Chloe gazes on Daphnis bathing (and washes him) at 1.13:[14]

Ἦν δὲ ἡ μὲν κόμη μέλαινα καὶ πολλή, τὸ δὲ σῶμα ἐπίκαυστον ἡλίῳ· εἴκασεν ἄν τις αὐτὸ χρῴζεσθαι τῇ σκιᾷ τῆς κόμης. Ἐδόκει δὲ τῇ Χλόῃ θεωμένῃ καλὸς ὁ Δάφνις, ὅτι δὲ τότε πρῶτον αὐτῇ καλὸς ἐδόκει τὸ λουτρὸν ἐνόμιζε τοῦ κάλλους αἴτιον. Καὶ τὰ νῶτα δὲ ἀπολουούσης ἡ σὰρξ ὑπέπιπτε μαλθακή, ὥστε λαθοῦσα ἑαυτῆς ἥψατο πολλάκις, εἰ τρυφερώτερος εἴη πειρωμένη.

His hair was black and long, his body tanned by the sun: one might have supposed it to be stained by the shadow of his hair. It seemed to Chloe as she was looking that Daphnis was beautiful, but because this was the first time he seemed beautiful to her she thought the bath the cause of the beauty. And washing his back the soft flesh yielded, so that she secretly touched herself many times, testing whether he might be more delicate than she was.

1.13.2

Although Chloe does not understand that her recognition of Daphnis' beauty is erotic (she thinks the bathing is making him seem beautiful), implicit in this passage is the narrator's intrusion into this scene, and the focalization through Chloe is repeatedly pointed out so that the narrator's superior understanding of what is happening is implicit too. Chloe touches herself 'secretly', to compare her texture to Daphnis', but the narrator and his narratee are allowed to witness this innocent exploration.[15] There is also the possibility that Longus is picking up on the bathing scene which occurs in Chariton's *Callirhoe*, (2.2–3: discussed above): there is similar focus on the colour and delicate texture of the bather's skin in each description. This would act to draw attention to the potential for voyeurism by recalling Callirhoe's reluctance to bathe in the presence of others and the reasons for this reluctance, factors which are absent from Daphnis' psychology due to his innocence. Comparison between the immediate viewers in *Callirhoe* and *Daphnis and Chloe* draws attention to the crucial differences: while the serving women who gaze on Callirhoe are astonished by the sight of her nude body, Chloe's reaction demonstrates a curiosity aroused by the beauty of Daphnis' body which goes beyond admiration and wonder and indicates to the reader that this is the beginning of infatuation. Consequently, this intertextuality implies that the reader is potentially more susceptible to enter into a voyeuristic response when reading the passage from Longus than when reading the passage from Chariton, particularly if the reader responds to the focalization through Chloe. Further, if the textual reconstruction based on the *Charmides* in that passage from Chariton is correct, then by recalling Chariton, Longus is also recalling this Platonic text and its crucial representation of the power of viewing beauty which is usually hidden. Just as when reading the passage from Chariton, the reader is invited to ask whether s/he can be like Socrates and regain composure after 'viewing' the beauty of the naked form of an ideal youth. Is this the kind of passage which made the Prologue narrator pray for *sōphrosunē*? This would go some way to explaining the occurrence of the plural participle in line with Morgan's argument: in reading the above passage the reader is just as liable as the author to suffer a loss of *sōphrosunē*.[16]

The question of why pray with hindsight remains. The narrator does not say 'I prayed for *sōphrosunē* before I wrote the four books', so the prayer is not a genuine prayer for the narrator's *sōphrosunē* while writing the coming books regarding 'the things of others': that writing process is already complete. Rather, the prayer is a warning for anyone engaging in similar writing and reading endeavours in the future, including the Prologue narrator himself. The implication is that once he produced these books, the narrator understood that the process of writing about what happens in the erotic lives of others requires the possession of *sōphrosunē*. There are challenges to this possession within the process of producing narrative, just as there are within the process of desiring. In addition, there is an immediacy and continuing relevance to the prayer which would be lost if it was conveyed in the past tense. Although the writing process itself is complete, the books exists and will be read in perpetuity, as the allusion to Thucydides playfully implies:[17] by every reader effectively repeating the prayer for *sōphrosunē* as s/he reads it, that prayer is made continually central to the act of reading the four books which follow. It is questionable whether this prayer is intended to be taken completely seriously: as discussed above, the voyeurism of the reader is, to a certain extent, unavoidable as particularly sensual scenes are evoked. There is surely some implicit humour in the idea that *sōphrosunē* can be completely maintained, and in the idea that the author would desire it to be maintained. The readerly *sōphrosunē*, which is encouraged by Longus, albeit perhaps with tongue in cheek, potentially acts to temper the desire which is inspired by the erotic content of the coming narrative: just as the narrator was seized by a πόθος to write, the beautiful sights which are translated into beautiful words should, it is implied, cause a πόθος in the reader on every reading. This desire on the part of the reader is to continually observe the 'things of others' which are narrated in the text. I suggest that *sōphrosunē* on the reader's part focuses on the *telos*, or 'destination' of the narrative, given that here, in *Daphnis and Chloe*, that involves marriage with chastity preserved.[18] The tension between these two poles creates a richer reading experience in other examples of the genre too, but it is in Longus' Prologue where the idea of metaliterary *sōphrosunē* is articulated most explicitly, and this articulation involves implicit humour as the narrator hints at the sexy text to come, while clothing his advertisement as a prayer for *sōphrosunē*.

There are parallels between the opening scenes of Achilles Tatius' and Longus' novels, and in what follows, I shall draw attention to how there is the possibility for direct ironic engagement with Longus by Achilles, specifically in the way in which voyeurism and erotic storytelling are nuanced and conveyed in the introductory chapters. In the opening frame of *Leucippe and Clitophon*, the reader is presented with an anonymous narrator who proceeds, after describing Sidon and after a brief explanation of the reason for his presence there, to give an ecphrasis of a votive picture which he saw of Europa being taken over the sea by Zeus, disguised as a bull. Scholars link this ecphrasis to the narrative of Clitophon which follows it, with Europa and Leucippe being equated to varying degrees.[19] Alvares compares the nature of the anonymous primary narrator to that of Clitophon, highlighting the similarities in their focus on sophistic stylization, voyeurism and aggressive sex and violence.[20] Longus' Prologue narrator and Achilles Tatius' primary narrator are each affected by the pictures they view, and by the erotic content of those pictures. The voyeurism of the primary narrator as he views the 'sexy' image of Europa is centre-stage in the opening frame of Achilles Tatius' novel, while the implied voyeurism in Longus' Prologue becomes obvious in the subsequent narrative, as I discussed above.

The part of the ecphrasis from the opening frame of Achilles Tatius' novel which is important for this discussion is the description which focuses on specific details of Europa's body as she sits on the bull:

Χιτὼν ἀμφὶ τὰ στέρνα τῆς παρθένου μέχρις εἰς αἰδῶ· τοὐντεῦθεν ἐπεκάλυπτε
χλαῖνα τὰ κάτω τοῦ σώματος· λευκὸς ὁ χιτών· ἡ χλαῖνα πορφυρᾶ· τὸ δὲ σῶμα
διὰ τῆς ἐσθῆτος ὑπεφαίνετο.[21] βαθὺς ὀμφαλός· γαστὴρ τεταμένη· λαπάρα
στενή· τὸ στενὸν εἰς ἰξὺν καταβαῖνον ηὐρύνετο. Μαζοὶ τῶν στέρνων ἠρέμα
προκύπτοντες· ἡ συνάγουσα ζώνη τὸν χιτῶνα καὶ τοὺς μαζοὺς ἔκλειε, καὶ
ἐγίνετο τοῦ σώματος κάτοπτρον ὁ χιτών.

A tunic enveloped the maiden's torso down to her most intimate part; from there
down, a skirt concealed the lower parts of her body. The tunic was white; the
skirt was purple. Her body was just about visible through her clothing: her navel
was deep, her belly taut, her waist slender, and the slenderness broadened
going down to her loins. Her breasts protruded gently from her chest (the girdle
that fastened her tunic also enclosed her breasts, and the tunic mirrored her
body).

                                                                1.1.10–11

The overt concentration from the narrator on what lies beneath Europa's clothing
clearly indicates his prurient interest in the female body.[22]

Europa's abduction by Zeus as it is described here may not allow insight
into Europa's emotions, but she is being kidnapped precisely because she
possesses the physical attributes which are so tightly focused upon, so that,
programmatically, the beauty of the female form potentially exists as an offering
for male acquisition. This object for the male gaze is offered by the primary
narrator potentially because he is *erōtikos* (1.2.1), so that the expression on
Europa's face is not described by him as his focus is on those parts of her body
which he is titillated by. The anonymous primary narrator's interest in the
objectification of the female form is aligned with Clitophon's,[23] so that the alert
reader should maintain a distance from these perspectives. I argue in the
previous chapter (section 1.4.4) that the author seems to want to belittle his
secondary narrator and characters in how they approach the virtue of *sōphrosunē*,
and, in the case of the primary narrator, I suggest that there is something similar
occurring: the way in which the primary narrator's salacious interest is
emphasized invites the reader to question this perspective, and to aim for a more
sōphrōn reading. There are titillating and sexually arousing readings on offer, but
these are not exclusively encouraged.[24] While in Achilles Tatius' novel, beauty,
sex and violence are closely associated with each other, the narrative set-up,
which does not allow for an omniscient overview of events, allows the possibility
for the reader to read beyond the limited perspectives of the narrators. Perhaps,
there is a subtle warning here about explicit content and the need to remain
sōphrōn, but Achilles Tatius' primary narrator does not direct his audience

as does Longus' narrator in his Prologue: for the reader of *Leucippe and Clitophon*, it is probably only on a second reading that s/he is able to appreciate fully the ethical limitations of the primary narrator, having witnessed the limitations of Clitophon as a narrator.

The narrator of Longus' Prologue was smitten with the images he viewed in the sacred grove, but as we saw above, he relates his reaction with the benefit of hindsight. He decides to pray for *sōphrosunē* following the production of the four books. While Longus' narrator recognizes the danger to *sōphrosunē* which is inherent in writing/reading about the love stories of others, the primary narrator in Achilles Tatius' frame seeks to indulge his desire for an erotic *logos*, which he states he will enjoy more if it is like *mythoi* (1.2.2):[25] implicit in his reaction to Clitophon is the fact that he is *erōtikos*, as mentioned already. Crucially, the reactions from the anonymous narrator do not involve his perspective as he is narrating (which is what we have in Longus' Prologue): both the status of being *erōtikos* and his direct speeches to Clitophon are firmly rooted in his experience as he was looking at the picture and as he was speaking to Clitophon. This differentiation between the temporal perspectives of Longus' Prologue narrator and Achilles' primary narrator has implications for reading protocols, including whether one can read on with *sōphrosunē*. The naturalistic orality which is present in *Leucippe and Clitophon* but which is necessarily a deception (we are reading a text, after all)[26] suggests an immediacy which goes beyond that present in Longus' Prologue. The reader is not, in Achilles Tatius' text, given an example of how to react to an erotically inspired creation with *sōphrosunē* following its production. Rather, if following the lead of the primary narrator, one is encouraged to indulge in the pleasure of the expectation of the coming narrative. Reading the openings of these two novels is to some extent like looking at two sides of the same coin: there is an emphasis on erotic themes as depicted in pictorial images and there is the representation of desire in the viewer of those images, but the discrepancies in how these aspects are conveyed point to different approaches to the same sphere. This in turn suggests that one author is reacting to the other, and, while it is difficult to assert confidently which way around this relationship is, Achilles Tatius' knowing irreverence elsewhere in his novel could easily suggest his playful reversal of Longus' concerns in his Prologue. The reader of Achilles Tatius' novel can appreciate the potential ironical use of Longus, and can note that the clear absence of a concern on the primary narrator's part to retain *sōphrosunē* does not indicate that the danger of losing it is not present, but indicates that this narrator is preoccupied with the pleasure of the erotic tale to come. Achilles Tatius conveys to the reader that his primary narrator, in being *erotikos*, has a limited understanding of the risks of erotic narrative, or he does not care about those risks, or he excitedly anticipates them (and his voyeuristic tendencies when viewing the picture of Europa could be indicative of any of these options). These possibilities ensure that any alert reader can potentially recognize that readerly *sōphrosunē* will be just as threatened in this novel as it is in *Daphnis and Chloe*.

2.3 Achilles Tatius: perpetuating readerly voyeurism?

Following on from the frame, voyeurism continues to be important in *Leucippe and Clitophon*, and there are several junctures in Clitophon's narrative where violence, often sexualized violence, on the female form is suggested and where the reader is forced to 'watch' this violence. First, I will explore the most graphic scene of violence in the novel, where Clitophon looks on as Leucippe is apparently eviscerated as a sacrificial victim (3.15), with a view to considering how voyeuristic the reader becomes at this point. Second, I shall look at the way in which Clitophon's representation of Leucippe and his suggestions about how verbal descriptions of her beauty bring about desire in certain characters imply the reader's susceptibility to voyeurism. I will then turn to those episodes where Leucippe invites those present to look at her body.

Morales' discussion of the scene at 3.15 suggests that the 'consumptive gaze' dominates in this episode as Leucippe is not just cut open but is also eaten, that this brings about an intensification of voyeurism, and that the way in which the scene is represented causes a lack of empathic or emotional response from the reader.[27] My concern is to consider the extent to which Clitophon's viewpoint can be seen to be programmatic for the reader in the way Morales suggests, and to analyse how his naïveté or lack of insight in his reaction to Leucippe's apparent mutilation compares with the reader's perception of the scene.

Clitophon narrates the sacrifice scene barely and with no emotional colouring (3.15.4–5). This is how he describes Leucippe being tied up:

... τῶν δὲ νεανίσκων ὁ ἕτερος ἀνακλίνας αὐτὴν ὑπτίαν ἔδησεν ἐκ παττάλων ἐπὶ τῆς γῆς ἐρηρεισμένων, οἷον ποιοῦσιν οἱ κοροπλάθοι τὸν Μαρσύαν ἐκ τοῦ φυτοῦ δεδεμένον.

One of the two young men laid her on her back and tied her down to some pegs driven into the earth (just as the artists represent Marsyas tied to a tree).

3.15.4

Repath notes that this comparison makes little sense both in terms of gender and in terms of what happens to Marsyas, and he suggests that it is even more puzzling a comparison given that the paintings of Andromeda chained to a rock and Prometheus having his liver eaten as described earlier in the book (3.7–8) would be much more appropriate as comparisons here.[28] These observations are crucial to how the reader reacts to the sacrifice scene, something which is often overlooked in scholarship:[29] we make connections where Clitophon does not, so, in contrast to Morales' argument, the reader, although offered only Clitophon's perspective, does not have to follow his interpretation.[30] This has implications for how voyeuristic the reader is in comparison to Clitophon, particularly bearing in mind the connection the reader is bound to make with the painting of Andromeda. While Clitophon, who connects Leucippe with Marsyas, focuses on the restriction of being tied up and the potential for physical suffering, the reader remembers Andromeda, terrified and all the more comely because of her terror, sexualized by being dressed in bridal clothes, and helpless in the face of an attack by a sea monster which is depicted with phallic overtones:[31] all of this means that Leucippe's sexuality is evoked for the reader, causing them to be more voyeuristic than Clitophon. Further, the reader might also recall Pantheia's dream at 2.23, where Leucippe is cut open with a sword in a sexually suggestive way, starting at her groin, which can be seen to prefigure her disembowelment at 3.15.[32]

The comparison of Clitophon's shock at the time of the sacrifice with that of Niobe can also be seen to be unexpected. Repath suggests that it feminizes Clitophon and makes him a passive victim of events, in contrast to the heroic representation of Perseus and Heracles which the reader will recall given the similarities between Leucippe and Andromeda and Prometheus.[33] This would demonstrate that Clitophon fails to include references which would draw attention to gender and the sexual implications of the scene, and which would emphasize the erotic nature of his relationship with Leucippe. Morales, in contrast, argues that the reference to Niobe's petrifaction, while ostensibly incongruous, implies an undercurrent of sexual arousal (by hinting at an erection) in Clitophon's response to Leucippe's ordeal.[34] Another line of interpretation regarding Clitophon's reaction to Leucippe's evisceration is put forward by King.[35] He suggests that Clitophon's allusion to Niobe can be read as a genuine expression of his shock and grief at seeing Leucippe murdered. This is surely how Clitophon as narrator intends his mythic paradigm to be taken. Also, although King seems not to reject Morales' sexualised interpretation of the Niobe reference, it is difficult to see both working simultaneously and

King's recognition of Clitophon's emotional state as the scene progresses is more convincing. However, in either case, Repath's point about the way in which Clitophon misses the opportunity to make connections to the paintings of Andromeda and Prometheus stands: it is still the case that readerly expectations are not fulfilled here. These expectations on the part of the reader (which are encouraged by the author, one could argue) mean that as s/he becomes a voyeur of this scene the reader is potentially more prurient than Clitophon, implying a loss of readerly *sōphrosunē* which is unavoidable.[36] Recalling the image of the sexualised Andromeda tied to a rock, threatened by the phallic monster, and the open wound of Prometheus probed by the beak of the bird, the implications are troubling for the reader: now unable to be superior to Clitophon in ethical terms, instead we are forced to connect directly Leucippe's apparent evisceration with the sexual act, something which Clitophon does not.

Achilles Tatius continues to foreground voyeurism in relation to Leucippe when she, both as the slave girl Lacaena at 5.17, and when reacting to threats from Thersander and Sosthenes at 6.21–22,[37] invites her immediate audience to view her body and envisage the tortures that have been, or could be, inflicted upon it. These invitations alone indicate that the reader is also a viewer of Leucippe and, moreover, that s/he can hardly resist picturing the potential or real violence done to her. However, the implications of these scenes are not straightforwardly voyeuristic: the internal characters who view Leucippe on these occasions do not view her as sexually objectified. At 5.17, Clitophon, as 'Lacaena' bares her back, is moved to compassion on hearing her story (but the viewing of her whip-scarred body seems to prompt his sympathy too): he is not turned on by her bared back, although at that point he is reminded of Leucippe. At 6.21, following on from Leucippe's repeated invitations to him and Sosthenes to look at her body and to wound it, which she makes in defiance of their efforts to make her submit to Thersander's sexual advances, Thersander reacts with mockery rather than showing that he is aroused by her actions and words. While it could be argued that this mockery is to a certain extent sexualized as he questions Leucippe's claims of virginity, it is not the case that her words result in an increase in his lust. Whether the reader aligns their response with these internal viewers is debatable. In what follows, I will focus on how the ideas of the power of hearsay and suggestibility in the text emphasize that real 'viewing' is not an essential prerequisite for causing (occasionally violent) desire for Leucippe, which has consequences for the reader, when reacting to the scenes at 5.17 and 6.21–22.[38]

Both Callisthenes and Thersander fall for Leucippe's charms on hearing about them, rather than on seeing them. When Clitophon narrates how Callisthenes desired Leucippe to be his wife on only hearing about her, his susceptibility is described as follows:

... τοσαύτη γὰρ τοῖς ἀκολάστοις ὕβρις, ὡς καὶ τοῖς ὠσὶν εἰς ἔρωτα τρυφᾶν καὶ ταῦτα πάσχειν ἀπὸ ῥημάτων, ἃ τῇ ψυχῇ διακονοῦσι τρωθέντες ὀφθαλμοί.

... the wantonness of the licentious is so great that even with their ears they wallow in erotic pleasure, and they suffer from words these things, which wounded eyes usually administer to the soul.

2.13.1

Clitophon's sententious condemnation of Callisthenes' perceived weakness implies that it is only the ἀκόλαστοι that suffer this erotic desire on hearsay.[39] Clitophon's opinion is outwardly sententious, but he bases it, we can presume, on his own experience: he had to see Leucippe to desire her, and he implies that he is not prodigal and wanton like Callisthenes.

A little later, Clitophon emphasizes how Callisthenes' passion increased once Sostratus had rejected his advances towards his daughter:

ἀναπλάττων γὰρ ἑαυτῷ τῆς παιδὸς τὸ κάλλος καὶ φανταζόμενος τὰ ἀόρατα ἔλαθε σφόδρα κακῶς διακείμενος.

For he imagined the beauty of the girl and picturing what he could not see he got into an exceedingly bad state unawares.

2.13.2

The verbs ἀναπλάττω and φαντάζω emphasize that Callisthenes makes Leucippe visible in his mind's eye, the fantasy image which he creates spurs him on to misguided action when he tries to kidnap the girl. Thus, words which he hears about how she looks help him to build her imagined beauty into something irresistible. Quite what Callisthenes heard about Leucippe and her beauty is not revealed, just as it is not clear how Clitophon has come by this inside information, although we may suppose it is from Sostratus, or from Callisthenes himself, given the supposed turnaround in Callisthenes' character and the consequences of this (8.17–19). The fact that Callisthenes mistakes Calligone for Leucippe implies that it is indeed an error to base one's desires on verbal description alone. While Calligone proves to be just as desirable to Callisthenes when she is seen by him as Leucippe was when only heard about, it is clear that the latter desire was not rooted in a genuine appreciation of the beauty of an individual girl, but on someone else's description of her. However, the important fact remains that, within this narrative, verbal description can initiate desire, which is just as powerful as those desires created by actual viewing of beauty.

Thersander also proves erotically vulnerable on hearing about Leucippe's beauty when Sosthenes praises her to him. Sosthenes' method is made clear by his own words:

... οὕτως αὐτὴν πιστεύσειας ἀκούων, ὡς ἰδών ...

... You must believe what you are hearing, as if you were seeing (it) ...

6.3.5

The slave's technique proves successful, and Thersander is convinced of the girl's beauty and so concurs with Sosthenes' plan to abduct Leucippe, who is now under the care of Melite's maids. Later, his reaction to Sosthenes' continued descriptions of Leucippe's beauty is made clear, in terms which echo those used in relation to Callisthenes' passion at 2.13:

Τοῦ δὲ Σωσθένους αὐτῷ μηνύσαντος τὰ περὶ τῆς Λευκίππης καὶ κατατραγῳδοῦντος αὐτῆς τὸ κάλλος, μεστὸς γενόμενος ἐκ τῶν εἰρημένων ὡσεὶ κάλλους φαντάσματος, φύσει καλοῦ ...

But when Sosthenes reported to him what had happened with Leucippe and dramatically exaggerating her beauty, he was filled as if by a fantasy of beauty from the words, a natural beauty ...

6.4.4

Again, the verb φαντάζω is present, and is in direct connection with words (ἐκ τῶν εἰρημένων) in this passage. In addition, there is the repeated use of κάλλος, κάλλους and καλοῦ. All of these elements emphasize how Thersander creates a vision of Leucippe's beauty from the words of Sosthenes. Thersander is represented as ethically reprehensible by Clitophon, and, while Clitophon does not spell the connection out, it is fairly clear that, as is the case with Callisthenes, it is Thersander's lack of self-restraint which allows him to lust after a slave girl he has never seen. However, as with Callisthenes at 2.13, the role of desire induced by hearsay is clear. There is sufficient *enargeia* at work in this narrative to ensure that the reader can respond emotionally to what is reported.[40] Thus, when Leucippe conspicuously displays herself at 5.17 and 6.21–22, the reader is already aware of her beauty from Clitophon's previous description of her face (1.4), and the repeated suggestions of his and other men's desire for her. I suggest that, just as words cause Callisthenes and Thersander to fall for Leucippe, Clitophon's narrative, with its emphasis on the beauty of Leucippe, invites the narratee to engage in voyeurism and to react emotionally, perhaps with desire, to the visions of Leucippe which are conjured up.[41]

While the potential for a sexualized enjoyment of these scenes on the part of the reader might seem to endanger any *sōphrosunē* on his part, I suggest that the way in which Leucippe invites her immediate audience to look at her body is ambiguous: she is both flaunting her beauty and inviting sympathy.[42] This works on the metanarrative level to complicate the viewing of Leucippe by the reader. While it is clear that the nature of the narrative is such that voyeurism is encouraged, not just because it is invited, but also because verbal representations of beauty are effective in bringing about unbridled desire in characters within the narrative, it is also possible for the reader to be different from the distinctly non-*sōphrōn* Callisthenes and Thersander, and to temper the voyeuristic approach with readerly *sōphrosunē* and so view Leucippe's potential and real suffering with empathy, rather than with prurience.[43]

This discussion on the role of *logos* and its effect upon the listener must take into account Clitophon's claim in Book 1 that 'an erotic story fuels desire' (1.5.6). By including a generalization here, Clitophon implies that everyone is subject to the erotic power of stories, which clearly has implications on a metaliterary level. While, as discussed above, it is often the most licentious who seem vulnerable to desire via hearsay alone, Clitophon's statement at 1.5.6 can be seen as programmatic for his narrative and its impact upon the reader. The power of language in the novel intensifies the potential for readerly voyeurism. However, as we saw above, Clitophon is not a reliable narrator, and his perspective is not necessarily programmatic for the reader. This factor allows the reader to resist the predominant erotic drive, particularly in those places where an alternative reading is on offer, such as one involving empathy for characters. It is a challenge for the reader to avoid the predominant erotic response, and so this kind of resistant reading involves *sōphrosunē* as we question the predominant nature of the male gaze.

*

It is perhaps part of Achilles Tatius' strategy to create an uncomfortable and unstable reaction in the reader: this text challenges our *sōphrosunē* and asks whether the perception of female sexuality and suffering follows the approach of the male narrators and characters or goes beyond those approaches. Ultimately, the reader is left to ponder these options and their ethical consequences. While *Leucippe and Clitophon* has passages seemingly designed to arouse, I hope I have made it clear that the work is aimed at a readership that would not be overwhelmed by the more titillating factors to the detriment of the intellectual reading experience on offer. Achilles Tatius' technique demonstrates that his original readership would have the perspicacity and intellectual ability to read beyond his narrator's perspectives, and that readerly *sōphrosunē* is intrinsically involved in the reading process.

2.4 Heliodorus: *sōphrosunē*, sexual dynamics and readerly voyeurism

There are two instances where the reader is invited to contemplate scenes of a sexual nature in Heliodorus' *Aethiopica*. The first is at 4.8, where Persinna sensitively narrates her intimacy with her husband in which Chariclea was conceived. I will discuss this passage later when I come to consider the role of the heroines of the novels as texts, so it is to the other instance that I now turn, namely that at 5.4.

It is made very clear that the reader is witnessing an intensely private scene between the protagonists at 5.4:

> τότε γὰρ πρῶτον ἰδίᾳ καὶ παντὸς ἀπηλλαγμένοι τοῦ ὀχλήσοντος ἀλλήλοις ἐντυόντες ἀπαραποδίστων καὶ ὁλοσχερῶν περιπλοκῶν τε καὶ φιλημάτων **ἐνεπίμπλαντο**. Καὶ πάντων ἅμα εἰς λήθην ἐμπεσόντες εἴχοντο ἐπὶ πλεῖστον ἀλλήλων οἱονεὶ **συμπεφυκότες**, <u>ἁγνεύοντος</u> μὲν ἔτι καὶ <u>παρθενεύοντος</u> ἔρωτος **κορεννύμενοι** δάκρυσι δὲ **ὑγροῖς καὶ θερμοῖς** εἰς ἀλλήλους **κεραννύμενοι** καὶ <u>καθαροῖς</u> μόνον **μιγνύμενοι** τοῖς φιλήμασιν· ἡ γὰρ Χαρίκλεια τὸν Θεαγένην εἴ τι παρακινοῦντα αἴσθοιτο καὶ **ἀνδριζόμενον** ὑπομνήσει τῶν ὅρκων ἀνέστελλεν, ὁ δὲ οὐ χαλεπῶς ἐπανήγετο καὶ <u>σωφρονεῖν</u> ῥᾳδίως ἠνείχετο ἔρωτος μὲν ἐλάττων ἡδονῆς δὲ κρείττων γινόμενος.

Finding themselves now for the first time together in private, free of anyone to interrupt them, they took their fill of unhindered and uninhibited embraces and kisses. Falling into oblivion of everything simultaneously, they clung to each other for a long time as if conjoined, consummating a still pure and virgin love, in a congress of moist warm tears, coupling only with chaste kisses. For if ever Chariclea found Theagenes becoming too passionate and playing the man, she would subdue him with a reminder of his oaths, and he would draw back without resentment and happily bear to be self-controlled, being weaker than love but stronger than pleasure.

5.4.4–5

I have put the sexually charged language into bold text,[44] and the language of restraint is underlined. The use of this language is not, I think, just intended to represent this scene in terms which represent Chariclea's and Theagenes' experience. As we have seen above, the lack of direct speech on both protagonists' part does not suggest that realism is the narrator's aim here.[45] If this scene is to be read as serving only to show a *sōphrōn* couple enjoying affectionate hugs and kisses, we must consider the effect of the sexualized language on the reader. Jones notes the similarity between how Heliodorus represents his protagonists' *sōphrosunē* while using sexually charged language and how Longus hints in his Prologue that there are prurient scenes to come, and that *sōphrosunē* must be maintained.[46] It is clearly important that both authors seem to challenge their readers to resist being titillated by the eroticism of their novels. The representation of the protagonists' embraces and kisses is not as 'chaste' as their apparent enjoyment of them. The sexualized language is surely designed to challenge the reader to maintain her/his *sōphrosunē*,[47] even as Theagenes and Chariclea maintain theirs. However, the use of language which represents sexual restraint and purity (underlined) implies that titillation is not the only aim of the narrator here. While there is a greater proportion of 'sexy' terms, the terms of restraint are placed centrally in the passage (ἁγνεύοντος, παρθενεύοντος, καθαροῖς), with σωφρονεῖν appearing towards the close of the passage, in a sense 'rounding off' this foray into intimacy. The reader is thus presented with a scene which can be read in a voyeuristic way, but equally, can be understood as the ultimate expression of *sōphrosunē*: even in such tempting circumstances, this couple acted with restraint, the narrator seems to suggest. The reader's desire for this couple to enjoy each other freely is a subversive one: this is as close as we will get, and, it is implied, we are not as *sōphrōn* as we should be if we read this scene voyeuristically. While the beauty of Chariclea is constantly on display, as if the reader is always being tempted, this scene invites readers to look at their own desire and question whether it is something which should be allowed free rein. At any rate, the primary narrator will not allow this scene the power it could have in respect of encouraging voyeuristic tendencies. It is similar to the scene between Persinna and Hydaspes at 4.8 in that sex is suggested, but prurience is avoided. The extent to which the reader adheres to the ethical parameters implied by the narrator is down to the individual, but they are there nevertheless.

Finally, there is the suggestion within this passage that Theagenes is not quite as *sōphrōn* as Chariclea: she has to restrain his ardour by reminding him of his oath. While the narrator emphasizes that Theagenes quickly corrects his behaviour, and is able to master his passion, there remains the fact that he had to be stopped by his beloved Chariclea: he did not manage to restrain himself instinctively, as Chariclea seems to. Is the reader similar to Theagenes at this point? Does s/he also have to pull back from enjoying the thought of what could happen here and thinking about the satisfaction to be gained from such an encounter with Chariclea? While Chariclea's standard of *sōphrosunē* might well be unattainable for most readers of this text, Theagenes' realistic desires are much more easily understood and the reader can empathize with the youth. This heightens the voyeuristic engagement on the reader's part, before s/he too is brought back into line as the sexual possibilities fade, and *sōphrosunē* is restored.

2.5 Heroine as text: Callirhoe, Chloe, Leucippe and Chariclea

In this section, I will build on my previous discussion by considering the extent to which the heroines of four of the novels are synonymous with the texts, and by focusing on how this influences our reading of the texts and the interaction between voyeurism and *sōphrosunē* in the reading experience. König's discussion of body and text addresses the way in which the protagonists of the Greek novels are aligned with the texts, and he states that:

> ... the mildly titillating air of compromised respectability which is such a central feature of all the surviving Greek novels ... is a direct consequence of the ambiguity between the seductiveness and virtuousness in their main characters' beauty.[48]

The extent to which the textuality of the heroines Callirhoe, Chloe, Leucippe and Chariclea involves this ethical ambiguity and how this influences the extent to which *sōphrosunē* is involved in our readings of the novels will be my main concern in this section.

There is much potential for a metaliterary reading of Chariton's novel if its original title is *Callirhoe*, which is very probable.[49] The name of the heroine is synonymous with the text itself, so that every time she is praised or causes astonishment, and as her reputation spreads across geographical boundaries, the text itself is being promoted. Further, if Callirhoe is to be directly associated with *Callirhoe*, it is possible that in addition to considering the beauty and fame of the girl and the text, we might also consider another attribute which is repeatedly assigned to the protagonist, namely her *sōphrosunē*.

Before considering how *sōphrosunē* might apply to the text itself, and how Callirhoe offers an alternative 'reading' of her story from the surface-level reading, it is worth considering two significant places where Callirhoe is clearly aligned with the narrative and exploring the consequences of these alignments. At 4.7.5–6, Callirhoe's fame is said to precede her as she travels from Ionia to Babylon:

> …προέτρεχε γὰρ τῆς γυναικὸς ἡ Φήμη, καταγγέλλουσα πᾶσιν ἀνθρώποις ὅτι Καλλιρόη παραγίνεται, **τὸ περιβόητον ὄνομα**, τὸ μέγα τῆς φύσεως κατόρθωμα …

> …Rumour ran ahead of the woman, announcing to everybody that Callirhoe was at hand, the much-talked of name, the great success of nature …

Ἡ Φήμη can be seen to be symbolic of the author, who conveys the tale *Callirhoe*.[50] The repute of both woman and text is being emphasized, with the result that the reader is left in no doubt about how wonderful this work of literature is. There is some irony in attributing Callirhoe's supremacy to nature: her creator is not nature, but Chariton, and his power is hinted at with this implicit alignment.

At 5.5.3–4, Callirhoe, having just been told by Dionysius that she must attend the trial, laments once more the fame that her beauty has brought her:

> …διήγημα καὶ τῆς Ἀσίας καὶ τῆς Εὐρώπης γέγονα … κάλλος ἐπίβουλον, εἰς τοῦτο μόνον ὑπὸ τῆς φύσεως δοθέν, ἵνα μου πλησθῇ γῆ διαβολῶν …

> …I have become the tale of Asia and Europe … treacherous beauty, given to me by nature only so that the earth be filled with slanders about me …

While lamenting, Callirhoe also draws attention to her fame, and the use of διήγημα aligns her with the narrative of which her experiences are a part.[51] The focalization allows for a clear perspective from the heroine, again emphasizing her displeasure at her predicament. This passage might well suggest that there is cruelty in 'nature' for providing Callirhoe with such beauty, which constantly challenges her hold on *sōphrosunē*. As noted above, 'nature' can be equated with Chariton, so there is a certain degree of self-referential censure here. Callirhoe might blame nature, but the reader should blame Chariton for the heroine's continuing misfortunes, but equally praise him for his ingenious narrative twists: the two are inseparable.

The above observations can be associated with the heroine's *sōphrosunē*, of which her modesty is a part. In a metaliterary analysis it could be said that while the text is made to astonish and be famous just like its heroine, its reader needs to react not just like the internal spectators of Callirhoe who flock to her just for a glimpse,[52] but also with a degree of *sōphrosunē* as suggested by the depiction of this complex figure. As readers we are exposed constantly to a certain view of Callirhoe, as supremely attractive, but we also have a view of her from her own perspective, as constantly harassed by crowds and individual men because of her beauty. Callirhoe's own 'reading' of her story differs considerably from the narrator's telling of it, but the reader is able to gain access to her perspective through her reiterated laments, and this adds breadth to the overall reading experience. This means that if we empathize with the heroine, if we enter into her own 'reading', then we potentially temper with *sōphrosunē* our desire to view her. Thus, through aligning the text with its heroine, and allowing differing perspectives on her story, Chariton succeeds in encouraging nuanced reactions from his readers.

Callirhoe is synonymous with the text concerning her, and there is a similar role for Chloe, which is made clear at Longus, 2.27, when Pan announces to the Methymnaeans, who have imprisoned Chloe on board the ship:

… ἀπεσπάσετε δὲ βωμῶν παρθένον ἐξ ἧς Ἔρως μῦθον ποιῆσαι θέλει …

… you have torn from a shrine a maiden from whom Love intends to make a story …

As Morgan notes, this is a self-referential moment, and the story, or myth, which Erōs will make from Chloe is the book we are reading.[53] What are the implications for the reader and her/his *sōphrosunē*? I have already discussed how there are opportunities for readerly voyeurism in Longus' text, and where these opportunities have Chloe as their focus, such as when she is focalized through Daphnis' desiring gaze at 1.25–26 and at 1.32, there is the additional factor of Chloe as text to consider. It is not the case that the reader is engaging in voyeurism which compromises her/his readerly *sōphrosunē* just because Chloe is the desired object: if she is identified with the text itself then the reader, in viewing Chloe on those occasions where she is sexualized, is effectively being 'seduced' by the text. While Chloe displays *aidōs* at certain points, as discussed above,[54] she would have sex with Daphnis if she could, and her behaviour reflects this willingness and desire. Chloe's lack of sexual knowledge does not prevent her behaviour from being erotic. Further, the reader's superior sexual knowledge imbues Chloe's behaviour with a deeper eroticism: we know what she wants to do with Daphnis, even though she does not know. The Prologue narrator when praying for *sōphrosunē* effectively implies the challenging nature of retaining this virtue while viewing this text: if the text is Chloe then the reader's *sōphrosunē* is potentially more difficult to retain. The generic pattern that encourages the protagonists and the reader to possess *sōphrosunē* in the midst of erotic narratives is somewhat subverted in Longus' text. It is highly challenging for readers to be *sōphrōn* when their superior sexual knowledge ensures that they respond to the erotic hints on display, especially when their sexual awareness and potential lasciviousness is thrown into sharp relief by the erotic innocence of Daphnis and Chloe.

There is also a textual role for Leucippe in Achilles Tatius' novel, particularly in one crucial scene. When Clitophon saw Leucippe in the guise of 'Lacaena', she told Clitophon and Melite of her mistreatment at the hands of Sosthenes, and she also displayed her whipped back to them:

> Καὶ ἅμα διανοίξασα τὸν χιτῶνα δείκνυσι τὰ νῶτα διαγεγραμμένα ἔτι οἰκτρότερον. Ὡς οὖν ταῦτα ἠκούσαμεν, ἐγὼ μὲν συνεχύθην· καὶ γὰρ τι ἐδόκει Λευκίππης ἔχειν· ...

> And at the same time opening her tunic she showed the marks etched onto her back, an even more pitiable sight. When we heard this, I for my part was confused, since she seemed to have something of Leucippe about her ...

> 5.17.6–7

It is significant that the term διαγεγραμμένα is used here to describe how Lacaena's back is scarred. By using this term which denotes artistic representation, and indeed writing itself, is Achilles Tatius inviting his reader to consider how 'Lacaena' has her own story to tell, one which is symbolized by the marks on her back?[55] This metatextual idea is strengthened by the fact that, albeit rarely, τὰ νῶτα can denote the back of a page.[56] The hint which follows about the slave girl's true identity, when Clitophon saw the resemblance to Leucippe, but failed to recognize her outright, suggests that the girl's self-exposure allowed Clitophon a degree of recognition which her presence and conversation did not allow. This in turn indicates that as the reader 'sees' the wounded back of Lacaena, s/he 'reads' a version of Leucippe's story which as yet has not been told. Voyeurism thus becomes a part of the reading process itself, and, in this case, it acts to cause greater understanding and empathy for this abused girl, rather than merely acting to further her objectification. Indeed, multiple reactions to this scene exist simultaneously (Clitophon's confusion, Melite's pity and compassionate response in her subsequent sympathetic treatment of 'Lacaena'), allowing for a spectrum of reactions from the reader. This is something which is apparent more forcefully as Clitophon reacts to Leucippe's letter at 5.19.[57] Repath links the scars 'written' on Lacaena/Leucippe's back to her letter, so that reactions to both signify Clitophon's and, potentially, the reader's confusion. Clitophon's reactions to the letter include shock, pleasure and distress. Repath asks 'can we help it?' when discussing whether the reader should imagine Leucippe being whipped, with sexualized overtones.[58] This point invites us to consider readerly ethics, and to question whether there is a more *sōphrōn* reading on offer that the one which titillates via the male gaze. King illustrates the 'multiple focalizations' involved in the letter reading scene, which problematize the reader's view of Leucippe's narrated pain.[59] I suggest that readerly *sōphrosunē* tempers the reader's response by allowing us to step back from Clitophon's muddled emotions as he reacts to the letter and to Lacaena's scars, and to resist his focalization, so that we can empathize more fully with Leucippe's experiences of abuse.

In Heliodorus' *Aethiopica*, the extent to which Chariclea is the embodiment of the text and how her primary virtue of *sōphrosunē* is involved in this potential embodiment are crucial considerations. Morgan argues for the idea of Chariclea as text, building on the trope of the alignment of text and (in particular, female) body in Roman elegy, and in Longus, Chariton, and Achilles Tatius.[60] In the remainder of this section, I will look at those passages which invite such a metatextual reading and in which this coincides with an emphasis on the *sōphrosunē* of Chariclea.

The passage at 4.8 is significant for any metaliterary reading of this text, and presents *sōphrosunē* as synonymous with the text's central *ethos*. This chapter is much discussed,[61] understandably given its central importance to Heliodorus' narrative arc: it looks back to the earliest point in the *histoire*, namely, Chariclea's conception, and provides crucial information about her unusual origins,[62] which implicitly point to her future *nostos*.[63] The role of *sōphrosunē* has also been discussed fairly thoroughly, both in regard to its role in Chariclea's characterization,[64] and in regard to its metaliterary role.[65] I will consider the way in which Persinna prescribes *sōphrosunē* for Chariclea, and how this highlights the centrality of *sōphrosunē* in our reading of the wider text. While the story that emerges involves marital sex and the unusual circumstances of Chariclea's conception, the purpose of the narrative is to ensure that, if she lives, Chariclea will understand her origins, and act in a manner which is appropriate for a princess of Ethiopia. A significant part of this central message is *sōphrosunē* (4.8.7). On Chariclea's birth, Persinna sets out the parameters by which her daughter should live. The reader learns that the very earliest part of Chariclea's life, which marks the earliest point in the *histoire*, is coloured by *sōphrosunē*, so that the virtue is at the very root of the narrative.

Chariclea's fate is bound up in this piece of text, in which she was wrapped as a baby, to the extent that she can be seen to be synonymous with it, as Morgan recognizes.[66] As Anderson notes, the *sōphrosunē* that Persinna is so keen to encourage in her daughter is intrinsic to Persinna's own characterization, and it is fear of people thinking she has diverged from her chastity that compels her to abandon her child.[67] The virtue is not encouraged merely for its own sake, or for the sake of propriety: the dangerous consequences of others perceiving one as a woman without *sōphrosunē* were uppermost in Persinna's mind as she composed these words. These words are compelling not just because they represent Chariclea's origins, but because they were produced *in extremis* and are imbued with emotion and wisdom borne of Persinna's expectation of and avoidance of impending disaster. Heliodorus endows Chariclea's *sōphrosunē* with gravitas and poignancy as it is that virtue which is central to the physical text that her mother created and wrapped around her. Chariclea owes not only her familial and ethnic identity to this mini-narrative, but also her ethical identity. Persinna's text is emblematic of Chariclea herself, and *sōphrosunē* is intrinsic to both that text, the heroine, and the wider text.

At 5.31, *sōphrosunē* and potential readerly voyeurism once more coincide, and this discussion will lead us on to considering Chariclea's role as a cipher for the text. At this point, Calasiris is narrating his experiences to Cnemon and Nausicles. He tells how Chariclea has attracted the amorous attentions of the pirate chief, Trachinus, who has boarded the Phoenician vessel on which the protagonists and Calasiris were passengers, and this pirate has gained Chariclea's (false) promise of marriage. Calasiris perceives an opportunity to free himself and his wards from this dire situation by means of manipulating the desire of Pelorus (Trachinus' deputy) for Chariclea in order to cause unrest. Calasiris, having told Chariclea to adorn herself as if for marriage, sends Pelorus to look at the girl in order to fuel his desire for her. His words to Pelorus are significant. He responds to the pirate's comment that he has not seen the girl in her full glory as follows:

Καὶ μὴν ἔξεστιν . . . εἰ λάθρα παρέλθοις εἰς τὴν ναῦν· οἶσθα γὰρ ὡς καὶ τοῦτο διεκώλυσεν ὁ Τραχῖνος· αὐτὴν τὴν Ἄρτεμιν ὄψει προκαθημένην. Ἀλλ᾽ ὅπως τὸ παρὸν θεάσῃ σωφρόνως, μὴ σαυτῷ τε κἀκείνῃ θάνατον προξενήσῃς.

Well, you can, if you sneak into the ship without being seen, for I know that Trachinus has forbidden even that. You will see Artemis herself sitting there! But make sure that for now you look chastely, lest you be the agent of death for yourself and her.

5.31.1

The passage which follows this speech is also important:

Ὁ δὲ μηδὲν μελλήσας ὥς τινος τῶν ἀναγκαίων ἐπείγοντος ἀνίσταται καὶ λαθὼν
εἰστρέχει τε εἰς τὴν ὁλκάδα καὶ ἰδὼν τὴν Χαρίκλειαν δάφνης τε φέρουσαν ἐπὶ
τῆς κεφαλῆς στέφανον καὶ χρυσουφεῖ στολῇ καταυγάζουσαν (τὴν γὰρ ἐκ
Δελφῶν ἱερὰν ἐσθῆτα ἠμφίεστο ὡς ἢ νικητήριον ἢ ἐντάφιον ἐσομένην) καὶ
τἆλλα περὶ αὐτὴν φαιδρυνόμενα καὶ σχῆμα παστάδος ἀπομιμούμενα, διακαίεται
ὡς εἰκὸς τῇ θέᾳ, πόθου τε ὁμοῦ καὶ ζήλου προσπεσόντων, καὶ δῆλος ἦν αὐτόθεν
ἐπανήκων ἀπὸ τοῦ βλέμματος ἐμμανές τι διανοούμενος.

Without delaying for a moment he rose to his feet as if there were some urgent
necessity of nature, and stole quickly into the merchantman, and seeing
Chariclea wearing a crown of laurel on her head, refulgent in her gown of golden
weave (she had dressed herself in her sacred clothes from Delphi, to be either a
victor's mantle or a burial shroud), and everything around her radiantly
beautiful, mimicking the appearance of a nuptial bedroom, he was, naturally
enough, consumed with fire at the sight, as desire and jealousy together assailed
him, and the moment he returned it was clear from his gaze that he was
purposing something demented.

                                                                    5.31.2

Of course, Calasiris' advice to Pelorus, that he should look with *sōphrosunē*, is
completely at odds with how irresistible Chariclea is in her finery. Calasiris
somewhat confuses matters by suggesting that Pelorus will see Artemis sitting
there: the virgin goddess should traditionally inspire pious respect and awe,
rather than sexual desire, and the consequences of any Actaeon-like viewing,
where the goddess suspects sexualized attention, are clear. Calasiris perhaps
includes this reference to Artemis to ensure that Pelorus is suitably intimidated
and so does indeed only *look* at Chariclea. Pelorus is representative of a certain
type of viewing: while he succeeds on a physical level in looking with *sōphrosunē*
(he does not make any attempt to seduce or rape Chariclea), he is completely
overwhelmed by the vision of beauty which he sees, to the extent that, on his
return to Calasiris, he seems possessed. Here, as the reader witnesses the stunning
impact of Chariclea on Pelorus, how is s/he supposed to react? Calasiris is an
authorial figure at this juncture, offering a view of Chariclea (potentially
synonymous with the text, as we have seen) to Pelorus, who, in being susceptible
to Chariclea's (the text's) erotic power, is like the reader. Potentially, Heliodorus
is offering a challenge to his readers similar to that offered by Longus in his
Prologue, and similarly difficult for the reader to achieve. Calasiris' manipulation
of Pelorus and his management of Chariclea imply an author who has firm

control of both his readers and his text. *Sōphrosunē*'s role in Pelorus' psychology is to temper his ardour so that he avoids violence against Chariclea, but Calasiris does not intend it to do any more than this, since his plan depends on Pelorus being 'maddened' by his desire. Does Heliodorus want his readers to be somewhat maddened too? Does the extent of the reader's *sōphrosunē* govern his craving for this text, and if so, would the author wish for that craving to be moderated by encouraging the virtue? I suggest that Pelorus is a non-ideal version of the reader. This type of reader would be too enthusiastic, perhaps rushing through the text, and would miss the deeper messages at work, which a more *sōphrōn* reader would pick up on.[68] The implications of this passage for readerly voyeurism are further strengthened by the fact that the scenes depicted by Calasiris at this juncture immediately precede the scene which opens the novel, when Chariclea is viewed by the bandits before they or the reader know her identity. There, the bandits do not desire her, but see her as divine, allowing us to perceive another way of viewing to that offered by Pelorus, one which allows for readerly *sōphrosunē*.

*

The previous sections on readerly *sōphrosunē* and voyeurism suggest that there is much interplay between these two aspects in the four extant examples of the Greek novel which I have discussed. Development can be traced in the extent and overall impact of this readerly protocol. In Chariton's text, it is through looking at instances of internally represented voyeurism that one becomes aware of how the reader's reaction is controlled or, at least, pushed in certain directions. In the novels of Longus and Achilles Tatius, the relationship between text and reader, and, specifically, between implied voyeurism towards those characters within the text and the reader's ability to resist this with *sōphrosunē* is made more explicit, and more complex. In Heliodorus' novel, *sōphrosunē* on the reader's part is challenged even as the narrator encourages his narratee to be as *sōphrōn* as Chariclea and Theagenes during their one narrated instance of physical intimacy: in the representation of such chaste desire, the sexualized language which interacts with phrases which emphasize *sōphrosunē* creates a heady and challenging mix for the *sōphrōn* reader. The role of the heroine as a cipher for the text is common to four of the extant novels, as I have discussed. As a consequence of the alignment of these heroines with the texts, readerly voyeurism is intensified and readerly *sōphrosunē* proves difficult to maintain. There is a clear tension between the lush and often eroticised visuality at work in these narratives and the implied promotion of *sōphrōn* behaviour and values which is also present to a significant extent. Voyeurism and *sōphrosunē* need not be mutually exclusive in the reader's approach to these texts, which are embodied in their heroines, who are at once alluring and resistant to the desiring gaze. The salient point that emerges from the discussion in the above sections is that the reader is invited to consider how s/he reacts to the opportunities for voyeurism: the challenges to readerly *sōphrosunē* reinvigorate the reading experience, and emphasize the importance of the concept on a metaliterary level. Although it is clear that the 'male gaze' is often dominant in terms of readerly response, that gaze is not monolithic, and each of the texts discussed in this chapter invites the potential for *sōphrōn* readings, which do not exclude the possibility of a female readership.

3

Readerly *Sōphrosunē*: Erōs and *Sōphrosunē*

There are different reading strategies available when reading any Greek novel,[1] but there is a balance needed between the desire for narrative convolutions and the focus on the desired *telos*, and I will argue that this involves the two concepts of *erōs* and *sōphrosunē*. While the role of readerly desire is discussed in relation to the novel, the role of readerly *sōphrosunē* is something that remains largely unexplored.[2] Just as the characters within the novels often experience internal conflict as their erotic experiences challenge their *sōphrosunē*, there is a similar tension in generically experienced readers as they enjoy the erotic ebb and flow of action while being aware that the conventional *telos* of marriage will come (albeit with varying degrees of closure), and while being aware that this requires a *sōphrōn* engagement with the ultimate aim of the narrative.

3.1 Erōs as metanarrative drive in Chariton's *Callirhoe*

Although Tychē and Aphrodite are also depicted as driving the narrative forward or changing its direction in Chariton's text,[3] Erōs is the divinity who instigates the action and fuels characters' desires in order to maintain narrative momentum.[4] Just as the role of Erōs within the narrative is balanced by *sōphrosunē* or self-control on the part of his victims (made explicit in Erōs' response to the internal *agōn* of Dionysius, discussed below), so his role on a metanarrative level can be seen to be similarly tempered by readerly *sōphrosunē*. In this section, I will trace how the balance between Erōs' metanarrative role and readerly *sōphrosunē* fluctuates within the text, allowing for a reading experience nuanced by constant tension between the two.

In the first chapter of Chariton's narrative, Erōs initiates the mutual attraction of the protagonists. At 1.1.3, following a brief overview of Callirhoe's exceptional beauty and the many suitors she attracts, the narrator states:

ὁ δὲ Ἔρως ζεῦγος ἴδιον ἠθέλησε συμπλέξαι.

But Erōs wanted to make a match of his own devising.

There follows a description of Chaereas and the political rivalry between his
father and Hermocrates (Callirhoe's father). This rivalry should prevent any
marriage between Callirhoe and Chaereas. Then Erōs' opportunity is described,
again emphasizing the god's role in bringing the lovers together, despite the odds.
It is at Erōs' prompting that Callirhoe's mother, who has previously kept her
beautiful daughter hidden from public view, allows her to go to Aphrodite's
temple (1.1.5). Callirhoe and Chaereas meet on a corner, a meeting contrived 'by
the god' (1.1.6), and they consequently fall in love at first sight. The frequency of
these references to Erōs in this small section of text leading up to the protagonists'
meeting is evidence of how responsibility for the action within the narrative at
this initial stage is attributed to this deity. In instigating the events represented in
this opening chapter, Erōs is the narrative force and his actions are essential for
the enjoyment of the reader. Desire is involved in the reading process: desire for
action, reaction and resolution. Indeed, at 1.1.4, the following statement is made:

φιλόνεικος[5] δέ ἐστιν ὁ Ἔρως καὶ χαίρει τοῖς παραδόξοις κατορθώμασιν· ...

But Erōs is strife-loving and rejoices in unexpected successes ...

It could be argued that Erōs is not only authorial in wanting to create a text full
of unexpected paradoxes, but he is also indicative of the desires of the implied
reader: a predictable narrative has little attraction for the reader. At this early
stage in the narrative, Erōs works to bring the protagonists together, and readerly
desire for excitement and the need for the union of Callirhoe and Chaereas are
not at this point divergent.

The events involving the rejected suitors change the narrative direction,
causing unpredictability. Thus, the reader's desire can align with the suitors': the
marriage of Chaereas and Callirhoe must be threatened for the sake of the
reader's enjoyment. Furthermore, in the ruler of Acragas' speech, Erōs is invoked
as an agent who will bring about Chaereas' downfall, along with Jealousy (1.2.5).
If Erōs' mutability is such that he can be both matchmaker for the protagonists
and a force working to separate them, then his role can already be seen as
complicated. Alternatively, given the focalization through one of the suitors, Erōs
could be being misrepresented here for the sake of instilling this speech with
persuasive power: if the ruler of Acragas can convince the others that he is
working with such an ally, then his plan is more likely to be adopted. While the

first plan to disrupt the marriage fails (1.3), the success of the second lends credence to the ruler of Acragas' intention to use Love and Jealousy against Chaereas: this is exactly what transpires, in the sense that the intensity of Chaereas' erotic desire for Callirhoe is intrinsic to his capacity for jealousy regarding her (1.4). While the role of the scheming suitors is crucial to the narrative drive at this stage, the susceptibility of Chaereas to their lies, and Erōs' implicit part in this disruption to the central relationship of this narrative are also important.

Erōs' role in punishing Chaereas is made clear at 8.1.3, when Aphrodite relents and turns against Tychē's continuing machinations against Chaereas:

... ἤδη γὰρ αὐτῷ διηλλάττετο, πρότερον ὀργισθεῖσα χαλεπῶς διὰ τὴν ἄκαιρον ζηλοτυπίαν, ὅτι δῶρον παρ'αὐτῆς λαβὼν τὸ κάλλιστον, οἷον οὐδὲ Ἀλέξανδρος ὁ Πάρις, ὕβρισεν εἰς τὴν χάριν. ἐπεὶ δὲ καλῶς ἀπελογήσατο τῷ Ἔρωτι Χαιρέας ἀπὸ δύσεως εἰς ἀνατολὰς διὰ μυρίων παθῶν πλανηθείς, ἠλέησεν αὐτὸν Ἀφροδίτη καὶ ὅπερ ἐξ ἀρχῆς δύο τῶν καλλίστων ἥρμοσε ζεῦγος, γυμνάσασα διὰ γῆς καὶ θαλάσσης, πάλιν ἠθέλησεν ἀποδοῦναι.

... by now she was becoming reconciled to Chaereas, though earlier she had been intensely angered at his ill-timed jealousy; for, having received from her the fairest of gifts, surpassing even that given to Alexander surnamed Paris, he had repaid her favour with insult. Since Chaereas had now made full amends to Love by his wanderings from west to east amid countless tribulations, Aphrodite took pity on him, and, as she had originally brought together this handsome pair, so now, having harassed them over land and sea, she resolved to unite them again.

While Aphrodite's role as seeking vengeance is foregrounded in this passage, Erōs' motivation is also referred to, so that the reader can return to the section where the events involving the suitors are narrated with a better understanding of the god's implicit role. One is invited to follow the trajectory of readerly desire at 1.2–4, and Erōs' actions, whether explicit or implicit, are crucial for narrative momentum. However, this does not mean that readerly *sōphrosunē* is completely unnecessary here: there is a tension between the reader's empathy for both Callirhoe and Chaereas, and her/his desire for narrative action.

The balance between readerly desire and *sōphrosunē* is upset after the *Liebespaar* are separated. Now the ideal reader wants the central couple to be reunited, but not yet. The twists of fortune to come are welcome because they continue to entertain, but at times they also threaten the narrative flow, so that there is a frisson of readerly anxiety that the resolution might not be satisfactory. The men other than Chaereas who desire Callirhoe are necessary in order to create diversion and interest in the text, and they are also the greatest threats to narrative teleology. While Mithridates and the Persian King both desire Callirhoe, the representation of Dionysius has the most complex implications on a metanarrative level, so that representation shall be my next concern.[6]

Dionysius' moral struggle is represented in such a way as to invite sympathy for his predicament, and the opposition between his *sōphrosunē* and Erōs is also spelt out (2.4.5), which clearly sets up the concept as conflicting with erotic desire.[7] I suggest that the desire on the part of the reader at this point is perhaps for Dionysius' desire to continue to be represented, rather than for his erotic success with Callirhoe. It is clear that Dionysius' desire for Callirhoe and his ability to be *sōphrōn* are held in balance to the extent that he does not commit an act of sexual *hubris*, but cannot escape from his overwhelming passion for the girl. But there is more to the opposition between desire and *sōphrosunē* here. Dionysius is characterized by his status as a *pepaideumenos*,[8] which may align him with the educated reader, and his ethical stance could be viewed as something worth aspiring to on the part of the reader. Therefore, it is easy to see the reader's *sōphrosunē* being encouraged by the portrayal of Dionysius. But the fact remains that Callirhoe's beauty affects this *pepaideumenos* to the extent that his behaviour is significantly altered and his life is transformed: the implication of this is that the text *Callirhoe* could be just as seductive as its eponymous heroine. Erōs is once more described as φιλόνεικος, which indicates his continuing role as both disrupting characters' ethical intent and spurring the narrative in new directions. His clear dismissal of Dionysius' *sōphrosunē* at 2.4.5 not only illustrates how the virtue is threatened by the god at this point, but also illustrates how the author (who is the real drive behind the text) will threaten his readers' *sōphrosunē* as the narrative develops and advances. Indeed, at this very point in the novel, the reader may think that Dionysius is a suitable replacement for Chaereas who perhaps does not deserve his wife and should be punished: this 'erotic' readerly desire for the union of Dionysius and Callirhoe is perhaps tempered with the knowledge that the initial attraction and love between Chaereas and Callirhoe was mutual and therefore supersedes all other potential relationships. But the desire for this union is rewarded when Dionysius marries Callirhoe: the divergent desires of the reader are encouraged by an author who lays the blame squarely at Erōs' door. Dionysius' struggle at 2.4, can be seen as emblematic of the reader's dilemma. While Dionysius tries to resist the erotic lure of Callirhoe by reminding himself of his status and *sōphrosunē*, the reader is at risk of losing her/his *sōphrōn* focus on the expected *telos* of Chaereas' and Callirhoe's reunion by means of this tempting alternative narrative trajectory: *Callirhoe* has the power to lead us where it will.

The tension between readerly desire and *sōphrosunē* is sustained throughout the subsequent narrative: it is not only when Callirhoe's chastity is threatened by rival lovers that the balance is affected, but also when events occur which seem to imply the protagonists' further separation or imminent reunion. This tension created for the reader by the misfortunes which occur for the protagonists is implicitly acknowledged towards the close of the novel where the following statement is made:

> Νομίζω δὲ καὶ τὸ τελευταῖον τοῦτο σύγγραμμα τοῖς ἀναγινώσκουσιν ἥδιστον γενήσεσθαι· καθάρσιον γάρ ἐστι τῶν ἐν τοῖς πρώτοις σκυθρωπῶν.

> And I think this last book will be most pleasureable to readers: for it is a purge of the misfortunes in the preceding ones.

8.1.4

Although there have been other authorial comments,[9] these could be seen as narratorial: this is the only instance where both text (σύγγραμμα) and readers (τοῖς ἀναγινώσκουσιν) are mentioned.[10] This self-conscious sentence suggests that pleasure is to come in this final book for the readers, which will be a purge (καθάρσιον) of the troubles portrayed in the previous books.[11] While I will not focus in detail on the use of καθάρσιον and its potential allusivity, it is, for my purposes, important to point out that the idea of purification by means of replacing trial and tribulation with happy events for the protagonists carries with it the clear message that this novel has an aesthetic drive, which the author is keen to emphasize. He reveals himself to be not objective and dispassionate, but desirous of the 'right' ending for the central couple. Inherent in this desire for a 'purge' for his readers is the judgement that the illicit desires directed at Callirhoe will no longer feature and, thus, authorial *sōphrosunē* steps in now that Erōs has been appeased (8.1.3). This passage tells us how the author constructs his readers' desires: they should not want any more misfortune or turbulence, he suggests, rather they should now want happy resolution, and this is what they shall have. This is spelt out:

> οὐκέτι λῃστεία καὶ δουλεία καὶ δίκη καὶ μάχη καὶ ἀποκαρτέρησις καὶ πόλεμος καὶ ἅλωσις ἐν τούτῳ, ἀλλὰ ἔρωτες δίκαιοι <καὶ> νόμιμοι γάμοι.

> No longer piracy and slavery and trials and fighting and suicide and war and captivity in this one, but just love <and> lawful marriage.

As I stated earlier in this section, readerly desire is encouraged to align with the novel's trajectory, and, in this final book, the author leaves the reader in no doubt as to where that trajectory is leading. The prolepsis indicating that just love and lawful marriage will be the focus of this book assumes, or insists, that this is what the reader now desires. This relies upon the reader now rejecting his desire for narrative twists and turns: now readerly *sōphrosunē*, leading us to the pleasure of the ending, supersedes readerly *erōs*.

Despite the above considerations, there is the sense of shifting narrative potential both just prior to and just beyond this bold authorial statement. At 8.1.2 the narrator states that Fortune intended Chaereas to leave Aradus without Callirhoe, abandoning her to his enemies. This near disaster need not be mentioned, but the narrator is clearly intending to demonstrate his awareness of an alternative narrative direction, in order to reject it, and to draw attention to the supremacy of Aphrodite's will over Tychē's.[12] At 8.1.6, the apparent willingness of Chaereas to enter into a new relationship with a captive beauty before he recognizes her to be Callirhoe is indicative of how his *sōphrosunē* is almost compromised.[13] The reader's perspective here allows her/him to enjoy this humorous interlude of Chaereas' near infidelity, safe in the knowledge that the prisoner is Callirhoe, but the potential for how the hero's character might be perceived suggests that, in this chapter, Chariton is still allowing dangerous perspectives to be entertained. This belies the statement at 8.1.4, and indicates that, while assured of the 'happy ending' to come, the reader is not resigned to this, and her/his expectations are still being manipulated to a certain extent by an author, who even when revealing his intentions, does so in the midst of continuing tension. Even at the very close of the novel, the reader is given a hint that, beyond the final lines, all may not be well forever: Callirhoe's prayer to Aphrodite at least entertains the possibility that there could be more trouble ahead for our couple (8.8.16). So the 'happy ending' is not unequivocally granted: the narrative is not absolutely 'closed'.[14]

3.2 Longus' Erōs and the reader's *sōphrosunē*

The implied *sōphrosunē* of the reader of Longus' text acts in a similar way to that demonstrated in Chariton's, tempering the erotic drive in order to focus on the desired *telos*. In further considering the metanarrative implications of Longus' Prologue narrator's prayer for *sōphrosunē*, as discussed above,[15] it is necessary to consider the role of Erōs as the narrative force of the subsequent text.[16] While

Erōs' universality is clear from the Prologue, and his power is a metanarrative comment on the potency of the author, the Prologue narrator's prayer for *sōphrosunē* indicates an anxiety about how to control a narrative that is governed by Love. Simultaneously, there are clear signs in the Prologue that Erōs is already at the heart of what the narrator sees in the painting, and the subsequent comments regarding the usefulness of the following text and its role as an offering to the god reinforce the sense that Erōs spurs on the production of the four books.

Erōs' role as a cipher for the author is crucial, and gives a twist to the function of *sōphrosunē* in this text. Given that at 2.27, Pan states that Erōs wants to make a *mythos* out of Chloe, and that at 1.11 Erōs 'plots something serious' as Daphnis and Chloe play, it is clear that the god drives this narrative forward, with the consummation of desire being the obvious goal for this 'author'. Philetas' tale at 2.3–7 further emphasizes Erōs' plans for Daphnis and Chloe: the god's intention is illustrated for the young couple, and their reaction to the story indicates to the reader that while Erōs drives the action, Daphnis' and Chloe's innocence somewhat tempers that erotic drive. As the youths' efforts at 'curing' their lovesickness fail, the reader, with their superior sexual knowledge, and their awareness of the need for *sōphrosunē* as indicated in the Prologue, is pulled in two directions. In places, their desires align with Daphnis' and Chloe's, so that there is empathy for their continual erotic frustration. Elsewhere, the reader's knowledge that Daphnis' and Chloe's continuing failure to consummate their relationship should ensure that no generic transgression will take place is prioritised. This *sōphrōn* inclination is perhaps strongest once Daphnis has acquired superior sexual knowledge to Chloe (see particularly, 3.24).[17] Now that Daphnis has gained some of the sexual knowledge needed for acculturation, and maintains a continuing compassion for Chloe, it is clearer to the reader that the generic trajectory need not be disrupted. Our desires can be restrained in line with Daphnis': although the reader's motivation is clearly divergent from the youth's, there is a similar concern for the preservation of Chloe's virginity for those readers who want the conventional happy ending.

Just as there is contrast between the plans of Erōs and the innocence of the protagonists in *Daphnis and Chloe*, there is also a contrast between the reader's erotic desires for anti-generic developments and her/his *sōphrosunē* as encouraged by the Prologue narrator. The reader's implicit superiority in terms of sexual knowledge and erotic awareness allows scope for a variety of reactions, which depend on the implications and tone of those passages that encapsulate the actions, words and emotions of Daphnis and Chloe.

3.3 Readerly *sōphrosunē* in *Leucippe and Clitophon*: resisting the narrator(s)

Erōs' direct involvement in the action of Longus' novel contrasts with the oblique way in which the god's influence is portrayed in Achilles Tatius', but I will demonstrate in this section that the role of Erōs is just as crucial on a metanarrative level in *Leucippe and Clitophon* as it is in *Daphnis and Chloe*. In the initial frame of Achilles Tatius' novel, the anonymous primary narrator focuses on Erōs' power as depicted in the painting of Europa's abduction:

> Ἔρως εἷλκε τὸν βοῦν· Ἔρως, μικρὸν παιδίον, ἡπλώκει τὸ πτερόν, ἤρτητο φαρέτραν, ἐκράτει τὸ πῦρ· μετέστραπτο δὲ ὡς ἐπὶ τὸν Δία καὶ ὑπεμειδία, ὥσπερ αὐτοῦ καταγελῶν, ὅτι δι' αὐτὸν γέγονε βοῦς.

> Erōs was leading the bull: Erōs, a little boy, had unfurled his wings, had strapped on his quiver, and was wielding his torch. He turned himself around towards Zeus and he was smiling surreptitiously as though mocking him because through him he had become a bull.
>
> 1.1.13

The lengthy ecphrasis of the mythological scene ends with this representation of Erōs, and the god's role in the abduction of Europa is emphasized. The delayed explanation for Zeus' infatuation serves as a crucial link to the introduction of Clitophon, who, while the primary narrator wonders at the power of the god, asserts that he knows about Erōs' power:

> Οἷον', εἶπον, 'ἄρχει βρέφος οὐρανοῦ καὶ γῆς καὶ θαλάττης.' Ταῦτά μου λέγοντος νεανίσκος καὶ αὐτὸς παρεστώς, 'Ἐγὼ ταῦτα ἂν εἰδείην', ἔφη, 'τοσαύτας ὕβρεις ἐξ ἔρωτος παθών.

> How that baby rules over heaven, earth and sea!' I said. When I said these things, a young man standing nearby also spoke: 'I should know these things, having suffered such assaults from Erōs.
>
> 1.2.1

The representation of Erōs as a god in the picture can be seen to be continued in the conversation which follows it. However, whether Clitophon refers to Erōs or *erōs* is debatable. In line with Repath's recent comments, I suggest that it is the god Erōs who is referred to here,[18] and therefore, if we trust Clitophon's hint, Erōs is the driver of Clitophon's narrative.[19] It is the 'assaults' from Erōs that Clitophon will go on to narrate, and, in what follows, I will discuss how Erōs' role is important for the reader and his response to the narrative, and how *sōphrosunē* is involved in this response. To comply with Erōs' will is Clitophon's only option, it seems. Any resistance is swiftly overcome, and his pursuit of Leucippe and his submission to Melite are both evidence of the god's power. In Clitophon's representation, then, Erōs propels the narrative forward, and this is clear in the first two books in particular.[20] However, within these first two books, there is subtlety and variation in how the god's power is implied by Clitophon and how he responds to that power. This in turn affects how the reader responds to his narrative.

The first place in Clitophon's narrative where the roles of *erōs* and *sōphrosunē* are represented as coming into conflict is at 1.5. Here, Clitophon responds, both as narrator and as character, to the song which relates Apollo's pursuit of Daphne:

τοῦτο μου μᾶλλον ἀσθὲν τὴν ψυχὴν ἐξέκαυσεν· ὑπέκκαυμα γὰρ ἐπιθυμίας λόγος ἐρωτικός. Κἂν εἰς σωφροσύνην τις ἑαυτὸν νουθετῇ, τῷ παραδείγματι πρὸς τὴν μίμησιν ἐρεθίζεται, μάλισθ' ὅταν ἐκ τοῦ κρείττονος ᾖ τὸ παράδειγμα· ἡ γὰρ ὧν ἁμαρτάνει τις αἰδὼς τῷ τοῦ βελτίονος ἀξιώματι παρρησία γίνεται· καὶ ταῦτα πρὸς ἐμαυτὸν ἔλεγον ʻἸδοὺ καὶ Ἀπόλλων ἐρᾷ, κἀκεῖνος παρθένου, καὶ ἐρῶν οὐκ αἰσχύνεται, ἀλλὰ διώκει τὴν παρθένον· σὺ δὲ ὀκνεῖς καὶ αἰδῇ καὶ ἀκαίρως σωφρονεῖς· μὴ κρείττων εἶ τοῦ θεοῦ;ʼ

The song inflamed my soul all the more, for an erotic story is the fuel of desire. Even if someone steers his mind towards self-control, he is roused towards imitation by an example, especially when that example is a divine one; in which case, any shame that you feel at your moral errors becomes an outspoken affront to the reputation of a higher being. This was what I said to myself: 'You see, Apollo too loves, and he too loves a maiden. *He* feels no shame at his love, but chases the maiden; whereas *you*, you are hesitant and embarrassed, and you practise an untimely self-control. Do you think yourself superior to a god?'

1.5.5–7

While the role of Erōs here is implicit rather than explicit (the god is not mentioned by name, although the use of ἔρων (1.5.7) alerts the reader to his role),[21] the emphasis on how erotic stories encourage imitation has clear metaliterary implications:[22] is the reader just as susceptible to erotic suggestion as is Clitophon? Also, is Clitophon emphasizing the lure of erotic narrative in order to suggest that his own narrative is equally seductive? The answer to both these questions is 'yes'.[23] At this point in the narrative the reader wants Clitophon's pursuit of Leucippe to advance, so that the *sōphrosunē* which he practised as a character, in the view of the reader, was indeed 'ἀκαίρως', because it is in danger of stalling the action which the reader wants to hear about. I suggest that

Clitophon is encouraging an engagement with the erotic elements of his narrative from his narratee by using sententious phrasing (ὑπέκκαυμα γὰρ ἐπιθυμίας λόγος ἐρωτικός), which emphasizes the erotic power of such narrative. Just as Clitophon as a character and as a narrator suggests that to be *sōphrōn* when faced with a story which exemplifies the unbridled power of Erōs over even the gods would be wrong, he is also implying, as narrator, that should the narratee respond with *sōphrosunē* at this point, by repressing his desire for erotic narrative convolutions, he would also be wrong. As Goldhill suggests, there is self-confessed 'slippage' in Clitophon's *sōphrosunē* here, which is then undercut by his comment regarding how one should not try to be greater than a divine paradigm,[24] and this has consequences for the reader. While Clitophon's motivation in emphasing the power of erotic narrative is to elevate his own desire for Leucippe to the level of a famous myth involving Apollo, and also to ensure that his narratee does not resist the erotic flow of his story, we must consider whether it is entirely wise to follow Clitophon's lead in this respect. I have already discussed how this episode suggests that Clitophon has a limited grasp of *sōphrosunē*, particularly in terms of his understanding of its ethical import,[25] so how does this work on a metaliterary level? If the reader does not trust Clitophon's ethical judgement, does this imply that the reader should also be wary of conforming to the manner of his reception of and reaction to erotic stories at 1.5? I would argue that despite Clitophon's lack of ethical awareness as narrator, and despite his evident naïveté, he does understand that erotic narrative has the potential to excite and stimulate those who hear it: he is, to frame it in simple terms, more interested in *erōs* than *sōphrosunē*, but at 1.5, I maintain, so is the reader.

Erōs' role as driver of the narrative, or, more accurately, Clitophon's representation of that role, continues to be important in the second book, but the emphasis changes somewhat, as the conflict between Erōs and *sōphrosunē* has potentially more crucial implications. At 2.5, the opposition between Erōs and *sōphrosunē* is clear when Clitophon's internalized debate regarding his desire for Leucippe and his obligations towards Calligone is narrated. While, just as at 1.5, the role of *sōphrosunē* is one which seems to stall the narrative drive, Erōs' victory over Clitophon's implied *sōphrosunē* at this point ultimately leads to the protagonist's attempt on Leucippe's virginity which occurs at 2.23. So, while at 2.5, the reader might still desire the victory of Erōs so that Clitophon's adventures are not restrained, by the time we see the consequences of Erōs' drive when Clitophon enters Leucippe's room, there is the potential for the reader to question his erotically motivated desire for action. The fact that Clitophon fails to consummate his desire for Leucippe, when that act could endanger the teleological thrust of the narrative, could provide the reader with some satisfaction, although the occurrence of the early consummation of the protagonists' passion might also be viewed as a subversive, but stimulating development. There remains a conflict within any reader between the desire for exciting narrative events, such as the possibility of a sexual encounter, and the *sōphrōn* hope that the generic *telos* will not be undermined.

The terminology which Clitophon as narrator employs when introducing Erōs' words at 2.5.2 – ὥσπερ ἐκ τῆς καρδίας – suggests a further level of interpretation: there is a hint here that Clitophon's representation of Erōs is perhaps self-serving, or that he is attributing his desire for Leucippe to the god, whom he perceived as dwelling within him, while his logical understanding of his duty is, in this representation, all his own. While as narrator he seems to imply the god's direct involvement in the events of the narrative, as readers we have to question whether this representation of Erōs does not in fact tell us more about Clitophon's own motivation. He represents himself as a character responding to emotional duress, suggesting that in placing the responsibility at Erōs' door, he personified his internal desire to ignore *sōphrosunē* and press on with his pursuit of Leucippe. The consequences for how the reader responds to this episode are complicated: there is the implication that, even if we accept his representation of the god's verbal intervention, Erōs tells Clitophon the character exactly what he wants to hear. However, there is the alternative consideration that Clitophon genuinely believed that Erōs was telling him what to do: this is not, therefore, necessarily the cynical apportioning of blame to an external agent, but rather, the naïve understanding of an erotically inexperienced young man.[26]

The above discussion indicates that the alert reader may question whether Clitophon's representation of Erōs can be taken seriously, which leads on to a consideration of how the god's metaliterary role is affected. If Erōs is like that aspect of Clitophon which wants to pursue his desire to its climax, perhaps the ἐπιθυμία mentioned at 1.5, the reader might now be suspicious of whether the purely erotic reading is sensible, if that reading is aligned with Clitophon's epithumetic tendency. *Sōphrosunē* at 2.5.2 is closely associated with filial duty and the negation of impulsive desire, which might imply that it has no place in the narrative at this point for a reader who is focused on the erotic. However, given that the reader should appreciate Clitophon's limited and prejudicial representation of both Erōs and *sōphrosunē*, we can surmise that Clitophon's *sōphrosunē* need not be identical with the reader's. I suggest that there is authorial play at work, so that the reader is superior to Clitophon as narrator and can, especially on a second reading, see that readerly *sōphrosunē* can provide some balance to Clitophon's erotic impulsiveness as narrator, and to Erōs' role, which, at least at 2.5, is aligned with narratorial intent. The reader might be aware of Clitophon's ethical transgressions (his implicit rejection of his betrothed, Calligone, and his pursuit of Leucippe with no explicit mention of marriage) and read with resistance against his narratorial flow, but it remains the case that generic expectations are such that Clitophon must win his beloved. The means may be transgressive and not particularly palatable to every reader's taste, but the desired *telos*, which all generically experienced readers expect, if not want, is potentially the most important motivating factor in the reader's mind. This means that a complex situation arises for the reader who has reservations about Clitophon's epithumetic tendencies: he might not want Clitophon to pursue his desire to its consummation *yet*, but he does want him to pursue his desire to its *eventual* consummation, within marriage. There is, then, an inherent tension in the reader's mind as s/he vacillates between conforming to Clitophon's narratorial intent and resisting it, which makes the reading experience all the more exciting.

Erōs and *sōphrosunē* also interact on a metaliterary level beyond the first two books: at 5.25–27, Melite accuses Clitophon of resisting Erōs' will and finally succeeds in seducing him, as discussed earlier.[27] *Sōphrosunē* is notable by its absence from the text throughout Books 5, 6 and 7, but its absence as a term does not necessarily imply its absolute absence as a concept or virtue. Indeed, Clitophon later suggests that he needs to emphasize his *sōphrosunē* in relation to Melite when telling his story to Sostratus (8.5), so that there is the implication that he saw himself as being in possession of the virtue to a certain extent when 'married' to Melite: in his view, he needs to exaggerate his *sōphrosunē*, but not to invent it.

So, what does the reader want at the point where Melite succeeds in seducing Clitophon? Should we align our readerly desire with that of Melite's *erōs*? Or, should we opt for a more *sōphrōn* reading? Are we to be subversively pleased at this new twist, or shocked at the anti-generic turn of events? Melite's role complicates how the reader responds to the text because it is not a straightforward role: she is an alternative lover for Clitophon but she is not vindictive towards her rival Leucippe; she wants to seduce the protagonist but tries to do so in a socially acceptable way (when married, and while Leucippe is 'dead'), before all her hope is lost and she resorts to emotional pleading for a no-strings attached sexual act; she is secondary to Leucippe, but in places her passion for Clitophon is more heartfelt than that of Leucippe, at least as far as Clitophon represents their respective passion. However, all of this is according to Clitophon, so that we are never sure if Melite is too good to be true, in terms of her consistent desire for the narrator and in terms of her attractiveness and intelligence. Whether we accept Clitophon's apportioning of blame for his sexual submission on his fear of Erōs is also debatable. However, in terms of Clitophon's narrative strategy, it is plausible to see that there is an implied role for Erōs' strategies, as Clitophon represents them: it is clear that every plan of Erōs' comes to fruition to some extent in this narrative, and the *sōphrōn* aspect of the reader's motivation is balanced by this awareness.

Clitophon attributes his adventures to Erōs, but, of course, it is Achilles Tatius who is really responsible for events in the novel. As Clitophon argues against the god at 2.5.2, this can be read as a demonstration of authorial power, as the author aligns himself with a divinity. This explains why there is more emphasis on Erōs in the earlier part of the novel, when the narrative is being initiated. In the final two books it could be argued that the implied presence of authorial control which is denoted by the role of Erōs is now less necessary because the narrative drive is well established. The ideal reader's concerns are also less 'erotic' in these two books, where the primary concern is for the welfare, and, indeed, for the survival of the protagonists rather than for their marriage.[28] However, the reader's attention is refocused on the issue of the protagonists' marriage at the close of the novel. The narrative does not end unequivocally with the marriage of the protagonists: the wedding is performed in Byzantium, before the couple travel to Tyre, where Callisthenes and Calligone wed, and where they all spend the winter, but trouble is implied by the unresumed frame, and by Clitophon's presence alone in Sidon and his downcast mood as he speaks of the *hubreis* he has suffered at the hands of Erōs, which brings us back to 1.2.1.[29] There is tension beyond the close of the novel between erotic readerly desire and *sōphrosunē*. This tension indicates the lack of complete satisfaction for the reader, who only attains a limited version of the narrative consummation which s/he expects and wants. While the reader has been allowed some relief from erotic tension in the last two books, at 8.19 the tension resurfaces, never to be resolved. The lack of knowledge that the reader possesses about exactly why Clitophon is unhappy, why he does not have Leucippe with him, and why he is in Sidon in the frame, suggests that Achilles Tatius, in pushing against the boundaries of the genre,[30] also subverts the purpose of having tension between the different reading strategies by allowing it no release at the climax of the novel. Readers are left with only their own imaginations to try and figure out what happened between events at the close of Clitophon's narration and his appearance in the frame. There is no chance for the reader to be wholly satisfied with the *telos* of marriage. By denying his readers complete satisfaction in generic terms, the author succeeds in creating a new kind of response from his reader, who can appreciate this inherently humorous manipulation of the boundaries of the genre. Achilles Tatius invites us to reflect on the fact that we never really finish reading his novel: we are constantly forced to reconsider the frame, then the close, and to speculate on potential solutions to the eternal problem of how Clitophon ended up as he did.

3.4 Tempering Erōs in the *Aethiopica*

In Heliodorus' *Aethiopica*, Erōs' role is not overt: he is never present in the action as a personified entity, and the lovesickness suffered by Chariclea and Theagenes is not couched as vengeance on the god's behalf. The primary narrator does not refer to the god, which implies that he is not concerned with reproducing the earlier novels' pattern of representing Erōs as a principal narrative drive. However, there are some implicit references to Erōs by Calasiris, which suggest that his role is to be considered as significant, and are notable particularly given that it is in Calasiris' narrative that the onset of love between the protagonists is described.

One of the places where Erōs is mentioned by Calasiris is at 4.10.5–6, where Calasiris responds to Chariclea's reluctance to speak about her desire for Theagenes:[31]

> Ἀλλ' ἐπειδήπερ ἅπαξ ἔρωτος ἐπήσθου καὶ φανείς σε Θεαγένης ᾕρηκε, τοῦτο γὰρ ὀμφή μοι θεῶν ἐμήνυσε, σὺ μὲν ἴσθι μὴ μόνη καὶ πρώτη τὸ πάθος ὑποστᾶσα ἀλλὰ σὺν πολλαῖς μὲν γυναιξὶ τῶν ἐπισήμων σὺν πολλαῖς δὲ παρθένοις τῶν τὰ ἄλλα σωφρόνων· μέγιστος γὰρ θεῶν ὁ Ἔρως καὶ ἤδη καὶ θεῶν αὐτῶν ποτε κρατεῖν λεγόμενος.

> But since you have once felt love, and Theagenes has captured you at first sight, for a voice from the gods informed me of this, understand that you are not the only woman or the first to experience this passion, but you are in the company of many distinguished ladies and many virgins who are otherwise virtuous. Love is the greatest of the gods and is even said sometimes to master the gods themselves.

This passage is designed by Calasiris to comfort Chariclea and he follows it with his recommendation for her to preserve her *sōphrōn* nature by thinking of marriage (4.10.6). However, there is also a metaliterary hint here with the mention of how the power of Erōs is described in stories, where he is said to conquer gods. A similar phrase is used in Chariton's *Callirhoe*, where the Persian King suggests that he has heard stories about how Erōs overpowers gods, but that he nevertheless always considered himself unconquerable:

> τίς γὰρ ἐστιν Ἔρως πρότερον ἤκουον ἐν μύθοις τε καὶ ποιήμασιν, ὅτι κρατεῖ πάντων τῶν θεῶν καὶ αὐτοῦ τοῦ Διός· ἠπίστουν δὲ ὅμως ὅτι δύναταί τις παρ'ἐμὲ γενέσθαι δυνατώτερος.

> Long ago I heard in stories and poems who Love is, and that he rules all the gods, even Zeus himself. However, I did not believe that in a match with me anyone could come out on top.

> Char. 6.3.2

I suggest that there is intertextuality present here: there is the use of forms of κρατέω in both texts in regard to Erōs' power over the gods; there is also the use of the term λεγόμενος in Heliodorus' text which implies the widespread familiarity with sayings or stories about Erōs, evoking Chariton's King's words. Perhaps this is a deliberate ploy on the part of the novelists to draw attention to the extent of this genre's power, which, as we shall see, is aligned with Erōs' on a metanarrative level. While both Calasiris and the King seem to demonstrate their familiarity with literary tradition here, it is also clear that the narratives of which they are a part are also concerned with the victories of Erōs. Generic self-assertion is surely a factor here: although it may be principally in other genres (epic, tragedy) that Erōs' power over gods is presented, this genre's concern with the erotic experience on the mortal plane is just as important, perhaps even more so.

In Calasiris' speech, he is trying to make Chariclea accept the inevitability of Erōs' success, while offering her a way of not falling victim to loss of reputation and feelings of shame. This involves the recognition of the fact that other *sōphrōn* maidens have suffered in this way and that marriage is a *sōphrōn* reaction to erotic desire. *Sōphrosunē* is not presented as working in absolute opposition to Erōs in this instance (it is rather that *sōphrōn* women will submit to Erōs by marrying the objects of their desire). However, there is clearly a dichotomy between the two in that those who possess the virtue see their erotic desire as a shameful emotion (τὸ ἐπιθυμίας αἰσχρὸν: 4.10.6). This dichotomy can be approached from a metaliterary angle: these erotic stories brought about by Erōs' power demand a response from the reader that reflects their content. It is not just that the reading process involves play between delay and resolution which mirrors the process of desiring: here, in this text, implicitly, Erōs drives one element of the narrative (the mutual desire between the protagonists), which invites comparison between this genre and others which are concerned with the deeds of Erōs. Just as the presence of desire can be reconciled to a *sōphrōn* lifestyle by the introduction of the promise of a long-delayed marriage, so the ethical concept can work as a tempering force on the desire of the reader. The reader's desire is not dismissed, just as Chariclea's is not; but the *sōphrosunē* inherent in the text, just as it is inherent in Chariclea, particularly from this point on, is a crucial factor, and the reader must reconcile her/himself to its power, as well as to Erōs'. The implication does not negate the superior power of Erōs over mortals and gods alike, and even over the reader, but it suggests subtly that the reader can maintain her/his *sōphrosunē* even while following the lead of 'erotic' desire for the consummation of the narrative. Just like Chariclea, the reader can be both desirous and *sōphrōn*: narrative power is aligned with erotic power and the presence of *sōphrosunē* is allowed as a force enabling a balanced appreciation of the ebb and flow of the reading experience.

*

In the previous four sections, I have explored how a tension is created in the reading experience, as the desire to follow the erotic drive of the narrative is balanced by the potential for readerly *sōphrosunē* to varying degrees. In the next three sections, the role of embedded narratives and internal narratees in the *Ephesiaca*, *Leucippe and Clitophon* and the *Aethiopica* will be the focus, with a view to considering how these elements affect the reader's response and with a view to considering the extent to which readerly *sōphrosunē* is involved in this response.

3.5 Embedded narrative in the *Ephesiaca*

There are instances in Xenophon of Ephesus' text where secondary narratives are told in order to preserve *sōphrosunē*. While these are indicative of the persuasive power of the narratives in question, they also display in clear terms how narrative inherently possesses the potential for impact on the narratee. These occurrences of *mise-en-abyme* suggest that the primary narrative possesses the same potential to impress and influence. While the aims of Anthia's 'stories' are to avert sexual advances and to preserve *sōphrosunē*, the 'aims' of the wider narrative are not so clearly demarcated. However, in a text so concerned with displaying sexual fidelity (often termed *sōphrosunē*) and the *technē* needed to do this, the extent to which the narrator's intention is to make his reader accept this virtue as part of the reading process is an important consideration.

To look at one of Anthia's inset narratives: on two occasions (2.9.4; 3.5.6) these narratives are apparently honest versions of the wider narrative so far, albeit from Anthia's perspective. Neither of these is told in direct speech, and the reader has only the briefest of summaries. While the episode at 3.5.6 is an example of how Anthia uses her story in order to gain help from a stranger (the doctor, Eudoxus),[32] it is the reaction to the mini-narrative at 2.9.4 which is important for a metaliterary reading involving *sōphrosunē*: this narration and the reaction to it not only demonstrate the power of narrative to persuade, but the episode also involves an averted sexual act by means of narrative skill. When Lampo reacts to Anthia's pleading and to her story by not forcing her into sex, she has used the power of narrative to persuade a simple goatherd to disobey his masters and resist the temptation to seduce or rape her. While this achievement relies in part on Lampo's character, it is still the case that Anthia needs to persuade him: she is not confident that the goatherd will automatically treat her with the respect she believes she deserves. Further, there is the suggestion, albeit implicit, that Anthia replaces the sexual act with narrative, something which is parallel to the scene in *Apollonius, King of Tyre* (34),[33] where Tarsia, who has been forced into a brothel, tells the story of her misfortunes to each new client, thus causing them to cease their sexual advances towards her due to their feelings of pity. There, just as in the representation of Anthia's narration here, Tarsia's words are not conveyed in direct speech, so that the reader is left to speculate as to the content of her story. It is implicit that both Anthia and Tarsia relate what the narrators of the main narratives have already related to us, hinting at the power of the wider narratives. While Tarsia's narrative is equated with the sexual act more directly than Anthia's (she is in a brothel and she is paid for her storytelling, albeit before her clients realise that stories are what they shall get), there is still the implication that a 'higher' form of human contact is achieved by Anthia's tale and its effect on Lampo, than that of a sexual act which would have the potential of pleasure for only one participant. Thus, the act of narrative is not merely aligned with the act of sex, but is raised above it, and the preservation of Anthia's *sōphrosunē* is brought about by Lampo's sympathy for her woes: these aspects suggest that the reader may achieve a heightened engagement with the text, which allows for a range of reactions, some of which, like Lampo's, involve an implicit *sōphrosunē* in their empathetic response.

3.6 Achilles Tatius: pleasure, erotic narratives and the reader's response

At *Leucippe and Clitophon*, 8.4, Clitophon narrates how there was an awkward silence as he, Leucippe and Sostratus came to terms with their reunion and Thersander's violent assault on Clitophon. They were in Artemis' temple at Ephesus, with the priest, who had provided them with refuge. Eventually, with the wine taking effect, the priest broke the silence, and addressed Sostratus as follows:

> Τί οὐ λέγεις, ὦ ξένε, τὸν περὶ ὑμᾶς μῦθον ὅστις ἐστί; Δοκεῖ γὰρ μοι περιπλοκάς τινας ἔχειν οὐκ ἀηδεῖς· οἴνῳ δὲ μάλιστα πρέπουσιν οἱ τοιοῦτοι λόγοι.

> Why not tell, my guest, the story in which you are involved? For it seems to me the twists and turns would be not unpleasurable. Speeches of that sort go particularly well with wine.

8.4.2

The idea of the convoluted story being pleasurable reminds the reader of the frame, where the primary narrator indicated that Clitophon's experiences would be more pleasurable to him in being like *mythois* (1.2.2),[34] and of his desire to hear erotic tales in a pleasant setting (1.2.3). The use of the term περιπλοκάς at 8.4 indicates that the priest, like the anonymous narrator, is keen on erotic stories.[35] The *mise-en-abyme* effect of Clitophon's narration at 8.5, as noted by Repath,[36] implies that the priest is like the primary narrator, with pleasure as the goal of the reception of narrative: the reaction of the reader will obviously also involve pleasure, but is that all it will involve?

Sostratus, after briefly introducing himself and his role in the story, continues as follows:

> τὸ δὲ λοιπόν, ὅπερ ἐστὶ μῦθος, λέγε τέκνον Κλειτοφῶν, μηδὲν αἰδούμενος. Καὶ γὰρ εἴ τί μοι συμβέβηκε λυπηρόν, μάλιστα μὲν οὐ σόν ἐστιν, ἀλλὰ τῆς Τύχης· ἔπειτα τῶν ἔργων παρελθόντων ἡ διήγησις τὸν οὐκέτι πάσχοντα ψυχαγωγεῖ[37] μᾶλλον ἢ λυπεῖ.

> As for the rest, which is the real story, speak Clitophon my boy, and don't be ashamed. After all, if events have caused me a certain amount of grief, it is certainly not your fault, but Fortune's. And, anyway, a narrative of events past for one whose sufferings are over entertains rather than grieves.

8.4.3–4

While the translation from Whitmarsh (which I have modified above) suggests that Sostratus is allaying Clitophon's concerns for Sostratus' feelings about the story, it is also plausible that the generalised statement which Sostratus makes concerning the entertaining potential of the narrative of past events for one whose sufferings are over refers to Clitophon too, and, indeed, Leucippe (although their suffering, or at least the potential for more suffering and humiliation, is not yet over). There is pleasure, then, for both narrators and narratees, and there is the suggestion that narrative which is told when the events narrated have been resolved is a pleasure to all concerned: the sufferings experienced are transformed into an entertainment.

The role of readerly *sōphrosunē*, which, as I discussed earlier, is nuanced according to which part of the narrative is being read, at this point in the final book should act to make readers reflect on how they compare with the internal narratees: are they interested, like the priest and Sostratus, exclusively in erotic narrative pleasure, or is their approach more subtle? Sostratus' and the priest's characterization is important here: are these narratees models to imitate or to avoid? Sostratus proves himself to be a rather naïve narratee later in the final book when he tells Clitophon about Callisthenes' moral transformation (8.17–18): clearly he has believed Callisthenes' version of events without question, and he is equally credulous regarding Clitophon's account, which the reader is aware is doctored (8.5.2). At 8.10, the priest's speech against Thersander is peppered with vulgarity, which demonstrates that he has an unpriestly interest in sexual gossip.[38] Neither Sostratus nor the priest are particularly 'ideal' narratees: their respective naïveté (which indicates a lack of moral judgement) and their efforts at slander demonstrate this, and the reader would do well to consider the consequences of being like these narratees, who are ethically unsound. This consideration, coupled with the reader's awareness of the subversion of the ideas put forward in the *Republic*, which was explicit at 1.5, as I discuss above,[39] but which is also evident here, means that there is a significant role for readerly *sōphrosunē* at this point in the narrative, which can temper the implied desire for exclusively pleasurable narrative to a certain extent. A reader interested in ethics may well regard narrative as having multiple purposes, pleasure being only one among these, and the roles of Sostratus and the priest at 8.4 may alert this type of reader to the risk in reading purely for hedonistic ends.

While the above discussion suggests the ethical risks of enjoying narrative too much, the role of readerly *sōphrosunē* could connect with some of the Platonic overtones evoked by the frame conversation between the anonymous primary narrator and Clitophon. While the pursuit of pleasure and the sexual connotations of a drinking-party suggest a lack of restraint in those wishing to be entertained by narrative, the Phaedran allusion at 1.2 suggests that there is a more complex set of implications for those wishing to be entertained. The allusion to Plato's *Phaedrus,* in the description of the place where the anonymous primary narrator led Clitophon so that he could tell his tale, is recognized and discussed.[40] Here I will consider the role of pleasure in the frame of *Leucippe and Clitophon,* and the effect of the Platonic allusion on the reader's perception of that pleasure. Clitophon is persuaded by the primary narrator to tell his erotic tale (1.2.2), which is 'like *mythoi*' (making the primary narrator all the more excited), and the setting for this narrative is described as follows:

> Καὶ ταῦτα δὴ λέγων δεξιοῦμαί τε αὐτὸν καὶ ἐπί τινος ἄλσους ἄγω γείτονος, ἔνθα πλάτανοι μὲν ἐπεφύκεσαν πολλαὶ καὶ πυκναί, παρέρρει δὲ ὕδωρ ψυχρόν τε καὶ διαυγές, οἷον ἀπὸ χιόνος ἄρτι λυθείσης ἔρχεται. Καθίσας οὖν αὐτὸν ἐπί τινος θώκου χαμαιζήλου καὶ αὐτὸς παρακαθισάμενος, "Ὥρα σοι', ἔφην, 'τῆς τῶν λόγων ἀκροάσεως· πάντως δὲ ὁ τοιοῦτος τόπος ἡδὺς καὶ μύθων ἄξιος ἐρωτικῶν.'

> And with these words, I took him by the hand and led him to a neighbouring grove, where the plane trees grew thick and plentiful, and the water flowed by cool and clear, just as it comes from freshly melted snow. I sat him down there on a low bench, and sat myself next to him. 'Well, it is time to hear your account,' I said, 'A setting such as this is delightful, and just right for erotic stories.'

> 1.2.3

The corresponding setting in the *Phaedrus* (230b–c) is described in the dialogue by Socrates. As we have seen in the discussion above, pleasure and narrative are closely connected in Achilles Tatius' text, and it is important to note that in the part of the *Phaedrus* to which the frame of *Leucippe and Clitophon* alludes, the spot at which Socrates and Phaedrus will choose to stop is described in the following way by Socrates, after he has noted the natural features and sacred aspects of the *topos*:

> εἰ δ᾽ αὖ βούλει, τὸ εὔπνουν τοῦ τόπου ὡς ἀγαπητὸν καὶ σφόδρα ἡδύ· ...

> Then again, if you like, how welcome it is, the fresh air of the place, and very pleasant ...

> 230c1–2: text and trans. Rowe 1986, as throughout: trans. adapted

Phaedrus responds to Socrates by suggesting that he is more like a visitor than a local in his appreciation of the surroundings. Socrates replies that it is learning in which he is interested and that such learning comes from the people in the city, rather than from the countryside and its trees, with the implication that he rarely leaves the city to go outside its walls: Phaedrus has succeeded in leading him here only by proferring speeches (230c6–e2). Pleasant surroundings are very much a secondary consideration for Socrates as he is portrayed here: it is for the sake of learning that he has followed Phaedrus to this place, and it is the hearing and discussion of speeches which is important to the philosopher. While the anonymous primary narrator in Achilles Tatius' text focuses on the potential pleasure of hearing Clitophon's erotic *mythos* in a pleasant spot, it is for the sake of learning from *logoi* that Socrates stops at the pleasant *topos*.

Later in the *Phaedrus*, when Socrates is making his first speech (which is his response to Lysias', mirroring the content but changing the argumentation), he mentions how everyone is ruled by two things: the 'inborn desire for pleasure' (ἡ . . . ἔμφυτος οὖσα ἐπιθυμία ἡδονῶν) and 'an acquired judgement which aims at the best' (δὲ ἐπίκτητος δόξα, ἐφιεμένη τοῦ ἀρίστου: 237d7–9). This is followed by a discussion of the potential conflict between these two things, which leads to the suggestion that *sōphrosunē* and desire for pleasure leading to *hubris* are in opposition:

> δόξης μὲν οὖν ἐπὶ τὸ ἄριστον λόγῳ ἀγούσης καὶ κρατούσης τῷ κράτει σωφροσύνη ὄνομα· ἐπιθυμίας δὲ ἀλόγως ἑλκούσης ἐπὶ ἡδονὰς καὶ ἀρξάσης ἐν ἡμῖν τῇ ἀρχῇ ὕβρις ἐπωνομάσθη.

> Now when judgement leads us by means of reason by what is best and is in control, its control over us has the name of restraint; when desire drags us irrationally towards pleasures and rules in us, its rule is called by the name of wantonness.

> 237e2–238a2

This speech is one Socrates will dismiss later in the dialogue, and therefore could be said to contain flawed assertions. However, the opposition between the desire for pleasure and *sōphrosunē* is picked up in Socrates' second speech, where he suggests that the charioteer of the soul can only control the soul's irrational part (represented by the bad horse), which tends towards sexual pleasure, by recalling the Form of *Sōphrosunē* which was viewed by the soul as it travelled around heaven (254b5–c3). What does all of this mean for pleasure in Achilles Tatius' text? I suggest that by recalling the *Phaedrus* in his frame, the author intends his readers to recognize that the pleasure to be gained from erotic narrative should be tempered by *sōphrosunē*. The reader should realise that Socrates' primary concern in the *Phaedrus* is not for erotic pleasure, but for understanding how the erotic can be made philosophically beautiful by *sōphrosunē*'s role in the soul of the lover. While it is quite possible to read this novel hedonistically, without concerning oneself with the questions evoked by the Phaedran allusion, or by seeing the allusion as ironic or as a parody, I think that Achilles allows the possibility that narrative can make the reader's *sōphrosunē* become a part of the reading experience. Far from negating the entertainment value of the text, this encourages 'high' entertainment. By recognizing that Clitophon's narrative and the various responses to it within the text (from the primary narrator before it begins, and from the priest and Sostratus) focus exclusively on the potential for pleasure, the reader can be more *sōphrōn* in his reading, and engage with the intertextual nuances rather than responding bathetically to the περίπλοκαι on offer.[41]

3.7 Heliodorus: Cnemon and the reader

Heliodorus' *Aethiopica* is the most complex in terms of narrative structure, and this means that it is richly rewarding for metanarrative analysis. Here, I will focus on the role of Cnemon as Calasiris' narratee, and analyse the extent to which he is a model or anti-model for the implied reader, and whether this affects the role of readerly *sōphrosunē*. There are several places in the text where Cnemon is presented as an erotically driven narratee,[42] whose insatiable appetite for narrative can be read as either suggesting that Cnemon's unrestrained desire for a certain type of narrative presents him as an anti-paradigmatic receiver of narrative,[43] or that the reader will also have this appetite, which is a generic expectation.[44] The addition of the idea of reading with *sōphrosunē* complicates the argument: does Cnemon's example mean that this is a valid or invalid option for the 'ideal' reader? Does a *sōphrōn* reading subvert the generic expectation, and how far is this a rewarding way of reading Heliodorus?

The passage which exemplifies Cnemon's position as an erotically driven narratee is that at 4.4.2–3, where he responds to Calasiris' bemusement at his continuing demands for more at the expense of sleep:

> Ἐγὼ καὶ Ὁμήρῳ μέμφομαι, ὦ πάτερ, ἄλλων τε καὶ φιλότητος κόρον εἶναι φήσαντι, πράγματος ὃ κατ' ἐμὲ κριτὴν οὐδεμίαν φέρει πλησμονὴν οὔτε καθ' ἡδονὴν ἀνυόμενον οὔτε εἰς ἀκοὴν ἐρχόμενον· εἰ δέ τις καὶ τοῦ Θεαγένους καὶ Χαρικλείας ἔρωτος μνημονεύοι, τίς οὕτως ἀδαμάντινος ἢ σιδηροῦς τὴν καρδίαν ὡς μὴ θέλγεσθαι καὶ εἰς ἐνιαυτὸν ἀκούων;

> …I blame even Homer, Father, when he says that there is satiety of all things, including love. Of this thing, in my judgement, one can never have one's fill, neither when it is accomplished by its pleasure nor when it comes into one's

hearing. And if someone may relate the love of Theagenes and Chariclea, who could be so inflexible, so steely-hearted, that he would not be spellbound by the tale, even if listening for a whole year?

4.4.3

There are three different implications involved in this passage, and they are worth considering before I move on to think about the metaliterary implications. First, Cnemon, literally, 'blames' Homer for stating that there is satiety in all things (*Iliad*, 13.636–637), and states that one can never have enough of love, or tales concerning it. Second, Cnemon aligns the pleasures of love with stories about love. Third, he puts the tale concerning Theagenes' and Chariclea's love above all others in terms of narrative power. There is some distance in how Cnemon presents these views: although the use of κατ' ἐμὲ personalizes his opinions, he does not use the first person singular, preferring to express things in semi-generalized terms. This could be because he is reflecting Menelaus' style of speaking in the *Iliad* (it is worth noting that Cnemon sees the viewpoint as that of Homer, rather than that of Menelaus), where the statement is presented as a widely held truth. This is somewhat pretentious of Cnemon, but it illustrates that he thinks that he is also presenting a statement that can be widely accepted. The context of the two statements could not be more different: Menelaus is making a speech exulting in his opponent's violent death at his hands, and berating the Trojans' seeming insatiability when it comes to war; Cnemon just wants to hear more of this intriguing and erotic story. There is, I think, some humour at work here at Cnemon's expense. The alignment of the pleasures of love with hearing stories about love is the most pertinent part of Cnemon's speech for perceiving his reception of Calasiris' narrative as 'erotic', so I will discuss this shortly. The final point that comes across is the recognition by Cnemon that this narrative about Theagenes and Chariclea is even more worthy of continued attention than other stories regarding love, and this seems like a wink from the primary narrator at his audience, clearly demonstrating the relative merit of his narrative.

To turn to the metaliterary implications of this passage: Cnemon's statements invite some consideration of readerly protocol. Is the reader meant to take Cnemon completely seriously? Should we also read without ever feeling we have had enough? How erotic is the reading process? Winkler argues that Cnemon is a naïve narratee,[45] and that he does not maintain the 'critical distance' required by novels and misses the nuances of Calasiris' duplicity,[46] and all of this implies that, as a model for reading, Cnemon fails. Looking at this passage alone, it is evident that this argument is not altogether watertight. In line with Morgan, I view Cnemon as a narratee who can be seen to reflect the demands of the genre: he wants to hear about love, and this is surely a major motivation behind wanting to read a Greek novel.[47] What does this mean for *sōphrosunē* as a tempering force on this erotic process? While Cnemon desires the continuation of this narrative, he clearly equates the entire process with the content of the story: his desire for narrative action is coloured by his desire for the depiction of desire. In addition to considering the motivations behind reading, it is necessary to discuss the different modes of reading available. Whitmarsh suggests that there is an opposition between 'teleological' and 'deviant' readings in the Greek novel, and how we read is dependent on our own desires as readers.[48] Which category does Cnemon fall into at this point as he reacts to Calasiris' narrative? Whitmarsh asserts, based on his analysis of the scene at 3.4.7, that Cnemon's reading can be seen to be 'deviant' in that it involves 'immoderate viewing' which is ultimately a sign of moral weakness.[49] Is this true at 4.4 too? Cnemon's reading could be seen as immoderate in the sense that he is so eager to hear about love that he ignores natural requirements such as the need for sleep, and in that he also rejects Homeric authority. However, it can be seen that his reading is also 'teleological' in that he clearly desires to keep listening in order to reach some kind of conclusion. Whitmarsh acknowledges the multiplicity of readings available,[50] and it is clear from Cnemon's example that no reading need adhere absolutely to one mode or another, and each can colour the other to a considerable extent.

Whether Cnemon's statement that one can never have one's fill of love or hearing about it is representative, in a metanarrative sense, of how, in this particular narrative, the end of desire is never reached, is an important factor to consider here too. Cnemon, and the reader, never get the fulfilment of their desire, because the love of Theagenes and Chariclea is chaste: it is possible that it is perpetually chaste, given the ending of this novel.[51] While the tease of this most beautiful couple who never have sex could frustrate a reader like Cnemon, it could be argued that this very frustration can be transformed into a self-fulfilling readerly *sōphrosunē*. There is perhaps a greater satisfaction available to the reader who can be *sōphrōn* in that the novel is not just about desire and its natural *telos*, it is about how this desire can be ever present and never ending. *Sōphrosunē* does not negate desire, but, at least in this novel, acts as a virtue which suggests one way of living with desire, and this can be seen to be part of the readerly protocol of Heliodorus, who perhaps pushes this idea to the very limit of what can be accepted by novel readers.

Another place where Cnemon expresses his desire for narrative in significant terms is at 5.1.4, where he responds to Calasiris' need for a break as follows:

Ἐπίσχες . . . ὦ πάτερ, οὐχ ὡς ἐμοῦ τὴν διήγησιν ἀποσκευαζομένου, δοκῶ γάρ μοι μηδ᾽ εἰ πολλὰς μὲν νύκτας πλείους δὲ ἡμέρας ἐπισυνάπτοις τοῦτο ἄν ποτε παθεῖν, οὕτως ἀκόρεστόν τι καὶ σειρήνειον τὸ κατ᾽ αὐτήν . . .

'Stop then, Father,' said Cnemon, 'though not because I am bored with your narrative, for I do not think that would ever happen to me, even if you were to continue for many more nights and a greater number of days, for there is something like the Sirens' song about it and one can never have too much of it.'

5.1.4

The alignment of Calasiris' narrative with the song of the Sirens implies the irresistible nature of the story, but the connotations of the Sirens also suggests a dangerous aspect. The effect of Cnemon's allusion is to further illustrate the power of narrative, or, at least, of this particular narrative. It also implies, once more, that the narrative is erotic in nature: the Sirens' power of seduction, however grisly the result, is of course legendary. Cnemon expresses his desire for this story in terms that reflect his hedonistic tendencies: he cares little for the inherent danger in the Sirens' song, but rather, like Odysseus, he just wants to hear it. The pleasure involved in the process outweighs the painful outcome in his view, or he disregards or overlooks it. But how can this narrative be said to be dangerous like the Sirens' song? The danger perhaps lies in the overwhelming temptation to put all other concerns on hold while listening to this narrative. Cnemon can be seen to be using melodramatic terminology in order to emphasize his need to hear Calasiris' story, but his statement can also be read as a hint that the story of Chariclea and Theagenes fills the audience, whether it is Cnemon or the reader, with an insatiable desire. Again, as I discussed above with reference to 4.4, we are faced with the issue of whether Cnemon represents the reader's desire, or whether he serves as a warning about the danger of over-desiring. While the Sirens allusion is meant to suggest a dangerous seductive quality to narrative, does it inspire fear in the reader or encourage him to press on regardless? Recalling the *Odyssey*, the choice is plain: Cnemon would clearly choose to tie himself to the mast and hear everything, tortured by longing for the consummation of this narrative, rather than opting for the beeswax like Odysseus' companions (*Od.* 12.39–54 (Circe's warning); 12.154–200). Cnemon's insatiable curiosity (and implicit courage) is thus aligned with Odysseus.[52] The reader can choose to align himself with Cnemon or not: his comment can be read ironically. Cnemon's perspective is limited and his desire is connected to his naïveté surrounding the nature of narrative. While I argued above that the reader is 'like' Cnemon in his desire for a love story, it also became clear that readerly *sōphrosunē* has an important role. Here, Cnemon's Siren-song reference emphasizes his focus on the pleasure of the process of storytelling, but the reader can choose another mode of reading, one involving a balance between the desire for the ending and the prolongation of the pleasure of reading, as discussed by Morgan.[53] This does not mean that the reader is not susceptible to the Siren-like spell cast by Heliodorus' text, but it means that s/he can approach the text in a more knowing way than Cnemon does at 5.1. The reader is aware that the novel will lead to a more pleasurable ending than that associated with the Sirens, so that s/he can surrender to the process of reading without anxiety, which is surely Heliodorus' intention.

*

There is a clear role for *sōphrosunē* on the level of readerly response in the extant examples of this genre. While the way in which this role operates varies between texts and within them, the overall effects of readerly *sōphrosunē* are to temper voyeurism and allow for a teleological emphasis in the reading experience. In places, particularly in the novels of Longus, Achilles Tatius and Heliodorus, there are complex and, on occasion, contradictory implications for the reader and her/his reading. It is not the aim of this book to establish rules for reading: this would assume that the authors of these texts had precise intentions regarding how one should appreciate their novels, which would be to assume too much. Moreover, to suggest that one need obey any rule when reading would surely take the joy from the activity. What I do suggest is that *sōphrosunē* is intrinsically involved in any reading of these texts. The emphasis on the virtue as erotic restraint within the action of the narratives encourages *sōphrosunē* in the reader. If the characters are subject to *erōs*, yet maintain their *sōphrosunē* to varying degrees, then how can a reader who engages with the erotic process of reading ignore her/his own readerly *sōphrosunē*? Just as the virtue is central to the psychological make-up of the protagonists, then it is arguably also central to the psychological make-up of the implied reader. This is not to say that every reader is *sōphrōn*, or that s/he would be made so by reading these novels; rather, the implication is that reading these texts may encourage one's recognition of the need for the virtue at certain points in the reading experience. An understanding of *sōphrosunē*, rather than necessarily the possession of it, is essential for a fully appreciative reading of these novels.

Conclusion

A representation of an erotic relationship is at the heart of each of the extant Greek novels, and these relationships are treated differently according to each author's intent and motivation. This book has explored and analysed the ways in which, because of the erotic theme of these texts, *sōphrosunē* is central to characterization and is central on the level of readerly response, as it regulates the erotic impetus in characters and in readers. While this concern with *sōphrosunē* can be viewed as generic, the variety of approaches to the concept represented in these five texts and how these approaches advance our understanding of these individual works proved to be the most significant and exciting aspects of my findings. In each chapter and section of this book, focus has been on those passages that encapsulated the way in which the representations of *sōphrosunē* influence our view of characterizations or influence how we may read these novels. An important aspect, which recurred in these analyses of each of the novels, was that of self-definition: many of the most significant usages of σωφρ- root terms relate to the character/narrator who expresses them, with fewer usages, particularly by characters (as opposed to narrators), relating directly to another character. Equally, where such self-definition does not occur, such as in Longus' *Daphnis and Chloe*, this proved to be highly significant in terms of what it reveals about the motivation behind the text. The various types of identity implied by this technique of self-definition invite some further discussion. Therefore, in this conclusion, I will address the extent to which those who claim *sōphrosunē* for themselves (be that a character, a narrator or an implied reader) suggest something about how they perceive and represent not only their respective ethical merit, but also their gender, social status or ethnicity.

In Chariton's *Callirhoe*, the eponymous heroine and her second husband, Dionysius, both use σωφρ- root terms in relation to themselves, whereas, tellingly, Chaereas does not. In the *Ephesiaca* the vast majority of usages are by either Habrocomes or Anthia referring to their own possession of *sōphrosunē*. Neither Daphnis nor Chloe describes himself or herself as *sōphrōn* at any juncture in Longus' text, and this is entirely congruous with the technique of focalization which is used in that novel. Achilles Tatius' Clitophon defines his earlier self in terms relating to *sōphrosunē*; while Leucippe, whose characterization is very much at the mercy of Clitophon as narrator, never uses such terminology of herself, but does vaunt her commitment to virginity at key points in the narrative, which is suggestive of Clitophon's wish to present Leucippe as chaste and devoted to him. In Heliodorus' *Aethiopica*, Chariclea repeatedly refers to her own *sōphrosunē* and to her *sōphrōn* desire for Theagenes. Theagenes does not refer to his own *sōphrosunē* at any point, but does refer to his and Chariclea's love as being *sōphrōn*, and he implicitly refers to his and Chariclea's mutual *sōphrosunē* while questioning the reward it earns them in Ethiopia as they are about to be sacrificed.

A pattern emerges from the above summary regarding who employs *sōphrōn* self-definition and in which novels this occurs. Those characters who self-define are also those in whom the motivation to be *sōphrōn*, or at least to appear to be, is well demarcated. Those who do not define themselves as *sōphrōn* are those in whom a development is necessary in order to attain the virtue, or those whose *sōphrosunē* tends to be defined in terms of their relationship to their beloved, rather than in terms of their individual approach. In relation to gender, those male characters and narrators who employ self-definition often do so while emphasizing their social status or education, or, at least, their claims of *sōphrosunē* come after the reader knows of their elite status (Dionysius: Chariton 2.6.3; Habrocomes, Xenophon of Ephesus 1.4.4; 2.1.4; Longus' Prologue narrator: Longus Pr.3; Clitophon: Achilles Tatius 1.5.6). While this factor is more central to Dionysius' characterization than it is for Clitophon's, it is important to recognise that masculine self-definition as both socially elevated and *sōphrōn* clearly indicates that the two characteristics are related. Furthermore, Dionysius, Habrocomes and Clitophon all claim (obliquely in Clitophon's case) to have been *sōphrōn* prior to meeting, respectively, Callirhoe, Anthia and Leucippe. The virtue is therefore active in these characters, according to their own self-definition, before the onset of *erōs*. A sustained *sōphrosunē* in the pre-narrative lives of these male characters which stems primarily from their social status and education contrasts quite markedly with their female counterparts, as we shall see below.

Callirhoe, Anthia and Chariclea are all aristocratic maidens, and this is emphasized in Chariton's and Xenophon of Ephesus' novels from the outset. However, when they first mention their respective *sōphrosunē*, it is not to claim that their social status or education has led them to possess it. Callirhoe refers to her chastity when stating how she imagines Chaereas bears witness to her virtue when he thinks that she is dead (Chariton, 1.14.10). Anthia refers (although in indirect speech) to the oaths of fidelity she made to Habrocomes (Xenophon of

Ephesus, 3.5.6). Chariclea's first mention (in terms of both the *histoire* and the *récit*) of *sōphrosunē* in direct relation to her possession of the virtue is connected closely to her relationship with Theagenes (Heliodorus, 1.8.3). For those female characters who use *sōphrosunē* as a part of their self-definition, these initial instances demonstrate that this self-definition involves their relationship with the male protagonist: this indicates that they represent their motivation in displaying *sōphrosunē* as stemming from this relationship. Each subsequent reaffirmation of their chastity or fidelity (where σωφρ- root terms are used) supports this initial self-definition, so that the authorial intention behind his representation of self-proclaimed female *sōphrosunē* is to imply that the central erotic relationship encourages Callirhoe, Anthia and Chariclea to display their *sōphrosunē* as a factor that binds them to their husband or lover.

From the discussion above, it is clear that there is a stark contrast between male and female characters' use of *sōphrosunē* to self-define. The male characters claim a sustained possession of the virtue, a possession that is challenged by their erotic desire, whereas, for the female characters, *sōphrosunē* is a crucial marker of their emotional commitment to their husband or lover. This is not to deny that there is a certain degree of equivalence between how *sōphrosunē* is for both male and female characters symptomatic of the depth of their fidelity towards one another. However, Callirhoe, Anthia and Chariclea emphasize this aspect as soon as they refer to their own *sōphrosunē*, while the male characters' focus is, at least to begin with, on *sōphrosunē* as a symbol of their social status and education. *Sōphrosunē* is symbolic of an aristocratic education in both males and females in the novels, but is emphasized in this respect in the representation of males. While the central erotic relationship is preserved by the *sōphrosunē* of both heroes and heroines, in the female characters their private erotic world is explicitly governed by their approach to *sōphrosunē*, and the public perception of their *sōphrosunē* is secondary to this. For the males, their *sōphrosunē* indicates that they have a certain social status, before they necessarily need to display it in relation to *erōs*. However, their experience of *erōs* profoundly affects their *sōphrosunē* and ensures that it is focused on their relationship with the heroine.

Longus is a different case, as he does not have his characters self-define as *sōphrōn* at any point as I mention above. However, nor does Longus' narrator use σωφρ- root terms when he describes the emotions and actions of Daphnis and Chloe: this perhaps implies that, for Longus, if Daphnis and Chloe do not see themselves as *sōphrōn*, he will not allow his narrator to intrude on their innocence in this respect by commenting on their possession or dearth of the virtue. In place of emphasis by frequent usage, Longus introduces the term at two highly significant points. The use of the participle form of σωφρονέω by the Prologue narrator implies that he, as an educated man struck by the beauty of the scenes depicted in the cave, is using the term as a form of self-definition. Although he does not claim possession of the virtue outright, he implies its potential role in his psychology, albeit perhaps with a degree of irony, as I discussed in Chapter 2 (section 2.2). Furthermore, the plural participle clearly broadens this classification to include similarly educated contemporaries: the types of people who may read this text, or as the vocabulary suggests, write related texts. For Longus' narrator, *sōphrosunē* is limited to those who have attained an erotic education. There is the implication, in the final book, by Clearistē's reference to the serving woman named Sōphrosunē, that Daphnis, once he knows his elite status and identity and is ready to marry Chloe, has gained the necessary erotic awareness and will be in possession of the virtue. The bookending of the novel with terms relating to *sōphrosunē* potentially demonstrates Longus' intention to relate Daphnis to the Prologue narrator. The role of *sōphrosunē* for the Prologue narrator refers to his response to the coming four books, and Daphnis' implied self-restraint will presumably be exercised to ensure his future fidelity to Chloe. However, there is the implication that *sōphrosunē*, in whatever capacity, is the preserve of those who are erotically aware and who are members of the social elite.

Ethnicity is another factor which governs how *sōphrosunē* is represented both in the self-definition of certain characters, or in how they are defined by others. Greek ethnicity is a marker of status in Chariton's and Xenophon of Ephesus' texts, and no non-Greek in these novels possesses *sōphrosunē* in the erotic sphere (see above, 1.1.3 for my observations regarding Chariton's Persian King and his self-control). Ethnicity as a moral indicator is less important in Longus' novel, where the rural/urban divide is much more crucial. Achilles Tatius' text has such a mix of narrative voices that ethnicity as an identifying category is severely disrupted.[1] In Heliodorus' text, Hellenic identity and ethical superiority is transferred to a utopian Ethiopia.[2] *Sōphrosunē* is of course inherently 'Greek' as a concept, and its representation in the Greek novels does not lead me to conclude that it is in any way divorced from this ethnic category.

Finally, does the reader self-define as *sōphrōn*? As I discussed above, Longus' Prologue offers a glimpse into authorial and narratorial assumptions regarding the reader of the subsequent narrative: the Prologue narrator's self-definition is potentially reflected by his narratee's self-definition, and the role of *sōphrosunē* in this is central. While Longus' readerly hints are more explicit than those of the other novel-authors, I have shown that there is much scope for analysis of the role of *sōphrosunē* on the level of the reader in all five of the extant examples. Any reader of a Greek novel has chosen to read that novel because of their interest in erotic stories, but it is what happens once that choice has been made which defines the reader further. A reader who empathizes fully with the characters must appreciate those characters' susceptibility to the initiation of erotic desire for one other person, and crucially, s/he must also appreciate those characters' *sōphrosunē*, which ensures the preservation of the central relationship. While the tension between the two poles of *erōs* and *sōphrosunē* varies between each novel, and within each novel, this tension provides the most pleasure and excitement in reading these texts. The Greek novels, in which treatments of *sōphrosunē* range from the relative uniformity of the *Ephesiaca* to the ethical elasticity of *Leucippe and Clitophon*, invite readers who can engage with the broad spectrum of imaginative approaches to this key virtue. They may not explicitly self-define as *sōphrōn*, but their reading must involve a tangible awareness of how the concept of *sōphrosunē* is intrinsic to the reading process.

From the above conclusions, certain implications arise regarding the virtue of *sōphrosunē* and the culture in which these novels were produced. While the novels cannot be said to be ethical treatises which direct the behaviour of their readers, one can infer that it would be very likely that the educated, male elite should possess *sōphrosunē* from adolescence onwards, and this should govern their behaviour and relationships. It can also be inferred that women of good social standing should prize *sōphrosunē* as the virtue that ensures that they remain virginal prior to and faithful within marriage. These claims can be made despite the novels' status as fictional works, and despite the label of 'ideal' which has been applied to these works. As De Temmerman suggests, there is too much 'ambiguity, playfulness, and awareness of psychologically motivated behavioural patterns' in the characterization within these novels for them to deserve the label of 'ideal'.[3] Consequently, there is a case to be made for a degree of realistic characterization within these texts. While the behaviour of the heroes and heroines is often at the extreme end of virtuous, this very extremity warrants us to perceive that in the world of the readers of these novels, it is imperative to strive for the possession of the virtues displayed by the protagonists, and chief among these is *sōphrosunē*. While the virtue is crucial whatever one's gender, it is clear that classical and philosophical ideas surrounding the primacy of male *sōphrosunē* have not been dismissed in the first few centuries of the Common Era. Women ought to possess *sōphrosunē* in relation to their lover/husband, while men should possess it regardless of their relationship status.

Despite the distinction above regarding male and female *sōphrosunē*, in the Greek novels, one character trumps others as regards this virtue: Chariclea. Her zealous and religiously informed possession of this virtue goes beyond that displayed by other novelistic characters. This extraordinary piece of characterization by Heliodorus has the tonality of the depiction of an early Christian heroine, such as Thecla or Agnes. If one accepts the dating of Heliodorus as early fourth century, then the Christian overtones can be read as direct engagement on Heliodorus' part with early Christian ideology. Culturally, then, Chariclea could be representative of a new kind of feminine approach to *sōphrosunē*. Women could reclaim the virtue and glory in it. While Chariclea succumbs to marriage, she certainly does so on her own terms. The influence of Christianity would erode that aspect of Greco-Romanic culture in which marriage was the only happy ending for a *sōphrōn* woman. While the Greek novel's narrative trajectory must involve marriage, and while in general this concern is socially normative, Heliodorus puts his *sōphrōn* heroine, rather than her marriage, centre stage, and this could be seen as a hint at the changes already underway in Greek society, or at least at the changes underway in literary representations of women.

My reading of the five extant Greek novels puts the concept of *sōphrosunē* at their heart. The survival of each central relationship requires *sōphrosunē*. Readers must understand how their own possession or lack of this cardinal virtue fundamentally governs how they read these novels. While marriage is the socially endorsed 'end' of each novel, the 'means' is often more important for narrative literature, and that 'means' is *sōphrosunē*.

Notes

Introduction

1 On the justification for and advantages of reading the five extant Greek novels as a genre, see Morgan (1995); Goldhill (2008). For recent further discussion see Whitmarsh (2011), 12–21; Jones (2012), 3–4; De Temmerman (2014), 2–3. For my purposes, the commonality of the erotic theme to each of the five texts (Chariton's *Callirhoe*, Xenophon of Ephesus' *Ephesiaca*, Longus' *Daphnis and Chloe*, Achilles Tatius' *Leucippe and Clitophon*, Heliodorus' *Aethiopica*) and the importance therein of the virtue of *sōphrosunē*, in addition to their categorisation as examples of extended prose fiction, leads me to agree with the majority of recent commentators in considering these works to be a generic corpus. This is not to suggest that the fragments categorised as novelistic do not belong to this genre, but I omit discussion of these principally because *sōphrosunē* and its cognates are absent from them, and also because these brief pieces of text do not lend themselves to any proper evaluation of implied *sōphrosunē* due to the lack of narrative development.

2 Goldhill (1995); Chew (2000); Kasprzsk (2009); Jones (2012); De Temmerman (2014).

3 (1990).

4 See particularly Konstan (1994) and Goldhill (1995).

5 Konstan (1994).

6 Goldhill (1995), 4.

7 Goldhill (1995), 8.

8 (2003).

9 (2004).

10 (2012).

11 Haynes, (2003), 161–162.

12 Morales (2004), 156–220.

13 Mulvey (1989).

14 Morgan (2004a).

15 Whitmarsh (2011), in particular, 168–169, but also throughout part 2.

16 De Temmerman (2014).

17 Rademaker (2005), 7.

18 North (1966), 78–84.

19 Rademaker (2005), 161–189.

20 See Rademaker (2005), 163–169.

21 North (1966), 80.

22 Rademaker (2005), 173.

23 North (1966), 73.

24 Rademaker (2005), 183–184.

25 North (1966), 74.

26 Rademaker (2005), 185, n.38.

27 Rademaker (2005), 188.

28 Philostratus (*VS*. 524) refers to the text *Araspas the lover of Panthea*, which, he states, is usually ascribed to Dionysius of Miletus, but is actually the work of Celer 'the writer on rhetoric'. This reference suggests that Xenophon's text was influential during the period, and that the episodes involving Panthea in particular were subject to sophistic adaptation.

29 See Tatum (1994), 15–28, for an overview of how the *Cyropaedia* is relevant for Greek fiction. Broader engagement by Chariton with the Xenophontic corpus, particularly with the *Anabasis*, is discussed: Laplace (1997), 51–53; Smith (2007) 163–176; Trzaskoma (2011); (2012). De Temmerman argues that Xenophon of Ephesus practises the stylistic device of *apheleia* in the manner of Xenophon of Athens: De Temmerman (2014), 118–151.

30 Tatum (1989), 168; Laplace (1997), 65–67; Smith (2007), 163–172; Montiglio (2013), 19–20.

31 Capra (2009); De Temmerman (2014), 120–121.

32 For brief discussion on the *Cyropaedia* as a general influence on the genre, see Anderson (1982), 4.

33 Nausicaa's conspicuous superiority when seen among her handmaidens is recalled when Araspas describes Panthea among her attendants (5.1.5). This allusion, or at least the use of a topos which is rooted in the representation of the Odyssean maiden, evokes the role of *aidōs* in Nausicaa's psychology, demonstrated when she avoids attracting the slander of the locals by not escorting Odysseus to the palace of her father (*Od*. 6.273–289).

34 I do not suggest that no other Platonic dialogue was read by the authors of the Greek novels (Achilles Tatius and Longus seem to show awareness of ideas from the *Meno* and the *Protagoras*, for example). However, it is allusion and influence from the four dialogues mentioned above which are significant for my purposes here.

35 North (1966), 150.

36 Rademaker (2005), 325.

37 See North (1966), 169; Rademaker (2005), 340, n.69.

38 This episode is also alluded to by Petronius (*Sat*. 128).

39 Text and translation from Emlyn-Jones and Preddy (2013), adapted in places.

40 Repath (2007a).

41 Herrmann (2007a)

42 See North ((1966)), 174–175 for further discussion of *Rep.* 5–7, focusing on
    sōphrosunē.

43 σώφρονα: 245b4; 273e6. σωφρονεῖ: 244a5. σωφρονεῖν: 231d5. σωφρονοῦντος:
    245a8. σωφρονοῦσαι: 244b2. σωφροσύνη: 237e3; 256b6. σωφροσύνῃ: 256e5.
    σωφροσύνην: 241a3; 247d6. σωφροσύνης: 244d4; 250b2; 253d6; 254b7. σώφρων:
    279c3.

44 North (1966), 179, n.57, sees this kind of *sōphrosunē* as comparable to that
    demonstrated by Socrates according to Alcibiades' speech in the *Symposium*.

45 This definition fits within the description of popular *sōphrosunē* in the *Republic*, as
    discussed above.

46 Trapp (1990).

47 I do not deny the importance of the *Phaedrus* in Longus' text, something which is
    discussed by Hunter (1997), and Repath (2011), but for Longus' approach to
    sōphrosunē, I think the dialogue is less crucial.

48 Hunter (1983), 109, n.43; (1997); (2012); Trapp (1990).

49 North (1966), 199.

50 North (1966), 200.

51 North (1966), 200–201.

52 North (1966), 201, and n.14.

53 North (1966), 203.

54 North (1966), 206.

55 An important source book for Hellenistic philosophy including Stoicism is Long and
    Sedley (1987).

56 Long (1974), 115.

57 North (1966), 217–218.

58 North (1966), 218.

59 North (1966), 219. She also states that Chrysippus was responsible for the
    'proliferation of virtues in the Old Stoa'. The subordinate virtues to *sōphrosunē* were:
    eutaxia ('proper arrangement'), *kosmiotēs* ('orderliness'), *aidēmosynē* ('sense of
    shame'), and *enkrateia* ('self-restraint'). All carry the sense of controlling or ordering
    the impulses.

60 North (1966), 220–221.

61 See North (1966), 222–223.

62 North (1966), 227–228.

63 North (1966), 229–230. See also 230, n.97.

64 North (1966), 231.

65 For a detailed analysis of this text and its role as a commentary on Plato's dialogues
    on love, see Rist (2001). For further discussion on the Platonic influence on this
    dialogue, see Trapp (1990), 157–161; Hunter (2012), 185–222.

66 Goldhill (1995), 144, suggests that the *Amatorius* provides the theory to the practice of the novel.

67 This structure recalls, to differing degrees, the structure of Plato's *Symposium* and the structure of the *Theaetetus*: see Hunter (2012), 202–204. The opening of Achilles Tatius' *Leucippe and Clitophon*, where Clitophon strikes up a conversation with the primary narrator and subsequently tells his story, is not dissimilar. Also, (Ps.-)Lucian's *Amores* is layered in a very similar fashion, with one dialogue being filtered through another: Lycinus narrates an earlier debate on love to his companion, Theomnestus. This structural parallel with Achilles Tatius' text becomes important for my purposes when the debate regarding the relative merits of love of women and love of boys begins (750c), a debate which is recalled at *Leucippe and Clitophon*, 2.35–38, and which is also recalled in (Ps.-)Lucian's *Amores* (see below and Rist 2001, 557 n.4).

68 There are 14 occurrences of *sōphrosunē* and its cognates in the *Amatorius*: 752a; 752c; 753b; 753c (2); 759a; 764f; 765b; 766a; 767b; 767e; 769b; 769d (2).

69 When referring to the persona speaking within the dialogue, rather than the author, I shall put his name into inverted commas.

70 Goldhill (1995), 158–161.

71 Goldhill (1995), 152–154.

72 See Trapp (1990), 157–161; Hunter (2012), 185–222.

73 See also Max.Tyr. 19, for similar evocation of Phaedran imagery.

74 On this passage, see Rist (2001), 566, n.25.

75 I also acknowledge the significance of Alciphron's *Letters of the Courtesans*, but do not offer detailed analysis here as the implications are very close to those of Lucian's *Dialogi Meretricii*, with humour and irony inviting the reader to reflect on the nature of the *sōphrosunē* in sexual contexts which is evoked in these texts.

76 For a recent appraisal of this dialogue and the claim for its authenticity as the work of Lucian, see Jope (2011). I find Jope's arguments for Lucianic authorship convincing, and this of course makes the dialogue relevant for those novels composed in the second century CE.

77 See North (1966), 312–377.

78 De Temmerman (2014).

79 The exception is Goldhill (1995) on Longus.

80 Whitmarsh (2011), 168–176: building on Brooks (1984). See also Carson (1986), 85.

81 König (2008); Morgan (2013).

1 Characterized *Sōphrosunē*

1 Balot (1998), 146–148; Scourfield (2003), 169–71; Repath (2007), 65–68; Alexander (2008), 187–188; 193 Montiglio (2010), 27–34 (her discussion involves comparisons

between Dionysius' and Artaxerxes' struggles, rather than direct analysis of Dionysius' *agōn*); Jones (2012), 55–60.

2 Reardon has φιλόνικος at all times where φιλόνεικος is suggested by F (Reardon (2004), 2 n.17). It is not a serious concern for my purposes here.

3 See Scourfield (2010), 303, n.53: He suggests that the alignment of *sōphrosunē* and *hubris* is also implicit at Eur. *Hipp.* 474–75.

4 Text taken from Reardon (2004); translations from Goold (1995), adapted in places.

5 The two concepts are traditionally opposed, by e.g. Theognis, Aeschylus, Euripides, Isocrates, Plato and Plutarch. See North (1966), *passim*, for discussion of this opposition.

6 Smith (2007), 165: he also points to Chariton's innovative use of Xenophon's representation of Cyrus' response to Panthea in the *Cyropaedia*. See also Tatum (1989), 168. In view of Chariton's apparent knowledge of Xenophon's text, it is clear that the possession of a similarly nuanced *sōphrosunē* to Cyrus' is shown to be inadequate to the challenge of Erōs. Just as Cyrus recognises (*Cyr.* 5.1.8), the sight of an unsurpassably beautiful woman denies the *sōphrōn* man his usual self-control. It is implied that Dionysius' *sōphrosunē*, while identical to Cyrus' in how it should temper the erotic drive, comes into force too late: Erōs' power cannot be avoided in this text, where no character is able to offer sufficient resistance.

7 Balot (1998), 148.

8 See Balot (1998), 149–150: Balot illustrates how erotic passion has altered Dionysius as demonstrated by his behaviour at 3.9.4 to 3.10.2. He makes the observation that he is transformed '. . . into a competitive, paranoid lover, who has almost forgotten the moral way of looking at things.'

9 At 5.7.2, a similar claim is made by Mithridates, who is seen within the narrative to succumb to his desire without any real evidence of *sōphrosunē*. The reader has no valid reason to believe Mithridates' claim.

10 See n.5 above.

11 Jones (2012), 48.

12 Dionysius' words and actions indicate that he aims to conform to Stoic behavioural ideals, but his moral struggles demonstrate that he fails to reach these standards.

13 Montiglio (2010), 27–28.

14 6.3.8; Montiglio (2010), 28–29.

15 Montiglio (2010), 29.

16 See Alvares (2002), 112.

17 For discussion on Chaereas' angry jealousy and lack of self-mastery see Balot (1998), 155; Alvares (2002), 107–110; Scourfield (2003), 165; Jones (2012), 84–88; De Temmerman (2014), 83–88. See also Kanavou (2015), for discussion of *sōphrosunē* in relation to Chaereas (in addition to broader discussion regarding the virtue's place in Chariton's novel).

18 On this see Balot (1998), 160; Alvares (2002), 115; also, although more focused on anger rather than jealousy, Scourfield (2003), 175.

19 See Whitmarsh (2011) 167: he suggests that Callirhoe's actions of writing to Dionysius and mentioning the child and keeping it a secret from Chaereas because of his jealousy and former violence act as 'intratextual signals' that the joyous ending is somewhat tempered by a 'morally complex past that cannot be entirely effaced'.

20 Scourfield (2003), 173–174; De Temmerman (2014), 91–92.

21 Jones (2012), 139–140.

22 For a detailed study of Chaereas' rhetorical technique and ability in this speech, see De Temmerman (2014), 100–104.

23 Cairns (1993), 2.

24 See e.g. 78–81, where Hippolytus refers to *Aidōs* tending the meadow where only those *sōphrōn* by nature can pluck the flowers. See North (1966), 78, for her comments regarding Euripides' view of *sōphrosunē* and its kinship with *aidōs*.

25 See also Rademaker (2005), 12–13, where he suggests that *aidōs* is one of the 'moral' uses of the term *sōphrosunē*, but that these uses define the virtue negatively, implying the repression of certain types of behaviour. I will discuss other significant uses of *aidōs* and its cognates in the later novels: in Longus' representation of Chloe (below: 1.3.4); and when Clitophon connects *sōphrosunē* with *aidōs* at Ach. Tat. 1.5 (below 1.4.1).

26 Callirhoe's prayer at 8.8.16 suggests that there is still a certain level of anxiety about the future on her part.

27 Schmeling (1974), 103; Egger (1994a), 41–42; Goldhill (1995), 128–129; Haynes (2003), 49–50; Scourfield (2003), 177–178; Smith (2007), 111–116; Trzaskoma (2010), 220–224; Tilg (2010), 275–277; Whitmarsh (2011), 165–167; De Temmerman (2014), 50–51, 61–65.

28 See De Temmerman (2014), 61–62: he sees this allusion as important primarily because it implies a similar kind of 'objective' characterization for Callirhoe as for tragic figures through the use of internal dialogues as devices for assessing moral character (he cites Gill 1996, 216–226). This kind of internalized moral dilemma is also present in Chariton for Dionysius and for the Persian King, as De Temmerman notes (see above 1.1.1, 1.1.2).

29 Trzaskoma (2010), 221–222.

30 See Kanavou (2015) on the impact and consequences of Callirhoe's decisions surrounding her child. Kanavou also discusses the role of *sōphrosunē* as a feature of Chariton's 'narrative artistry' with interesting results.

31 The suggestion that the text as we have it may be an epitome was originally put forward by Bürger (1892), and was widely accepted for many years, but is dismissed by Hägg (1966) and (1983), 21, and subsequently by several others: Schmeling (1980), 21, 76–77; Anderson (1982), 148; Konstan (1994b), 49; Holzberg (1995), 52–53;

Chew (1997–98); (1998); Kytzler (2003), 348–350. There are also scholars who suggest that the text stems from an oral composition rather than a literary one: Ruiz-Montero (1982); O'Sullivan (1995); König (2007). I concur with much of Chew's analysis (1997–98) which focuses on how the text may work on its own terms, rather than by blaming external circumstances for the inconsistencies within it, as do the epitome theorists and those who would claim that the text stems from an oral composition. One of Chew's objections to the epitome theory is that the text seems complete in the first book, something which led Bürger to think it was retained unabridged, which makes little sense, as Chew points out (205). The obvious problem with Chew's recognition of this as problematic for the epitome theory is that it is just as problematic for those wishing to suggest that this is a novel in its complete form: why write the first book in a similar style and with a similar literary quality to Chariton's text, and then abandon this endeavour for the remaining four books? Tagliabue (2017) argues that the text can be reclassed as 'paraliterary' in line with Couégnas' definition (1992) of the term. However, there are some inconsistencies in Tagliabue's argument as he argues for character progression and intertextual complexity in Xenophon's text, while also suggesting that the text is paraliterary.

32 There are 22. See De Temmerman (2014), 126: he states that *sōphrosunē* is by far the most heavily emphasized characteristic in this novel.

33 Of Habrocomes: 1.4.4; 2.1.3; 2.1.4; 2.1.4; 2.5.7; 2.10.3; 3.12.4; 5.14.3. Of Anthia: 1.9.3; 3.10.1; 4.3.4; 5.4.6; 5.5.5; 5.5.6; 5.7.2; 5.8.7; 5.8.9; 5.14.2. Of both: 3.5.6. Exceptions are 1.2.6, where σώφρων appears in a simile used to describe Anthia's eyes (see below sub-section 1.1); 2.6.4, where σώφρων describes Manto, ironically; 5.9.10, where the verb σωφρονέω is used in indirect speech from Anthia to describe retrospectively the behaviour of Anchialus, who tried to rape her (4.5.5). See Tagliabue (2017), 93–95 for relevant discussion of the central thematic role of *sōphrosunē* in the *Ephesiaca*.

34 Text from O'Sullivan (2005), throughout. Translation from Henderson (2009) throughout, adapted in places.

35 Another significant factor in Anthia's representation at this early point in the narrative, is that she is dressed in hunting-gear, followed by dogs, and, the narrator states, when she worships at the temple, she is often taken to be Artemis herself by the populace (1.2.6–7), something which recalls Chariton's representation of Callirhoe in the King of Persia's imagination at *Callirhoe* 6.4.5–6, which in turn recalls the representation of Nausicaa in the *Odyssey*.

36 Haynes (2003), 53.

37 LSJ⁹: s.v. φοβερός indicates the active/passive uses.

38 1.12.4; 1.13.3; [1.15.4]; 2.6.4; 4.6.4; 5.7.8 (φοβερώτερος: 1.11.6).

39 This and related terms also occur at Ach. Tat. 1.4.7; 3.7.7; Hld. 1.21.3.

40 See, particularly, 1.3.2, where Anthia reveals parts of her body for Habrocomes to view. Also, her speech at 1.4.6–7 indicates that her anxiety about her desire is not

based on ethical considerations: she is anxious to see Habrocomes and regrets her limited ability to achieve this due to her status as an underaged maiden; she does not regret her intense desire for Habrocomes.

41 There is plenty of scope to see the thematic connection with the tragic figure in Xenophon's novel. Hippolytus is alluded to in Chariton's introduction of Chaereas (1.1.3), which could be indicative of a generic interest in the tragic hero, or in the Euripidean play as a whole, perhaps picked up by Heliodorus in his Phaedra-like depictions of Demaenete (see particularly 1.10) and Arsace (8.15) and Theagenes' encounter with a bull (10.28–30). I argue for Heliodorus' engagement with the tragedy in the characterization of Chariclea in section 1.5.5.

42 Chariton, 1.1.3.

43 For recent appraisals of the debate regarding the relative dating of Xenophon of Ephesus and Chariton, see Tilg (2010), 88–90, where he maintains that Chariton precedes Xenophon, and Tagliabue (2017), 213–215. I agree with Tagliabue's general conclusion that relative dating of these two novels is not presently definitive. However, my point about the intertextuality here points towards Xenophon's being the later text, and this is not convincingly discounted by any scholar, in my view.

44 See below section 1.2.4 for discussion of Anthia's frequent self-definition as *sōphrōn* in Book 5.

45 See Cueva (2004), 39; De Temmerman (2014), 142. See above n.41. Cf. Tagliabue (2017), 105–112: he argues that Habrocomes is implicitly compared to a Platonic *erōmenos* in his introduction, rather than to Hippolytus. I suggest that the two implicit comparisons are not mutually exclusive, but the argument for the implied Platonic undertones is less convincing.

46 See Tagliabue (2017), 116–118. Habrocomes' passivity is widely recognized. See Schmeling (1980), 119–121; Haynes (2003), 91; Henderson (2009), 203.

47 Tagliabue (2017), 116–118.

48 It occurs in the *Ephesiaca* seven times. First here, then at: 2.9.4; 2.13.8; 4.3.3; 5.2.5; 5.4.7; 5.14.2. The only other occurrence of the adjective in the other four extant novels, is in Heliodorus' *Aethiopica* (9.25.5). The verb ἁγνεύω is used twice in Heliodorus (5.4.5; 10.7.7), but is not found elsewhere in the extant corpus.

49 See the entry in *LSJ* ⁹s.v, particularly II, where it is suggested that post-Homer, when used to describe persons as 'undefiled, chaste' it is principally applied to maidens, except at Eur. *Hipp.* 102, where it is used of Hippolytus. The ritual and religious overtones are clear from this entry.

50 Fidelity: Longus, 2.39; Chastity until marriage: Heliodorus, 4.18.

51 See Jones (2012), 203–205.

52 Schmeling (1980), 116, notes that in Xenophon's text there is a 'great, almost single-minded, emphasis on chastity', which can be read as 'an obsession rather than as a virtue'. I would not go as far in suggesting that *sōphrosunē*'s status as a virtue is

challenged in this novel, but there is the suggestion of obsession in the protagonists' regard for it, particularly, as I note above, in Habrocomes'.

53 Anthia: 2.4.6; 3.5.6; 3.6.2–3; 4.3.3–4; 4.5.3; 5.5.6; 5.8.8.–9. Habrocomes: 3.10.1–2.

54 Another passage where love and death are explicitly connected comes in Book 5, where Habrocomes meets the aged fisherman Aegialeus, who relates his tale of forbidden love and exile, and keeps the mummified corpse of his beloved Thelxinoe with him (5.1). For discussion of this passage see Whitmarsh (2011), 1–2; Morgan (2004d), 491; Tagliabue (2017), 50–52; 133–138.

55 See also 3.11, when she resists sex with Psammis.

56 Compare this passage to that discussed in the previous sub-section, 3.12.4, where Habrocomes' considerations are along similar lines, but with a different result. Cf. Konstan (1994a), 48–50.

57 See above, n.43.

58 Schmeling (2003), 542.

59 I do not include it here, but Anthia also tells a false tale to Psammis regarding her consecration to Isis, thus avoiding his advances (3.11).

60 As Montiglio (2013), 62–63, suggests, Anthia only displays inventiveness in order to defend her virtue, unlike Callirhoe, Leucippe and Chariclea, who innovate for other reasons. I would add that it is always in view of their erotic attachments that the heroines show innovation, so that Anthia's displays of intelligence only in the service of *sōphrosunē* are not as limited as Montiglio suggests: *sōphrosunē* for Anthia is intimately bound up with her love and devotion to Habrocomes.

61 Gold (1993), 90–92.

62 See Tagliabue (2017), 93–94, where he argues that Anthia's strategy in the brothel demonstrates how her 'growth in personality' has progressed.

63 Alvares (1995); Watanabe (2003); Jones (2012), 186–99; Tagliabue (2017), 159–161.

64 Schmeling (1980), 54–55; Konstan (1994a), 26–28; (1994b), 50–51; Alvares (1995), 394; Jones (2012), 189; 191–92.

65 A similar episode occurs in Achilles Tatius' *Leucippe and Clitophon* (1.7–14), where Clitophon's friend Clinias has a comparable pederastic affair with the same tragic outcome.

66 See Alvares (1995), 395–397.

67 Schmeling (1980), 107.

68 See De Temmerman (2014), 136, where he suggests that Manto, Apsyrtus and Hippothous demonstrate the narrator's view that a lack of self-control in decision-making processes has negative consequences. I concur with this idea, but do not agree with De Temmerman's subsequent assertion that Habrocomes' implicit alignment with these characters implies a lack of *sōphrosunē* on his part.

69 For a thorough analysis of the reciprocal nature of this 'pederastic' love and the implications of this see Jones (2012), 187–194. See also Watanabe (2003), 14–15, for

discussion of Hippothous' status as an *erastēs* and how this reinforces his masculinity.

70 1.2.1; 1.3.1; 1.3.2; 1.4.1; 1.4.2; 1.4.4; 1.4.5; 1.11.5; 2.1.2.

71 Except for in the initial description of her eyes at 1.2.6.

72 I do not see De Temmerman's (2014, 126–127) differentiation between Anthia's *sōphrosunē* as 'marital fidelity' and Habrocomes' as 'a refusal to have sex with people other than his wife' as valid: there is no discernible difference in terms of motivation and consequence between the two in this novel.

73 There is a textual issue regarding this name. Morgan (2004a), 238, opts for 'Sōphronē', which is a conjecture based on the use of this name in Menander's *Epitrepontes*, and Terence's *Eunuch* and *Phormio*. The MSS, however, have 'Sōphrosunē', which occurs, Morgan notes, in a letter of Aristaenetus. I concur with Herrmann (2007a), 226, where he suggests that the MSS are correct, but the alternative naming does not prevent it being significant for my purposes, as it still evokes the virtue of *sōphrosunē*.

74 Names are often allegorical in Longus. 'Daphnis' has mythical and Theocritan connotations; 'Chloe' is connected with Demeter; 'Philetas' recalls the Hellenistic poet, Philitas; 'Dionysophanes' is obviously linked to Dionysus. On names in Longus, see Morgan (2004a), 3, 5–6, 231–232.

75 Herrmann (2007a), 226. I frequently refer to the challenges to *sōphrosunē* faced by the protagonists of earlier and later novels in the course of this chapter.

76 Ach. Tat. 1.5.6; 2.5.2. See also the *agōn* of Dionysius in Chariton at 2.4.5, where Erōs dismisses Dionysius' attempt to overcome his passion with *sōphrosunē*.

77 Herrmann (2007a), 226.

78 See Herrmann (2007a), 206–209 for discussion of the role of Platonic allusion in the Philetas episode: the *Protagoras* is evoked by the contrast between *logos* and *mythos* in an educational context, and the question from Daphnis and Chloe about 'whatever Erōs is' (2.7.1) recalls the use of 'τί ποτ' ἐστί' by Socrates in several Platonic dialogues.

79 The story of Echo at 3.23, which marks the culmination of the increasingly violent content of each of the inset tales involving nymphs (Phatta, Syrinx, Echo), will be discussed in the sub-section on Daphnis' restraint.

80 For detailed discussion of Philetas' role at 2.3–7, see McCulloh (1970), 93–100, and Morgan (2004a), 177–182.

81 Text and translation taken from Morgan (2004a), throughout: translations adapted in places.

82 It is important to note that they do not lie down together with naked bodies until 3.24, by which stage Daphnis understands the mechanics of sex. The implicit suggestion behind their reluctance to enact this part of Philetas' advice is that they are somehow inhibited: they are said to 'shrink from the third cure, undressing and

lying down' (τὸ δὲ τρίτον ὤκνουν φάρμακον, ἀποδυθέντες κατακλιθῆναι) a response which could stem from *aidōs*, but this motivation is not given by the narrator, even though the emotion does occur in the narrative: he instead suggests that such behaviour would be too bold not only for maidens, but also for young goatherds (θρασύτερον γὰρ οὐ μόνον παρθένων ἀλλὰ καὶ νέων αἰπόλων).

83 He does act with more aggression than Chloe at 2.11, where he pulls Chloe rather forcefully (βιαιότερον) towards him as they kiss, an episode in which the narrator indicates the natural erotic impulse which encourages Daphnis to act with a degree of domination.

84 On Lycaenion's role in the novel, see Repath (2019).

85 See Montiglio (2010), 46: she argues that the couple have 'internalised' an awareness of fidelity following on from Philetas' lesson about the name of love, but she does not address exactly how this fidelity is perceived by them.

86 See Goldhill (1995), esp. 23–30.

87 While Morgan's translation conveys the probable sense of this sentence, given the focalization through Daphnis which precedes it, there is the issue of whether to read Lycaenion as nominative, which would mean that it is her pleasure which is being recalled rather than Daphnis'.

88 For discussion of the contrast between Daphnis' and Dorcon's behaviour, see Repath (2019), 181–182, 184–188.

89 Cf. Montiglio (2009), 47–48.

90 Repath (2011), 116–118: see Plato, *Symp.* 219b–d, where Alcibiades refers directly to Socrates' *sōphrosunē*.

91 Repath (2011), 117–118.

92 Repath (2011), 117.

93 Morgan (2004a), 221–222.

94 This does not explain why the narrator of the main narrative hardly uses the term, while he often comments on the effects and role of *erōs*, which are also beyond the comprehension of his protagonists for much of the narrative. The narrator's silence on *sōphrosunē* in the main narrative could be explained by his lack of concern regarding the virtue: his focus is on *erōs* and its consequences. Therefore, there is some slippage between Longus' intentions and his narrator's concerning *sōphrosunē*, which fits with the argument of Morgan (2004a), 17–20.

95 There is perhaps a parallel with the idea of the protagonist being separated from his virtue, or a symbol of it, in Apuleius' *Metamorphoses*, where Lucius is separated from his pure-bred white horse (described at 1.2) when transformed into an ass, and reunited (when the horse is named 'Candidus') once he has regained his human form (11.20). See Winkle (2014), 107–125 on potential allusion in the representation of the white horse to the 'good horse' of Plato's *Phaedrus*, with Lucius being potentially equated with the 'bad horse'.

96 1.3.1; 1.3.2; 1.21.3; 1.25.1; 1.31.2; 2.27.2; 3.24.3; 4.14.1.

97 4.17.2.

98 To note the other instances: 1.3.1 and 1.3.2 refer to Lamon's shame at the thought of leaving the abandoned child, Daphnis, where he lay; 1.21.3 refers to Dorcon's shame when he is discovered in wolf's clothing during his rape-attempt on Chloe; 1.25.1 refers to Daphnis' lack of embarrassment as he gazes on Chloe asleep; the instance at 2.27.2 is used by Pan of the Methymnaean captain Bryaxis' lack of respect towards the Nymphs in abducting Chloe.

99 De Temmerman (2014), 218–219, reads Chloe's reticence at this point as evidence for the emotional asymmetry between Chloe and Daphnis (Chloe exercises control over Daphnis' access to information at this point), which is reversed the novel as Daphnis acquires greater erotic maturity.

100 De Temmerman (2014), 225.

101 Text is taken from Garnaud (2013) and translations are from Whitmarsh (2001) (adapted in places).

102 On the question of Clitophon's reliability and manipulation, see Whitmarsh (2003); (2011), 90–93; Morales (2004), 48–56; Repath (2015); on how this potential for unreliability affects Clitophon's *sōphrosunē*, see De Temmerman (2014), 159–176. The role of the anonymous primary narrator in terms of how he receives or influences Clitophon's narration is also problematic, due to the complete lack of interruptions from him for the duration of the secondary narration and the fact that the frame is never resumed. On the complexities raised by Achilles' narrative set-up, see Morgan (2004c); (2007a); Whitmarsh (2011), 77–85; De Temmerman (2014), 152–158. Where I refer to 'Clitophon's narration/narrative' etc., I am not denying the primary narrator's potential influence, but it is difficult to assert with any certainty exactly where that influence is active and where it can be separated from the influence of the author.

103 For a recent analysis of Clitophon's characterization see De Temmerman (2014). Other notable studies include Whitmarsh (2003) and (2011); Haynes (2003); Morales (2004); Jones (2012); Repath (2015).

104 See Goldhill (1995), 67–76: his discussion includes consideration of the metaliterary implications of the use of *logoi erotikoi*, something which I will focus on in Chapter 3. Morales (2004), 80–81, also briefly discusses this passage, noting the force of example which brings about *mimēsis*.

105 See Morales (2004), 109–110, for a list of sententious statements (although incomplete).

106 Ἁμαρτάνω occurs only here and at 8.10.8 in Achilles Tatius' text: at 8.10.8 the verb refers to the alleged multiple hidden adulterous acts committed by Melite against Thersander, in the direct speech of the advocate, Sopater. The verb is rare in the examples of the extant corpus, only occurring at these two points in *Leucippe and*

Clitophon, then once in Xenophon of Ephesus', Longus', and Heliodorus' texts respectively. It is worth mentioning here that the term is clearly linked to ethical offences, in particular those connected with sex, in each of its occurrences, excepting that in Longus (1.24.4), which refers to the mistakes Chloe might make while playing the flute.

107 Translation from Emlyn-Jones and Preddy (2013).

108 Erotic desire is also the dominant factor in the psychological make-up of the tyrant in Book 9 (573e4; 574d5–575a6).

109 On the use of military imagery as a *topos* in Achilles Tatius, see Goldhill (1995), 75–76. For a detailed treatment of this passage, see De Temmerman (2014), 162–165.

110 De Temmerman (2014), 164–165.

111 For an extended version of this discussion of this allusion, and of other allusions by Achilles Tatius to Chariton, see Bird (2019a).

112 See above 1.1.1 for discussion of this passage.

113 See Kasprzyk (2009), 106–107: he focuses on how Clitophon uses Erōs as part of his narrative strategy, as opposed to how Chariton's omniscient narrator introduces the god into the 'real' action of his narrative.

114 There is the possibility that Clitophon as narrator is trying to recall Dionysius' moral struggle, but this very much depends on the date in which the action of the novel is set. See Whitmarsh and Morales (2001), xiv–xvi for a brief discussion of both the dating of the novel and of the dating of its action. For discussion of Clitophon's 'novelization' see Whitmarsh (2003), 194–195. For a recent appraisal of the potential to read intertextuality in Achilles' novel as Clitophon's own, see Repath (2013), 260–261.

115 De Temmerman (2014), 163–165. See also, Kasprzyk (2009), 106.

116 De Temmerman (2014), 164–165.

117 As with the discussion above regarding Chariton, there is the possibility that Clitophon himself is alluding to Xenophon, but further speculation along these lines is not my concern here.

118 De Temmerman (2014), 163.

119 De Temmerman (2014), 163–164.

120 The metanarrative erotic drive of this novel and of the other examples of the genre will be discussed below, in Chapter 3.

121 For recent discussion of this troubling scene see Ormand (2010), 174–175. Also, Morales (2004), 207–208; De Temmerman (2014), 166–168.

122 I translate αἰδῶ as 'shame' here in line with Morgan (2007a), 110, n.16.

123 On the contemporary meaning and implications of the term μοιχός, see Schwartz (2001), 102–103. She points out that Clitophon's use of the term at this point makes no legalistic sense: a male adulterer is so defined by his having sexual contact with

another man's wife, so he is not an adulterer in relation to Leucippe, even
supposing he had slept with Melite by this juncture; he is only an adulterer when he
sleeps with Melite knowing she is married to Thersander, which makes this
comment proleptic of the sexual act.

124 See Goldhill (1995), 100.

125 See also, for uses of φιλοσοφέω 1.12.1; 5.23.7; 8.5.7; for φιλόσοφος, see 2.21.5;
6.21.3.

126 It could also be the case that Clitophon, as narrator, uses the term to denote
convincing argumentation, which is just as mistaken in its understanding of the
meaning of philosophy.

127 Erōs' sophistry is also mentioned by Clinias in his lesson to Clitophon at 1.10.1. See
Whitmarsh's note (Whitmarsh 2001, 148): he draws attention to the possible
influence of Euripides and Plato on the comments at 1.10.1 and 5.27.1. There could
also be an echo of Xenophon's *Cyropaedia* (6.1.41) here: Araspas' comment draws
attention to Erōs' capacity for deviousness, something which is clearly relevant in
Achilles Tatius' text.

128 Cf. 5.16.

129 For further discussion of Erōs' role at 5.25–27 with focus on the metaliterary
implications, see Chapter 3 (section 3.3).

130 These instances of claims of virginity can be read with the awareness that during
the *sunkrisis* at 2.35–38, Clitophon displays extensive knowledge regarding sex with
women, but suggests he is inexperienced in sexual matters, apart from his
encounters with prostitutes (2.37.5): his duplicity here is recognized by Menelaus,
who suggests that Clitophon is a veteran, rather than a novice, in sexual matters
(2.38.1).

131 See Ormand (2010),163; Brethes (2012); Ciocani (2013).

132 Sissa (1990).

133 I concur with O'Sullivan's emendation (1980, 349), making the verb here future
tense, instead of the MSS present: I have therefore emended Whitmarsh's
translation, which follows the MSS.

134 Repath (2013), 255–256.

135 See Goldhill (1995), 95, where he notes that this remark is particularly fascinating
given Clitophon's experience with prostitutes. See n.130 above.

136 Repath (2013), 254–255.

137 Jones (2012), 243–245. Also, see Goldhill (1995), 98, and the discussion of Ormand
(2010), 171–176.

138 See Goldhill (1995), 99–100.

139 Repath (2007a), 116–118.

140 Kasprzyk (2009), 112–113.

141 As illustrated by Kasprzyk (2009), 113–114.

142 Kasprzyk (2009), 107. See above section 1.3, for my discussion of Longus' protagonists' lack of self-definition as *sōphrōn*.

143 Jardine (1985), 25.

144 Gold (1993), 86.

145 E.g. Morales (2004), 206; Whitmarsh (2011), 149–150; De Temmerman (2014), 170.

146 See Morgan (2007a), 108, regarding Clitophon's narration of events in Book 6; De Temmerman (2014), 188, makes the point that Leucippe's intentions are hard to gauge, and his further discussion regarding how Clitophon depicts Leucippe's reaction to his advances supports my argument regarding the unknowability of Leucippe's emotions at 2.19 and 2.23.

147 For discussion of this dream see Bartsch (1989), 89–91; Morales (2004), 125–126; 206. Also, MacAlister (1996), 123; Haynes (2003), 60; Whitmarsh (2011), 149–150.

148 See Bartsch (1989), 91–93; Morales (2004), 221–222.

149 Morales (2004), 203–206. On parallels/ the relationship between the novel and Christian martyrologies, see also Cooper (1996), 43–44; Shaw (1996); Chew (2003).

150 Morales (2004), 203; Chew (2003), 135.

151 Chew (2003), 136.

152 Chew (2003), 138.

153 See Haynes (2003), 60; Ormand (2010), 167.

154 It should also not be discounted that Leucippe, when telling Clitophon, may have embellished her account of her experiences with Thersander in order to appear more committed to her future husband: her letter at 5.18 demonstrates her ability to produce a skilfully engineered version of events, although, of course, this is conveyed through Clitophon's narration too. See Repath (2013) on this.

155 See Morgan (2007a), 110–111.

156 De Temmerman (2014), 190.

157 See Kasprzyk (2009), 108, n.32, on the uses of the term to denote 'intellectual' restraint in the extant examples of the Greek novel.

158 4.9.7 (x2); 4.10.6; 4.17.2; 4.17.3; 4.17.5.

159 Charmides even suggests he will pay Menelaus and Leucippe for their respective 'services', thus assuming that Leucippe will prostitute herself for the right price (4.6.2); he never alludes to marriage.

160 Repath (forthcoming).

161 The translation is from Sprague (1973).

162 Morales (2004), 195–196.

163 1.3.1; 1.8.3; 1.9.3; 1.10.4; 1.12.2; 1.20.2; 1.24.3; 1.25.4 (x2); 2.4.2; 2.7.1; 2.17.4; 4.8.7; 4.10.5; 4.10.6; 4.18.2; 5.4.5; 5.22.3; 5.29.6; 5.31.1; 6.9.3; 6.9.4; 7.2.2; 7.2.3; 8.6.4; 8.9.18; 8.9.22; 8.11.1; 8.13.2; 10.9.1; 10.9.4; 10.9.5; 10.10.4.

164 1.3.1; 1.8.3; 1.20.2; 1.25.4 (x2); 2.4.2; 4.8.7; 5.22.3; 6.9.3; 8.9.22 (with Theagenes); 8.11.1; 8.13.2 (with Theagenes); 10.9.4; 10.9.5.

165 Much of the content of what follows in the next two sections is reproduced from Bird (2017).

166 See subsection 1.5.5 below.

167 Text is from Rattenbury and Lumb (1960). Translations are from Morgan's forthcoming Loeb edition (in provisional form; adapted in places) for Books 1–7, and from Morgan (1989b) for Books 8–10 (adapted in places), unless otherwise stated.

168 For Habrocomes' rejection of Erōs, see Xen. Eph. 1.1.5–6. For his subsequent defeat at the hands of the god, see 1.4.1–5. For discussion of Habrocomes' *sōphrosunē* in his introduction, see above, 1.2.1.

169 De Temmerman (2014), 253.

170 See 1.5.6 below.

171 I discuss this chapter in terms of readerly response in Chapter 2 (section 2.4).

172 See Whitmarsh (2011), 170–171.

173 See 1.4.5 above.

174 See De Temmerman (2014), 273–275: he reads Theagenes' altered behaviour in becoming more duplicitous as evidence of his learning from Chariclea.

175 Morgan (1989b), 311.

176 See Winkler (1982), 146.

177 Repath (2007a), 78–79. He also notes similarities with Chariton's Dionysius, whose struggle is also depicted in these Platonic terms.

178 See Morgan (1991), 86–90, for a thorough analysis of the narrative dynamics involved in this opening *tableau*.

179 Cf. Char, 1.1.1; Xen. Eph. 1.2.5.

180 See e.g. Char. 5.4–7; Xen. Eph. 2.1.5.

181 See section 1.5.1 above.

182 Chariclea self-defines using σωφρ- root terms on four occasions (1.3.1; 1.8.3; 1.25.4 x 2), each of which occurs in the primary narrative, rather than in Calasiris', implying that Calasiris' focus is less on Chariclea's *sōphrosunē* as she represents it. Her possession of the virtue is emphasized with more subtlety by Calasiris, particularly via Persinna's embroidered message, and by his representation of Chariclea's consistently chaste behaviour.

183 Similarly, at 1.3.1, the bandits cannot understand what Chariclea says to them.

184 See also Charicles' comment at 2.33.6: 'πεῖσον ἢ λόγοις ἢ ἔργοις γνωρίσαι τὴν ἑαυτῆς φύσιν καὶ ὅτι γυνὴ γέγονεν εἰδέναι.' ('. . . induce her by word or deed to acknowledge her own nature and understand that she has grown into a woman.')

185 See Haynes (2003), 71: she sees the scene as appearing to allude to the 'fateful decision of a Hippolytus'.

186 See Eur. *Hipp.* 13. Also, Hippolytus' conversation with the *therapōn* is significant; particularly the youth's barbed comments at 102 and 106, which demonstrate his flagrant lack of respect for Aphrodite.

187 Xen.Eph. 1.1.5–6. The resort to magic and priestly advice also occurs in the *Ephesiaca* at 1.5, and again springs from parental anxiety. The key difference in Heliodorus is that Charicles asks for help before Chariclea becomes lovesick, as well as following the onset of her malady.

188 E.g. at 3.11.5, when he claims to have seen and received instructions from Artemis and Apollo in a night-vision, and at 4.12.3, when he claims to have learnt the whole truth regarding Chariclea's origins from the gods.

189 Erōs is not involved as a personified entity in the action of the narrative, as he is in Chariton's, Xenophon's and Longus' novels. Achilles Tatius' is more complex in its treatment of Erōs, who appears in the ecphrasis of the painting of Europa's abduction at 1.1.13, and is involved in Clitophon's narrative at 1.11.3 and 2.5.2, although only in Clitophon the character's internalised debates.

190 The frequent use of αἰσχρός, αἰσχύνη, and αἰσχύνω in the *Hippolytus* indicates the centrality of ideas relating to *aidōs*, particularly in relation to the characterization of Phaedra (on Phaedra's *aidōs* see Cairns (2003), 321–339). Adjectival forms (in addition to the occurrence discussed above at 404) are found at: 331, 411, 500, 503, 511, 721, 957, 999. The noun is found at: 246; 1332. Verbal forms (in addition to 408 discussed above) are found at: 420, 719, 1172, 1291.

191 Kovacs (1980), 303. He also notes *aidōs*' role in Phaedra's fateful decision to falsely condemn Hippolytus, which springs from her 'passionate devotion to honor', which he sees as synonymous with *aidōs*.

192 Allusion to the *Hippolytus* also occurs at 1.10.2, in Cnemon's narration regarding Demaenete, and at 8.15.2, when Arsace's suicide is couched in language reminiscent of Phaedra's. See Bird (2019b) for further discussion of the allusions to Euripides' *Hippolytus* in the representation of Chariclea.

193 See Morgan (1998), 68–72, on the difficulties of interpreting these two parallel scenes.

194 Dowden (1996), 274, draws a comparison between this scene and Xenophon of Ephesus, 4.2, where Habrocomes is swept from his pyre by the Nile due to divine intervention, and he highlights the contrasting hermeneutic intent of Heliodorus, who presents this miracle as something requiring explanation, rather than a self-evident miracle like Xenophon's. The same can be said of the comparison between this miracle in Heliodorus and that performed in the *Acts of Paul and Thecla* as discussed below.

195 For discussion of the metaliterary implications of 5.31, see section 2.5, below.

196 See Maguire (2005), 142–145: her argument includes the suggestion that Paul and Calasiris can be aligned as holy men whose power enables the heroines' escape. However, I think that the quasi-erotic infatuation which Thecla has for Paul makes

this alignment less likely, and the association would not work when considering the events at 8.9, as Calasiris died at 7.11.

197 The name of Thyamis in the *Aethiopica* perhaps alludes to Thamyris in the *Acts of Paul and Thecla*: Chariclea appears to accept Thyamis' offer of betrothal, then escapes it, and Thecla breaks her betrothal to Thamyris.

198 The bridal chamber full of light as a symbol for heaven is an image which recurs in Christian texts. One example is that which is evoked in the *Acts of Thomas*, both in Hymn 1, line 23 (Klijn (2003), 29, with commentary: 34) and in the Lord's speech to the married couple who are persuaded to reject sexual intercourse in chapter 12 (Klijn (2003), 53, with commentary, 55). This instance in Heliodorus raises Chariclea's experience to the level of a miracle, and the image of a bride in a fiery chamber is not found elsewhere in the genre. I suggest that Heliodorus is engaging with Christian imagery, and this engagement suggests that *sōphrōn* love aimed at marriage in a pagan setting is just as sacred as Christian abstinence. See Maguire (2005), 122–128, on the parallels between Heliodorus and the *Apocryphal Acts* more generally.

199 De Temmerman (2014), 293.

200 See 1.5.3 above.

201 For discussion of 4.8, see below, 2.5.

202 See 1.5.3 above.

203 See Morgan (1989c), 316, and Ormand (2010), 189–192.

204 Ormand (2010), 190.

205 Another instance of Chariclea's manipulation comes at 1.21–22, when she lies to Thyamis regarding her and Theagenes' past and relationship. See, above, 2.5.1 for Theagenes' reaction to her response to Thyamis. For detailed discussion see De Temmerman (2014), 260–264.

206 See Olsen (2012), 308–309, on this passage: she sees this passage as evidence for the asymmetry of Chariclea's and Theagenes' *sōphrosunē*, or, at least, for Chariclea's representation of it.

207 See above, 1.5.2, for discussion of Theagenes' role in this scene.

208 See Winkler (1982), 128–132, on Calasiris' duplicity in how he presents himself to Charicles and Theagenes, including his sententious speech on the evil eye, and his real (kindly) intentions towards Chariclea.

209 Theagenes' reaction to this is discussed above at 1.5.2.

210 (1989a), 111.

211 2.15.1; 2.15.2; 2.29.5; 3.3.8; 3.5.4; 3.5.6; 4.6.1; 4.9.1; 4.11.2; 10.16.2.

212 This idea is present at Hld. 3.5, when the protagonists first see each other during the festival.

213 See Morgan (1989c), 318–320; cf. Winkler (1982), 157; Whitmarsh (2011), 201–204.

214 1.29.4; 2.7.1; 2.33.1; 3.10.4; 5.13.4; 5.31.2; 7.19.1; 8.9.13; 10.7.3; 10.41.3: see Morgan and Repath (2019) on these puns and their implications, including this instance at the close of the narrative.

215 2.17.4, where Cnemon refers to the moderating influence of Thyamis over the Herdsmen; 6.9.3, where Calasiris refers to Chariclea's loss of self-control in her grief; 8.9.18, where Arsace tells the populace to be sensible; 8.13.2, where there is some ambiguity in Bagoas' description of Chariclea and Theagenes to Euphrates: he could mean 'chaste' or 'self-controlled'.

2 Readerly *Sōphrosunē*: Reader as Voyeur

1 Voyeurism is important in ancient literature related to the sphere of *Erōs*, beauty and *sōphrosunē*: the frame of Plato's *Charmides* is influential in this respect, and I will discuss the potential for its direct influence on Chariton's text below. Herodotus' story of Candaules and Gyges (1.8) is also important as an archetypal example of the subversive and dangerous potential of voyeurism.

2 The text is corrupt here, with several emendations by editors. For details see Reardon (2004), 25 (notes to lines 61–63). See the comment which follows on textual reconstruction dependent on the *Charmides*.

3 As we will see below (2.2), at Longus, 1.13, there is an episode which, although more sensual than this scene in Chariton's text, seems to share features with it, suggesting that Longus might well be engaging with Chariton here. The episode involving Erōs in the garden of Philetas (Longus, 2.4) also has verbal similarities to this scene.

4 See Egger (1994a), 37–39.

5 See Elsom (1992), 221–22: she sees the scene as clearly objectifying Callirhoe, with the women servants co-opted as male-identified viewers, and the idea of wounding carrying etymological overtones of penetration.

6 The translation is from Sprague (1973).

7 Sprague (1973), 61.

8 We see similar questions at 1.1.12, 5.4.4 and 5.8.2. There is a contrast between the way in which Chariton draws a veil over this night of passion and the way in which Xenophon of Ephesus treats Anthia's and Habrocomes' wedding-night, where the reader is allowed access to the couple's intimacy to a certain extent.

9 See Char. 1.1.4; 2.4.5.

10 E.g. McCulloh (1970), 31–32; 80–81; Hunter (1983), 38–52; Pandiri (1985), 116–118; Newlands (1987); Zeitlin (1990), 418; 431–436; 442–443; Goldhill (1995), 6–8; Morgan (2004a), 145–150: Paschalis (2005), 50–52; Herrmann (2007a), 210–216; Repath (2011), 100–105; Whitmarsh (2011), 93–97.

11 I will refer to the 'narrator' of the Prologue from this point on, but it is important to recognize that the narrator of the Prologue is the author of the subsequent narrative, something which is emphasized by the references to creating books and to writing in the Prologue.

12 Morgan (2004a), 148.

13 See Whitmarsh (2011), 94–97: he suggests that the process of viewing an artwork involves the viewer in a 'power relationship' which allows the educated (or 'empowered') viewer to 'signify' the images, that is, to give them proper meaning. Longus' narrator in the Prologue, as he states that he represented the pictorial in his narrative, thus engages in an act of intellectual control, which has repercussions for the social positioning of the subject. I will argue below that this kind of intellectual control is maintained throughout the narrative and involves the representation of *sōphrosunē* specifically.

14 It is also important at 1.26, where a cicada falls between Chloe's breasts and is retrieved by Daphnis (see Morgan (2004a), 171); at 3.13–14, where Daphnis attempts to imitate the goats and sheep in order to relieve his and Chloe's frustration (see Morgan (2004a), 207–208); at 3.18, where Lycaenion provides Daphnis with practical sexual tuition (see Goldhill (1995), 23–30).

15 Goldhill (1995, 10) discusses the voyeurism invited by this scene.

16 See Morgan (2004a), 150, Goldhill (1995), 8.

17 See Morgan (2004a), 16, on the Thucydidean allusion at Pr.3.

18 Daphnis is not entirely chaste in that he has had sex with Lycaenion. However, this aberration in terms of strict fidelity is made unconsciously on Daphnis' part. Also, the lesson he learns from Lycaenion not only ensures that Daphnis knows what to do on his and Chloe's wedding-night, but also ensures that he preserves his beloved's virginity because of his fear brought about by Lycaenion's hyperbolic warning about the pain and bloody consequences suffered by a girl's loss of virginity. See 1.3.3, above for further discussion of Lycaenion's warning and Daphnis' response to it.

19 Bartsch (1989), 48–55; Cf. Morales (2004), 37–48; Reeves (2007).

20 Alvares (2006), 19.

21 The image of a woman with transparent clothing recalls Xen. *Mem.* 2.1.22ff., where Heracles' choice at the parting of the ways is narrated. The female figure of vice is dressed provocatively with her attributes visible through her clothes (... ἐσθῆτα δὲ ἐξ ἧς ἂν μάλιστα ὥρα διαλάμποι ...). Although the terminology is not identical, the sense is the same. If the reader is intended to recall the figure of vice, then there are implications for how we perceive Europa's attitude as portrayed by the painter: she is perhaps represented as a very willing, maybe even shameless, abductee.

22 See Whitmarsh (2011), 89.

23 It could also be the case that the primary narrator interferes with Clitophon's version of events. For the issues created by the play of voices in Achilles Tatius' text, see Whitmarsh (2011), 82.

24 Cf. Morales (2004), 87.

25 The juxtaposition between *logos* and *mythos* goes back at least as far as Plato's *Protagoras*, where Protagoras acknowledges the increased pleasure associated with the latter as opposed to the former (320c).

26 On the lack of textuality in Achilles Tatius' text, and some of the implications of this, see Ní Mheallaigh (2007).

27 Morales (2004), 166–172. See also, Ballengee (2009), 74–90, where the emphasis in the analysis of this episode is on how gender ambiguity and male masochistic enjoyment of violence exercised on the female subject exists in what Bakhtin termed the 'adventure time' of the novel, where social norms and conventions are transgressed.

28 Repath (2015), 53–55.

29 e.g. Ballengee (2009), 80–81: she notes that at 3.15, the pictures of Andromeda and Prometheus are recalled, but she fails to discuss the fact that these connections are not made by Clitophon, and the implications of this failure on his part as viewer of the scene, and as narrator. Clitophon's 'mastery' and male dominance, which Ballengee suggests are factors in his viewing of Leucippe's apparent torture (81–83), are, I think, compromised by his failure to properly grasp the connections and consequent implications involved in his own story.

30 See Morgan (2007a), 114–115, where he suggests that Clitophon's use of mythological analogy at this juncture and others is indicative of his concern with sophistic self-presentation which clearly trumps any desire to convey his experiences accurately.

31 As per Ballengee (2009), 78.

32 Bartsch (1989), 87–89.

33 Repath (2015), 55.

34 Morales (2004), 170–172.

35 King (2017), 206–210.

36 This could potentially operate elsewhere: at 4.9, when Leucippe temporarily loses her sanity, she is tied up after exposing herself, and while Clitophon responds with apparent compassion, the reader could connect her bondage with that of Andromeda at 3.7, and the loss of modesty on Leucippe's part could be seen as titillating, as Morales notes (2004, 195–196). In what follows, it should become clear that a variety of perspectives is offered to the reader by Achilles Tatius.

37 See 1.4.5, above, for discussion of 6.21–22.

38 On the metanarrative role of visualization in the Greek novel see Goldhill (2001), 167–172, 178–180; Zeitlin (2003); Morales (2004); König (2008); Whitmarsh (2011); 171–176, Morgan (2013).

39 See Morales (2004), 88–95; Whitmarsh (2011), 172.

40 For the use of *enargeia* in the novels generally, with particular emphasis on Heliodorus, see Whitmarsh (2011), 171–176.

41 See Kauffmann (2015) on the 'unreality' of Leucippe's beauty. His argument rests on the unreliability of Clitophon's representation of Leucippe's attractions, emphasizing Clitophon's general unreliability as narrator, which is a major focus in my discussion:

see 1.4, above. However, although Clitophon's depictions of Leucippe's beauty are potentially hyperbolic, as Kauffmann suggests, this does not detract from the intention of Clitophon to invite voyeurism in his narratee.

42 I acknowledge, in agreement with King (2017), 211, that at 5.17, there is a hint of the striptease about Lacaena's revelation of her scarred back, noting the language used: διανοίξασα ... δείκνυσι. However, this invitation to view the naked back is nuanced by Leucippe's intention to seek pity from Melite.

43 Leucippe's revealing and drawing attention to her body can also be compared to the action of Iphigenia in allowing her saffron robe to fall to the ground on the point of being sacrificed (Aesch. *Ag.* 239): this action results in pity from onlookers, not desire, and this could also be how Leucippe intends her actions to be taken.

44 Following Jones' highlighting of 'semi-sexual' terminology – (2012), 154 – with my own addition of ἀνδριζόμενον.

45 See above, section 1.5.2.

46 Jones (2012), 155, n. 204.

47 See Jones (2012), 154–155.

48 König (2008), 138.

49 For discussion of the titles of the Greek novels in general see Whitmarsh (2005b). For the view that the title of Chariton's text is *Callirhoe* see e.g. Reardon (1996), 315–316, Morgan (2013), 227. See also Tilg (2010), 214–216 for his argument that the title is *Narratives About Callirhoe*, which emphasizes Callirhoe as the subject of the narrative, so does not detract from my argument here.

50 See Tilg (2010), 243–244.

51 See Tilg (2010), 228–229.

52 Cf. Kaimio (1996), 59–64. While I appreciate his argument, Kaimio's claim that the audience of Chariton's novel must react like the internal audiences depicted in the text belies the way in which the reader's experience of events differs considerably from that of those internal audiences. It is also flawed in seeming to impose limits on the reading experience, whereas I see the potential for a multiplicity of readerly reactions, as I hope to make clear.

53 Morgan (2004a), 16–17, 193.

54 See section 1.3.4.

55 As per Repath (2013), 251–252.

56 See *LSJ*⁹ s.v. citing Galen, 15.624 and *POxy.* 1725.9 (iii A.D.).

57 Repath (2013); King (2017), 211–214.

58 Repath (2013), 252.

59 King (2017), 214.

60 Morgan (2013).

61 Winkler (1982) 119–120, 127; Bartsch (1989), 48; Anderson (1997); Hilton (1998); Olsen (2012); De Temmerman (2014), 247, 251–252, 255, 258.

62 See Hilton (1998), 80.

63 Anderson (1997), 312, notes that this letter also functions as a catalyst in the courtship of Chariclea and Theagenes – the reading of the letter coincides precisely with Chariclea's revelation of her love for Theagenes 'to intertwine the discovery of identity with the awakening of desire'.

64 De Temmerman (2014), 257–258.

65 Anderson (1997), 313; Hilton (1998), 82–84; and Morgan (2013), 230.

66 Morgan (2013), 230.

67 Anderson (1997), 313–314.

68 See Whitmarsh (2002), 121–122: following his discussion on the central role of ecphrasis and *enargeia* in Heliodorus' text, Whitmarsh draws attention to how Heliodorus provides examples of incontinent viewers within the text, such as Demaenete and the 'vulgar women' in the Delphic parade. My view of Pelorus concurs with this theory, but I emphasize that the *sōphrōn* (or continent) reader can prevail, something which Whitmarsh views as inherently problematic.

3 Readerly *Sōphrosunē*: Erōs and *Sōphrosunē*

1 See Whitmarsh (2011), 168–169: he discusses Photius' epigram which suggests that the reader of Achilles Tatius' text should focus exclusively on the *sōphrōn* marriage of Leucippe and Clitophon, avoiding the more prurient elements which surround it. Whitmarsh rightly observes the 'wilful myopia' involved in such a reading of Achilles Tatius' novel, but I suggest that this does not exclude *sōphrosunē* from the reading process, not only in *Leucippe and Clitophon*, but in each of the extant examples of the genre.

2 Brooks (1984), 37–61; Carson (1986), 85; Whitmarsh (2011), 168–176. Also, there are interesting ideas regarding the ethics of the audience of archaic and classical Greek poetry in Walsh (1984): in discussing the way in which poetry influences the psychological state of its audience, he identifies the roles of *erōs* and *aidōs* in Pindar (55–60), discusses the implied morality of the audiences of Aeschylus and Euripides (91), suggests that a balance is struck between *erōs* and *aidōs* in Euripides' *Antiope* fragment (114–115), and also identifies a 'natural connection between *areta* and song' in Euripides *Heracles* and *Medea* (117). All of these observations and claims feed into debate around narrative and readerly experience in Greek literature, providing a foundation for similar ideas which are present in the novel, as discussed below. Walsh's identification of *aidōs* as a kind of restraint in the reading experience is paralleled by my own arguments surrounding *sōphrosunē* in the readers of the novels.

3 Tychē: 1.10.2; 1.13.4; 1.14.7–9; 2.8.3–4; 2.8.6; 3.3.8; 4.1.12; 4.4.2; 4.5.3; 4.7.3; 5.1.4–6; 5.5.2–3; 6.8.1; 8.1.2; 8.3.5. Aphrodite: 1.1.7; 2.2.7–8; 3.2.5; 3.2.12–14; 3.6.3; 3.8.3;

3.8.7; 3.10.6; 5.10.1; 7.5.2–5; 8.1.3; 8.4.10; 8.8.15. (Of these references to Aphrodite's controlling role, only 8.1.3 is narratorial: the others are either in the form of prayers or speeches by characters.)

4 This is overtly evident at 1.1.3–4;1.1.5; 1.1.12; 2.4.5; 4.7.5–6; 6.4.5; 8.1.3. Also, see Whitmarsh (2011), 34–37, and Chew (2012), 76.

5 Or φιλόνικος: See Reardon (2004), 2, n.17.

6 I discuss the implications of the scene involving the Persian King at 6.4.5 above in the first chapter (subsection 1.1.2).

7 See my discussion at subsection 1.1.2.

8 For detailed analysis of the *paideia* of Dionysius, see Jones (2012), 20–22, 41–43, 46–48, 50–53, 55–58, 60–64.

9 3.2.17; 5.8.3; 6.9.4 (and rhetorical questions at 1.1.12; 5.4.4; 5.8.2). There will be an authorial statement at the very close of the narrative: 8.8.16.

10 See Doulamis (2012), 25; Whitmarsh (2009), 47–48.

11 See Tilg (2010), 130–37. He argues for Chariton's engagement with Aristotle's *Poetics*, using καθάρσιον in this passage as his starting point.

12 Whitmarsh (2009), 47–48.

13 See Smith (2007), 207 and Montiglio (2013), 16–20.

14 See Fusillo (1997) on closure in the ancient novels, and specifically, 215–217, on Chariton's ending. See also Repath (2005), 264.

15 See section 2.2.

16 See Morgan (2004a), 16–17. See also Bowie (2005), 79 for comparison between Erōs' and Longus' creations.

17 For discussion of 3.24, and the consequences for our view of Daphnis' restraint, see above, subsection 1.3.3.

18 See Repath (2015), 59–60: he suggests that we should read 'Erōs' and not 'erōs', in agreement with O'Sullivan (1980), 160, and the translations of Gaselee (1969), Plepelits (1980), Winkler (1989), and Whitmarsh (2001).

19 Cf. Chew (2012): she argues that Tychē's role is more important than Erōs' in Clitophon's narrative, and that it is this divinity to whom responsibility for Clitophon's experiences and sufferings is assigned by Clitophon as narrator. While I recognize the considerable role of Tychē, I do not think that her role means that Erōs' is unimportant, and, as I argue in this chapter, Clitophon's representation of Erōs as a motivating force in the relationships between Clitophon and Leucippe and Clitophon and Melite is of central importance. Also, Chew fails to discuss fully the narrative set-up of the novel, and does not acknowledge the potential slippage between how Clitophon presents his story and how Achilles Tatius might intend it to be read.

20 For discussion of how Erōs' role diminishes in the second half of the novel, see Nakatani (2003).

21 The most famous version of the Apollo and Daphne myth which we have is from Ovid, *Metamorphoses*, 1.452–567. It is perhaps relevant that Ovid emphasizes Cupid's role in his version, making Apollo's patronising insults towards Cupid motivate the latter to target Apollo and make him lust after the nymph. We cannot be sure whether Achilles Tatius had this version or a similar one in mind when he refers to the myth. However, it is more than probable that Apollo's desire for Daphne is inflicted by a vengeful Erōs/Cupid, particularly given his lack of success (Daphne's subsequent transformation into a laurel tree denies the god any sexual enjoyment of the nymph, and this outcome is present in other versions, such as that of Parthenius (*Erōtica Pathēmata*, XV)). Therefore, Erōs/Cupid is potentially in the background here, and Achilles Tatius' reader would be well aware of the ironic connotations of Clitophon's view of the song as exemplary.

22 There are also inverted echoes of Plato's *Republic* in this passage: I discuss this above: 1.4.1.

23 See Goldhill (1995), 67–74; Morales (2004), 80–81.

24 Goldhill (1995), 73.

25 See above, 1.4.1.

26 For discussion of how cynically we should read Clitophon's apportioning of blame to Erōs, see Repath (2015), 59–60.

27 1.4.2.

28 The role of Tychē also decreases in the final two books, with her final appearance coming at 7.13.1. Nakatani (2003) discusses this point in some detail. See also Chew (2012).

29 For detailed discussion of the ending of *Leucippe and Clitophon*, see Repath (2005).

30 Repath (2005), 258.

31 For other references to Erōs in Calasiris' narrative, see 2.33 (where Chariclea is said to have rejected Erōs along with Aphrodite and all the accoutrements of marriage) and 4.18 (where Theagenes swears by various deities, including the Erotes, when promising to respect Chariclea's chastity).

32 See above, subsection 1.2.4.

33 I have already noted another parallel with the same chapter of this text in Chapter 1 (1.2.4): there it is the brothel-scene in the *Ephesiaca* which is compared to the episode from *Apollonius, King of Tyre*. I do not think that the doubling of these parallels is a problem, rather it suggests a common trope involving the implicit alignment of sex and the power of narrative.

34 There is a textual crux at this point, with ὀνήσειν being offered for ἥσειν in the manuscript tradition: see Garnaud (1991), 5. I think that ἥσειν is the more likely reading, given the phrasing at the close of the chapter where pleasure/delight is aligned with the *topos* and with *mythoi erotikoi*.

35 Repath (forthcoming) notes that other occurrences of this term in Achilles Tatius are erotically charged.

36 (Forthcoming).

37 I have retained Whitmarsh's translation of this term, a term that is problematic given its complex semantics: the two instances of the noun ψυχαγωγία (2.35.1; 5.8.1) in this text suggest pleasure or entertainment, so this translation seems to fit the context. The noun occurs once more in the extant corpus: at Heliodorus, 7.11.3, where it again seems to imply entertainment, with the additional consideration that it is used just prior to Calasiris' death, so that the 'leading of the soul' could entail both entertainment for Calasiris on his final night and a proleptic hint at his impending demise. See also Lucian, *VH.* 1.2, where the following is stated: 'γένοιτο δ᾽ ἂν ἐμμελὴς ἡ ἀνάπαυσις αὐτοῖς, εἰ τοῖς τοιούτοις τῶν ἀναγνωσμάτων ὁμιλοῖεν, ἃ μὴ μόνον ἐκ τοῦ ἀστείου τε καὶ χαρίεντος ψιλὴν παρέξει τὴν ψυχαγωγίαν, ἀλλά τινα καὶ θεωρίαν οὐκ ἄμουσον ἐπιδείξεται ...' ('They (literary people) will find this interlude agreeable if they choose as company such works as not only afford wit, charm, and distraction pure and simple, but also provoke some degree of cultured reflection.' Trans. Reardon (1989)) . This passage suggests an implicit contrast between 'amusement' (τὴν ψυχαγωγίαν) and more refined or cultured pursuits, which is important for my discussion regarding Achilles Tatius below.

38 At 8.8.11–12, Thersander suggests that the priest has spent the night with an adulterer (Clitophon) and a whore (Leucippe), turning the temple of Artemis into a brothel. This, of course, is a piece of cynical manipulation on the part of Thersander, but it stands as one of the many alternative versions of events which are presented in this trial scene, and indicates that the priest is not beyond the suggestion of this kind of ethical compromise.

39 1.4.1.

40 Martin (2002); Ní Mheallaigh (2007); Marinčič (2007); Repath (forthcoming).

41 Pleasure is an important theme in the *Phaedrus*, with ἡδονή and its cognates occurring 28 times in total. However, the emphasis for the philosopher is not on the pleasure to be gained from erotic attachments, but on the appreciation of beauty, of the good and of philosophical companionship.

42 3.4.11; 4.4.2–3; 5.1.4: see Hardie (1998), 30–31 on the role of 'sexual/textual desire' in Cnemon's representation as a narratee.

43 See Winkler (1982), 139–146.

44 See Morgan (1991), 95–99.

45 (1982), 142.

46 (1982), 144.

47 See Morgan (1991), 99.

48 Whitmarsh (2011), 169.

49 Whitmarsh (2011), 173.

50 Whitmarsh (2011), 176.
51 10.41.3: '...σὺν εὐφημίαις καὶ κρότοις καὶ χοροῖς ἐπὶ τὴν Μερόην παρεπέμποντο, τῶν ἐπὶ τῷ γάμῳ μυστικωτέρων κατὰ τὸ ἄστυ φαιδρότερον τελεσθησομένων.' ('... The people cheered and clapped and danced as they escorted them into the city, where the more mystic parts of the wedding ritual were to be performed with greater magnificence.' Trans. Morgan 1989). See above, 1.5.7.
52 Cnemon's cowardice is noted elsewhere: immediately following this exchange he demonstrates this shortcoming in his reaction to Thisbe's name being mentioned and her apparent presence in Nausicles' house (5.2: see also 2.7), so this comment at 5.1.4 could be read as a self-laudatory statement implying the young man's pomposity in bringing the hero Odysseus and his (apparent) courage to mind.
53 Morgan (1989c), 300.

Conclusion

1 Whitmarsh (2011), 77–85.
2 See Morgan (2009), 266–267; Whitmarsh (2011), 110; Morgan (2014).
3 De Temmerman (2014), 18.

Bibliography

Alexander, L.C.A. (2008), 'The Passions in Galen, Chariton and Xenophon', in J.T. Fitzgerald (ed.), *Passions and Moral Progress in Greco-Roman Thought*, London/New York.

Alvares, J. (1995), 'The Drama of Hippothous in Xenophon of Ephesus' *Ephesiaca*', *CJ* 90: 393–404.

Alvares, J. (2002), 'Love, Loss and Learning in Chariton's *Chaereas and Callirhoe*', *CW* 97: 107–115.

Alvares, J. (2006), 'Reading Longus' *Daphnis and Chloe* and Achilles Tatius' *Leucippe and Clitophon* in Counterpoint', in S.N. Byrne, E.P. Cueva, J. Alvares (eds), *Authors, Authority, and Interpreters in the Ancient Novel: Essays in Honor of Gareth L. Schmeling, AN* suppl. 5, Groningen: 1–33.

Alvares, J. (2012), 'Considering Desire in the Greek Romances Employing Lacanian Theory: Some Explorations', in M.P. Futre Pinheiro, M.B. Skinner, and F.I. Zeitlin (eds), *Narrating Desire: Eros, Sex, and Gender in the Ancient Novel*, Berlin/Boston: 11–28.

Anderson, G. (1976), *Studies in Lucian's Comic Fiction*, Leiden.

Anderson, G. (1982), *Eros Sophistes: Ancient Novelists at Play*, Chico.

Anderson, M.J. (1997), 'The ΣΩΦΡΟΣΥΝΗ of Persinna and the Romantic Strategy of Heliodorus' *Aethiopica*', *CP* 92: 303–322.

Anderson, M.J. (2009), 'The Silence of Semiramis: Shame and Desire in the Ninus Romance and Other Greek novels', *AN* 7: 1–27.

Babbitt, F.C. (ed. and trans.) (1928), *Plutarch, Moralia* Vol. II, London/Cambridge, Mass.

Babbitt, F.C. (ed. and trans.) (1931), *Plutarch, Moralia* Vol. III, London/Cambridge, Mass.

Ballengee, J.R. (2009), *The Wound and the Witness: The Rhetoric of Torture*, New York.

Balot, R.K. (1998), 'Foucault, Chariton, and the Masculine Self', *Helios* 25: 139–162.

Barrett, W.S. (1964), *Euripides Hippolytos*, Oxford.

Bartsch, S. (1989), *Decoding the Ancient Novel: The Reader and the Role of Description in Heliodorus and Achilles Tatius*, Princeton.

Bartsch, S. (2006), *The Mirror of the Self: Sexuality, Self-knowledge, and the Gaze in the Early Roman Empire*, Chicago.

Beresford, A. (trans.) (2005), *Plato, Protagoras and Meno*, London.

Bettini, M. (1999), *The Portrait of the Lover*, trans. L. Gibbs, Berkeley.

Bird, R. (2017), 'Virtue Obscured: Theagenes' *Sōphrosynē* in Heliodorus' *Aethiopica*', *Ancient Narrative* 14: 195–208.

Bird, R. (2019a), 'Achilles Tatius and Chariton: Reflections and Refractions', *Mnemosyne* 72: 471–487.

Bird, R. (2019b), 'Heliodorus' Charicleia and Euripides' *Hippolytus*: Surviving *Sōphrosynē*', in I.D. Repath and F-G. Herrmann, *Some Organic Readings in Narrative, Ancient and Modern*, Groningen: 193–210.

Borgeaud, P. (1988), *The Cult of Pan in Ancient Greece*, Chicago.

Bowersock, G.W. (1969), *Greek Sophists in the Roman Empire*, Oxford.

Bowie, E.L. (1994), 'The Readership of the Greek Novels in the Ancient World', in J. Tatum (ed.), *The Search for the Ancient Novel*, Baltimore/London: 435–459.

Bowie, E.L. (1996), 'The Ancient Readers of the Greek Novels', in G. Schmeling (ed.), *The Novel in the Ancient World*, Boston: 89–106.

Bowie, E.L. (2002), 'The Chronology of the Earlier Greek Novels since B.E. Perry: Revisions and Precisions', *AN* 2: 47–63.

Bowie, E.L. (2005), 'Metaphor in *Daphnis and Chloe*', in S. Harrison, M. Paschalis, S. Frangoulidis (eds), (2005), *Metaphor and the Ancient Novel*, *AN* suppl. 4, Groningen: 68–86.

Boys-Stones, G. (2001), *Post-Hellenistic Philosophy: A Study of its Development from the Stoics to Origen*, Oxford.

Brethes, R. (2012), 'How to Be a Man: Towards a Sexual Definition of the Self in Achilles Tatius', in M.P. Futre Pinheiro, M.B. Skinner, and F.I. Zeitlin (eds), *Narrating Desire: Eros, Sex, and Gender in the Ancient Novel*, Berlin/Boston: 127–146.

Brooks, P. (1984), *Reading for the Plot: Design and Intention in Narrative*, Oxford.

Brown, P. (1988), *The Body and Society*, New York.

Bürger, K. (1892), 'Zu Xenophon von Ephesos', *Hermes* 27: 36–67.

Burrus, V. (2005), 'Mimicking Virgins: Colonial Ambivalence and the Ancient Romance', *Arethusa* 38: 49–88.

Cairns, D. (1993), *Aidōs: The Psychology and Ethics of Honour and Shame in Ancient Greek Literature*, Oxford.

Capra, A. (2009), 'The (un)happy Romance of Curleo and Liliet: Xenophon of Ephesus, the *Cyropaedia* and the Birth of the 'Anti-tragic' Novel', *AN* 7: 29–50.

Carson, A. (1986), *Eros The Bittersweet: An Essay*, Princeton.

Carter, L.B. (1986), *The Quiet Athenian*, Oxford.

Chalk, H.H.O. (1960), 'Eros and the Lesbian Pastorals of Longus', *JHS* 80: 32–51.

Chew, K. (1997–98), 'Inconsistency and Creativity in Xenophon's *Ephesiaka*', *CW* 91: 203–213.

Chew, K. (1998), 'Focalisation in Xenophon of Ephesus' *Ephesiaka*', in R.F. Hock, J.B. Chance, and J. Perkins (eds), *Ancient Fiction and Early Christian Narrative*, Society of Biblical Literature Symposium Series 6, Atlanta: 47–60.

Chew, K. (2000), 'Achilles Tatius and Parody', *CJ* 96: 57–70.

Chew, K. (2003), 'The Representation of Violence in the Greek Novels and Martyr Accounts', in S. Panayotakis, M. Zimmerman, W. Keulen (2003) (eds), *The Ancient Novel and Beyond*, Leiden: 129–142.

Chew, K. (2012), 'A Novelistic Convention Reversed: Tyche vs. Eros in Achilles Tatius', *CPh* 107: 75–80.

Ciocani, V. (2013), 'Virginity and Representation in the Greek Novels and Early Greek Literature', Toronto: Diss.

Cohoon, J.W. (ed. and trans.) (1932), *Dio Chrysostom: Vol. I*, London/Cambridge, Mass.

Collard, C. (1981), *Euripides*, Oxford.

Conte, G.B. (1996), *The Hidden Author: An Interpretation of Petronius' Satyricon*, Berkeley.

Cooper, K. (1996), *The Virgin and the Bride: Idealised Womanhood in Late Antiquity*, Cambridge, MA.

Costa, C.D.N. (trans.) (2005), *Lucian: Selected Dialogues*, Oxford.

Couégnas, D. (1992), *Introduction a la paralittérature*, Paris.

Cueva, E.P. (1996), 'Plutarch's Ariadne in Chariton's *Chaereas and Callirhoe*', *AJPh* 117: 473–484.

Cueva, E.P. (2004), *The Myths of Fiction: Studies in the Canonical Greek Novels*, Michigan.

D'Alconzo, N. (2015), 'Works of Art in the Ancient Novel', Swansea: Diss.

De Temmerman, K. (2007), 'Blushing Beauty: Characterising Blushes in Chariton's *Callirhoe*', *Mnemosyne* 60: 235–252.

De Temmerman, K. (2009), 'Chaereas Revisited: Rhetorical Control in Chariton's 'Ideal' Novel *Callirhoe*', *CQ* 59: 247–262.

De Temmerman, K. (2014), *Crafting Characters: Heroes and Heroines in the Ancient Greek Novel*, Oxford.

Dillon, J. (1977), *Middle Platonists: A Study of Platonism 80BC to AD120*, London.

Doulamis, K. (2002), *The Rhetoric of Eros in Xenophon of Ephesus and Chariton: a Stylistic and Interpretative study*, Exeter: Diss.

Doulamis, K. (2007), 'Stoic Echoes and Style in Xenophon of Ephesus', in J.R. Morgan and M. Jones (eds), *Philosophical Presences in the Ancient Novel*, *AN* suppl. 10: 151–175.

Doulamis, K. (2012), 'All's Well that Ends Well: Storytelling, Predictive Signs, and the Voice of the Author in Chariton's *Callirhoe*', *Mnemosyne* 65: 18–39.

Dowden, K. (1996), 'Heliodorus: Serious Intentions', *CQ* 46: 267–285.

Dressler, A. (2011), 'The Sophist and the Swarm: Feminism, Platonism and Ancient Philosophy in Achilles Tatius' *Leucippe and Clitophon*', *Ramus* 40: 33–72.

Durham, D.B. (1938), 'Parody in Achilles Tatius', *CPh* 33: 1–19.

Egger, B. (1994a), 'Looking at Chariton's *Callirhoe*', in J.R. Morgan and R. Stoneman (eds), *Greek Fiction: The Greek Novel in Context*, London/New York: 31–48.

Egger, B. (1994b), 'Women and Marriage in the Greek Novel: the Boundaries of Romance', in J. Tatum (ed.), (1994), *The Search for the Ancient Novel*, Baltimore: 260–80.

Egger, B. (1999), 'The Role of Women in the Greek Novel: Woman as Heroine and Reader', in S. Swain (ed.), *Oxford Readings in the Greek Novel*, Oxford: 108–136.

Emlyn-Jones, C. and Preddy, W. (eds and trans.) (2013), *Plato, Republic*, London/
     Cambridge, Mass.
Elsom, H.E. (1992), 'Callirhoe: Displaying the Phallic Woman', in A. Richlin (ed.),
     Pornography and Representation in Greece and Rome, New York and Oxford: 212–230.
Epstein, S. (2002), 'The Education of Daphnis: the Goats, the Birds and the Bees',
     Phoenix 56: 25–39.
Finkelpearl, E.D. (1998), *Metamorphosis of Language in Apuleius*, Michigan.
Foucault, M. (1990), *The History of Sexuality*, iii. *The Care of the Self*, trans. R. Hurley,
     London.
Fowler, H.N. (ed. and trans.) (1936), *Plutarch, Moralia* Vol. X, London/Cambridge,
     Mass.
Funke, M. (2012), 'Female Sexuality in Longus and Alciphron', in M.P. Futre Pinheiro,
     M.B. Skinner, and F.I. Zeitlin (eds), *Narrating Desire: Eros, Sex, and Gender in the
     Ancient Novel*, Berlin/Boston: 181–198.
Fusillo, M. (1997), 'How Novels End: Some Patterns of Closure in Ancient Narrative', in
     D.H. Roberts, F.M. Dunn, and D. Fowler (eds), *Classical Closure: Reading the End in
     Greek and Latin Literature*, Princeton: 209–227.
Garnaud, J.-P. (ed. and trans.) rev. F. Frazier (2013), *Achille* Tatius, *Le Roman de Leucippé
     et Clitophon*, Paris.
Gaselee, S. (ed. and trans.) (2014), *Leucippe and Clitophon. Achilles Tatius*, London/
     Cambridge, Mass.
Gill, C. (1996), *Personality in Greek Epic, Tragedy, and Philosophy: The Self in Dialogue*,
     Oxford.
Gold, B.K. (1993), '"But Ariadne Was Never There in the First Place" Finding the
     Female in Roman Poetry', in N.I. Rabinowitz and A. Richlin (eds), *Feminist Theory
     and the Classics*, New York.
Goldhill, S. (1995), *Foucault's Virginity*, Cambridge.
Goldhill, S. (2001), 'The Erotic Eye: Visual Stimulation and Cultural Conflict', in S.
     Goldhill (ed.), *Being Greek Under Rome: Cultural Identity, the Second Sophistic and
     the Development of Empire*, Cambridge: 154–194.
Goldhill, S. (2008), 'Genre', in T. Whitmarsh (ed.), *The Cambridge Companion to the
     Greek and Roman Novel*, Cambridge: 185–200.
Goold, G.P. (ed. and trans.) (1995), *Chariton Callirhoe*, London/Cambridge, Mass.
Granholm, P. (2012), 'Alciphron: Letters of the Courtesans: Edited with Introduction,
     Translation and Commentary', Uppsala: Diss.
Grube, G.M.A. (trans.) rev. C.D.C. Reeve (1992), *Plato, Republic*, Indianapolis/
     Cambridge.
Hägg, T. (1966), 'Die Ephesiaka das Xenophon Ephesios: original oder Epitome?',
     CandM 27: 118–161; trans. T. Hägg as 'The *Ephesiaca* of Xenophon Ephesius –
     original or epitome?', in Hägg (2004): 159–198.
Hägg, T. (1971), *Narrative Technique in Ancient Greek Romance: Studies of Chariton,
     Xenophon of Ephesus, and Achilles Tatius*, Stockholm.

Hägg, T. (1983), *The Novel in Antiquity*, Oxford.

Hägg, T. (2004), *Parthenope: Selected Studies in Ancient Greek Fiction (1969–2004)*, L. Boje Mortensen and T. Eide (eds), Copenhagen.

Halperin, D.M., Winkler, J.J. and Zeitlin, F.I. (eds) (1990), *Before Sexuality: The Construction of Erotic Experience in the Ancient Greek World*, Princeton.

Hardie, P. (1998), 'A Reading of Heliodorus, *Aithiopika* 3.4.1–5.2', in R. Hunter (ed.), *Studies in Heliodorus*, PCPhS Suppl. 21, Cambridge: 19–39.

Haynes, K. (2003), *Fashioning the Feminine in the Greek Novel*, London and New York.

Helmbold, W.C. (ed. and trans.) (1939), *Plutarch, Moralia* Vol. VI, London/Cambridge, Mass.

Henderson, J. (2009), *Longus Daphnis and Chloe; Xenophon of Ephesus Anthia and Habrocomes*, London/ Cambridge: Mass.

Herrmann, F-G. (2007a), 'Longus' Imitation: *Mimēsis* in the Education of Daphnis and Chloe', in J.R. Morgan, M. Jones, (eds) (2007), *Philosophical Presences in the Ancient Novel*, AN suppl. 10, Groningen: 205–230.

Herrmann, F-G. (2007b), 'Greek Religion and Philosophy: the God of the Philosopher', in D. Ogden (ed.), *A Companion to Greek Religion*, Oxford: 385–397.

Herrmann, F-G. (2013), 'Dynamics of Vision in Plato's Thought', *Helios* 40: 281–307.

Herrmann, F-G. (2016), 'Plato and Critias', in A. Powell and J. Yvonneau (eds), *La Muse au long couteau: Critias, de la création littéraire à terreur de l'État*, Bordeaux.

Hilton, J. (1998), 'An Ethiopian Paradox: Heliodorus, *Aithiopika* 4.8', in R.L. Hunter (ed.), *Studies in Heliodorus*, PCPhS Suppl. 21, Cambridge: 79–92.

Hodkinson, O. (2012), 'Attic Idylls: Hierarchies of Herdsmen and Social Status in Alciphron and Longus', *JHS* 132: 41–53.

Holzberg, N. (1995), *The Ancient Novel: An Introduction*, trans. C. Jackson-Holzberg, London/New York.

Humble, N. (1999), '*Sōphrosynē* and the Spartans', in S. Hodkinson and A. Powell (eds), *Sparta: New Perspectives*, London: 339–353.

Humble, N. (2002), '*Sōphrosynē* Revisited: Was it Ever a Spartan Virtue?', in A. Powell and S. Hodkinson (eds), *Sparta: Beyond the Mirage*, London and Swansea: 85–109.

Hunter, R.L. (1983), *A Study of Daphnis and Chloe*, Cambridge.

Hunter, R.L. (1997), 'Longus and Plato' in M. Picone and B. Zimmerman (eds), *Der antike Roman und seine mittelalterliche Rezeption*, Basel: 15–28.

Hunter, R.L. (ed.) (1998), *Studies in Heliodorus*, PCPhS Suppl. 21, Cambridge.

Hunter, R.L. (2012), *Plato and the Traditions of Ancient Literature: The Silent Stream*, Cambridge.

Iacobitz, C. (ed.) (1913), *Luciani Samosatensis, Opera* Vol. III, Leipzig.

James, M.R. (1924), *The Apocryphal New Testament*, Oxford.

Jardine, A. (1985), *Gynesis: Configurations of Woman and Modernity*, Ithaca.

Jones, M. (2012), *Playing the Man: Performing Masculinities in the Ancient Greek Novel*, Oxford.

Jope, J. (2011), 'Interpretation and Authenticity of the Lucianic *Erotes*', *Helios* 38: 103–120.

Kaimio, J. (1996), 'How to Enjoy a Greek Novel: Chariton Guiding his Audience', *Arctos* 30: 49–73.

Kanavou, N. (2015), 'A Husband is More Important than a Child', *Mnemosyne* 68: 937–955.

Kasprzyk, D. (2009), 'Morale et sophistique: sur la notion de σωφροσύνη chez Achille Tatius', in B. Pouderon, C. Bost-Pouderon (eds), *Passions, vertus et vices dans l'ancien roman*, Lyon: 97–115.

Kauffmann, N. (2015), 'Beauty as Fiction in *Leucippe and Clitophon*', *AN* 12: 43–69.

King, D. (2012), 'Taking It Like a Man: Gender, Identity and the Body in Achilles Tatius' *Leucippe and Clitophon*', in M.P. Futre Pinheiro, M.B. Skinner, and F.I. Zeitlin (eds), *Narrating Desire: Eros, Sex, and Gender in the Ancient Novel*, Berlin/Boston: 147–60.

King, D. (2017), *Experiencing Pain in Imperial Greek Culture*, Oxford.

Klijn, A.F.J. (2003), *Acts of Thomas: Introduction, Text, Commentary*, Leiden/Boston.

König, J. (2007), 'Orality and Authority in Xenophon of Ephesus', V. Rimell (ed.), *Seeing Tongues, Hearing Scripts: Orality and Representation in the Ancient Novel, AN* suppl. 7: 1–22.

König, J. (2008), 'Body and Text' in, T. Whitmarsh (ed.), *The Cambridge Companion to the Greek and Roman Novel*, Cambridge: 127–144.

Konstan, D. (1994a), *Sexual Symmetry: Love in the Ancient Novel and Related Genres*, Princeton.

Konstan, D. (1994b), 'Xenophon of Ephesus: Eros and Narrative in the Novel', in J.R. Morgan and R. Stoneman (eds), *Greek Fiction: The Greek Novel in Context*, London and New York: 49–63.

Konstan, D. (1994c), 'Apollonius, King of Tyre and the Greek novel', in J. Tatum (ed.), *The Search for the Ancient Novel*, Baltimore and London: 173–182.

Konstan, D. (2007), 'Love and Murder: Two Textual Problems in Xenophon's *Ephesiaca*', *AN* 5: 31–40.

Kovacs, P.D. (1980), 'Shame, Pleasure, and Honor in Phaedra's Great Speech (Euripides, *Hippolytus* 375–87)', *AJP* 101, 287–303.

Kytzler, B. (2003), 'Xenophon of Ephesus', in G. Schmeling (ed.), *The Novel in the Ancient World*, Leiden: 336–359.

Laplace, M. (1997), 'Le Roman de Chariton et la tradition de l'éloquence et de la rhétorique: constitution d'un discours panégyrique', *RhM* 140: 38–71.

Levett, M.J. (trans.) rev. M. Burnyeat (1990), *Plato, Theaetetus*, Indianapolis.

Lateiner, D. (2012), 'Gendered Places in Two Later Ancient Novels (*Aithiopika, Historia Apollonii*)', in M.P. Futre Pinheiro, M.B. Skinner, and F.I. Zeitlin (eds), *Narrating Desire: Eros, Sex, and Gender in the Ancient Novel*, Berlin/Boston: 49–76

Long, A.A. (1974), *Hellenistic Philosophy: Stoics, Epicureans, Sceptics*, London.

Long, A.A. and Sedley, D.N. (1987), *The Hellenistic Philosophers (Volumes I and II)*, Cambridge.

Luginbill, R.D. (2002), 'A Delightful Possession: Longus' Prologue and Thucydides', *CJ* 97: 233–247.

MacAlister, S. (1996), *Dreams and Suicides: The Greek Novel from Antiquity to the Byzantine Empire*, London.

MacLeod, M.D. (1967), *Lucian Volume VIII*, London/Cambridge: Mass.

Maguire, S. (2005), 'Charikleia in Context', Swansea: Diss.

Marinčič, M. (2007), 'Advertising One's Own Story: Text and Speech in Achilles Tatius' *Leucippe and Clitophon*', in V. Rimell (ed.), *Seeing Tongues, Hearing Scripts: Orality and Representation in the Ancient Novel, AN* suppl. 7: 168–200.

Martin, R.M. (2002), 'A Good Place to Talk: Discourse and Topos in Achilles Tatius and Philostratus', in M. Paschalis, S. Frangoulidis (eds), *Space in the Ancient Novel, AN* suppl. 1, Groningen: 143–160.

McCulloh, W.E. (1970), *Longus*, New York.

Miller, W.B. (ed. and trans.) (1933), Xenophon, *Cyropaedia*, London/Cambridge, Mass.

Montague, H. (1992), 'Sweet and Pleasant Passion: Female and Male Fantasy in Ancient Romance Novels', in Richlin, A. (1992) (ed.), *Pornography and Representation in Greece and Rome*, Oxford: 231–249.

Montiglio, S. (2010), '"My Soul, Consider What You Should do": Psychological Conflicts and Moral Goodness in the Greek Novels', *AN* 8, 25–58.

Montiglio, S. (2012), 'The (Cultural) Harmony of Nature: Music, Love, and Order in *Daphnis and Chloe*', *TAPA* 141: 133–156.

Montiglio, S. (2013), *Love and Providence: Recognition in the Ancient Novel*, Oxford.

Morales, H. (2004), *Vision and Narrative in Achilles Tatius' Leucippe and Clitophon*, Cambridge.

Morgan, J.R. (1989a), 'The Story of Knemon in Heliodorus' *Aithiopika*', *JHS* 109: 99–113.

Morgan, J.R. (1989b), 'Heliodorus: An Ethiopian Story', in B.P. Reardon (ed.), *Collected Ancient Greek Novels*, Berkeley: 349–588.

Morgan, J.R. (1989c), 'A Sense of the Ending: the Conclusion of Heliodorus' *Aithiopika*', *APA* 119: 299–320.

Morgan, J.R. (1991), 'Reader and Audiences in the *Aithiopika* of Heliodorus', *GCN* 4: 85–103.

Morgan, J.R. (1993), 'Make-believe and Make Believe: The Fictionality of the Greek Novels', in C. Gill, T.P. Wiseman (eds), *Lies and Fiction in the Ancient World*, Exeter: 175–229.

Morgan, J.R. (1994), 'The *Aithiopika* of Heliodorus: Narrative as Riddle', in J.R. Morgan and R. Stoneman (eds), *The Greek Novel in Context*, London/New York: 97–113.

Morgan, J.R. (1995), 'The Greek Novel: Towards a Sociology of Production and Reception', in A. Powell (ed.), *The Greek World*, London: 130–152.

Morgan, J.R. (1998), 'Narrative Doublets in Heliodorus' *Aithiopika*', in R. Hunter (ed.), *Studies in Heliodorus, PCPhS* Suppl. 21: 60–78.

Morgan, J.R. (2003), 'Heliodorus', in G. Schmeling (ed.), *The Novel in the Ancient World*, Boston: 417–456.

Morgan, J.R. (2004a), *Longus: Daphnis and Chloe*, Oxford.

Morgan, J.R. (2004b), 'Chariton', in I. de Jong, R. Nünlist, A. Bowie (eds) *Narrators, Narratees, and Narratives in Ancient Greek Literature*, Leiden: 479–488.

Morgan, J.R. (2004c), 'Achilles Tatius', in De Jong, I., Nunlist, R., Bowie, A. (eds), *Narrators, Narratees, and Narratives in Ancient Greek Literature*, Leiden: 493–506.

Morgan, J.R. (2004d), 'Xenophon of Ephesus', in De Jong, I., Nunlist, R., Bowie, A. (eds), *Narrators, Narratees, and Narratives in Ancient Greek Literature*, Leiden: 489–493.

Morgan, J.R. (2007a), 'Kleitophon and Encolpius: Achilleus Tatius as Hidden Author', in M. Pachalis, S. Frangoulidis, S. Harrison, and M. Zimmerman (eds), *The Greek and Roman Novel: Parallel Readings*, AN suppl. 8: 105–120.

Morgan, J.R. (2007b), 'Chariton', in I. de Jong and R. Nunlist (eds), (2007), *Time in Ancient Greek Literature*, Leiden: 433–451.

Morgan, J.R. (2009), 'The Emesan Connection: Philostratus and Heliodorus', in K. Demoen and D. Praet, *Theios Sophistes: Essays on Flavius Philostratus' Vita Apollonii*, Leiden and Boston: 263–281.

Morgan, J.R. (2011), 'Poets and Shepherds: Philetas and Longus', in K. Doulamis, (ed.) (2011), *Echoing Narratives: Studies of Intertextuality in Greek and Roman Prose Fiction. AN* suppl. 13, Groningen: 139–160.

Morgan, J.R. (2013), 'The Erotics of Reading Fiction: Text and Body in Heliodorus' in in C. Bréchet, A. Videau, R. Webb (eds), *Théories et pratiques de la fiction à l'époque impériale*, Paris: 225–237.

Morgan, J.R. (2014), 'Heliodorus the Hellene', in D. Cairns and R. Scodel, *Defining Greek Narrative*, Edinburgh: 260–276.

Morgan, J.R. (ed. and trans.) (forthcoming), *Heliodorus Aethiopica*, London/Cambridge, Mass. (in provisional form Books 1–7 only, kindly provided by the translator).

Morgan, J.R. and Harrison, S.J. (2008), 'Intertextuality', in Whitmarsh, T. (ed.) (2008), *The Cambridge Companion to the Greek and Roman Novel*, Cambridge: 218–236.

Morgan, J.R. and Repath, I.D. (2019), 'Mistresses and Serving-Women, and the Slavery and Mastery of Love in Heliodoros' in: S. Panayotakis and M. Paschalis (eds), *Slaves and Masters in the Ancient Novel*, Ancient Narrative Supplementum 23, Groningen: 139–160.

Morwood, J. (ed. and trans.) (1997), *Euripides Medea, Hippolytus, Electra, Helen*, Oxford.

Mulvey, L. (1989), *Visual and Other Pleasures*, Basingstoke.

Nakatani, S. (2003), 'A Re-examination of Some Structural Problems in Achilles Tatius' *Leucippe and Clitophon'*, AN 3: 63–81.

Nehamas, A. and Woodruff, P. (trans.) (1989), *Plato, Symposium*, Indianapolis/Cambridge.

Newlands, C.E. (1987), '"Techne" and "Tuche" in Longus' *Daphnis and Chloe'*, *Pacific Coast Philology* 22: 52–58.

Ní Mheallaigh, K. (2007), 'Philosophical Framing: The Phaedran Setting of *Leucippe and Cleitophon'*, in J.R. Morgan, M. Jones (eds), *Philosophical Presences in the Ancient Novel*, AN suppl. 10, Groningen: 231–244.

Nimis, S. (1998), 'Memory and Description in the Ancient Novel', *Arethusa* 31: 99–122.

North, H. (1966), *Sōphrosynē: Self-Knowledge and Self-Restraint in Greek Literature*, Ithaca.

Olsen, S. (2012), 'Maculate Conception: Sexual Ideology and Creative Authority in Heliodorus' *Aethiopica*', *AJP* 133: 301–322.

Ormand, K. (2010), 'Testing Virginity in Achilles Tatius and Heliodorus', *Ramus* 39: 160–192.

Osborne, C. (1994), *Eros Unveiled: Plato and the God of Love*, Oxford.

O'Sullivan, J.N. (1978), 'Notes on the Text and Interpretation of Achilles Tatius I', *Classical Quarterly* 28: 312–329.

O'Sullivan, J.N. (1980), *A Lexicon to Achilles Tatius*, Berlin.

O'Sullivan, J.N. (1995), *Xenophon of Ephesus: His Compositional Technique and the Birth of the Novel*, Berlin.

O'Sullivan, J.N. (ed.) (2005), Xenophon Ephesius, *De Anthia et Habrocome Ephesiacorum Libri V*, Munich/Leipzig.

Page, T.E. et al. (eds) and W.C. Helmbold (trans.) (1961), *Plutarch Moralia* Vol. IX, London/ Cambridge, Mass.

Pandiri, T.A. (1985), '*Daphnis and Chloe:* The Art of Pastoral Play', *Ramus* 14: 116–141.

Paschalis, M. (2005), 'The Narrator as Hunter: Longus, Virgil and Theocritus', in S. Harrison, M. Paschalis, S. Frangoulidis, (eds), (2005), *Metaphor and the Ancient Novel*, *AN* suppl. 4, Groningen: 50–67.

Perkins, J. (1995), *The Suffering Self: Pain and Narrative Representation in the Early Christian Era*, London.

Phinney, E. 1979. 'Kernal Fantasy in Chariton's Romance, *Chaereas & Callirhoe*', *Pacific Coast Philology* 14, 68–75.

Plepelits, K. (1980), *Achilleos Tatios. Leukippe und Kleitophon*, Stuttgart.

Plepelits, K. (2003), 'Achilles Tatius', in G. Schmeling (ed.), *The Novel in the Ancient World*, Boston: 385–416.

Pletcher, J.A. (1998), 'Euripides in Heliodoros' *Aithiopika* 7 –8', *GCN* 9: 17–27.

Prince, G. (2003), *Dictionary of Narratology*, Lincoln/London.

Rademaker, A. (2005), *Sōphrosynē and the Rhetoric of Self-Restraint*, Leiden.

Rattenbury, R.M. and Lumb, T.W. (ed. and trans.) (1960), *Héliodore, Les Éthiopiques (Théagène et Chariclée)*, Paris.

Reardon, B.P. (1989), *Collected Ancient Greek Novels*, Berkeley.

Reardon, B.P. (1994), 'Achilles Tatius and ego-narrative', in J.R. Morgan and R. Stoneman (eds), *Greek Fiction: The Greek Novel in Context*, London: 80–96.

Reardon, B.P. (1996), 'Theme, Structure and Narrative in Chariton', in S. Swain (ed.) (1996), *Oxford Readings in the Greek Novel*, Oxford: 163–188.

Reardon, B.P. (2003), 'Chariton', in G. Schmeling (ed.), *The Novel in the Ancient World*, Boston: 309–335.

Reardon, B.P. (2004) (ed.), *Chariton: De Callirhoe Narrationes Amatoriae*, Leipzig.

Redondo Moyano, E. (2012), 'Space and Gender in the Ancient Greek Novel', in M.P. Futre Pinheiro, M.B. Skinner, and F.I. Zeitlin (eds), *Narrating Desire: Eros, Sex, and Gender in the Ancient Novel*, Berlin/Boston: 29–48.

Reeve, M.D. (ed.) (1982), *Longus Daphnis et Chloe*, Leipzig.

Reeves, B.T. (2007), 'The Role of Ekphrasis in Plot Development: the Painting of Europa and the Bull in Achilles Tatius' *Leucippe and Clitophon*, *Mnemosyne* 60: 87–101.

Repath, I.D. (2005), 'Achilles Tatius' *Leucippe and Cleitophon*: What Happened Next?', *CQ* 55: 250–265.

Repath, I.D. (2007a), 'Emotional Conflict and Platonic Psychology in the Greek novel', in J.R. Morgan and M. Jones (eds), *Philosophical Presences in the Ancient Novel*, *AN* suppl. 10, Groningen: 53–84.

Repath, I.D. (2007b), 'Callisthenes in Achilles Tatius' *Leucippe and Cleitophon*: double jeopardy?', *AN* 6: 101–29.

Repath, I.D. (2011), 'Platonic Love and Erotic Education in Longus' *Daphnis and Chloe*', in K. Doulamis, (ed.), *Echoing Narratives: Studies of Intertextuality in Greek and Roman Prose Fiction. Ancient Narrative* suppl. 13, Groningen: 99–122.

Repath, I.D. (2013), 'Yours Truly? Letters in Achilles Tatius', in O. Hodkinson, P.A. Rosenmeyer, E. Bracke (eds), *Epistolary Narratives in Ancient Greek Literature*, Leiden/Boston: 237–262.

Repath, I.D. (2015), 'Cleitophon the Charlatan', in S. Panayotakis, G. Schmeling, and M. Paschalis (eds), *Holy Men and Charlatans in the Ancient Novel*, Groningen: 47–68.

Repath, I.D. (2019), 'Longus: the Education of Dorcon', in I.D. Repath and F-G. Herrmann, *Some Organic Readings in Narrative, Ancient and Modern*, Groningen: 173–192.

Repath, I.D. (forthcoming), *Playing with Plato: Platonic Allusion in Achilles Tatius' Leucippe and Cleitophon*, Oxford.

Rist, J.M. (2001), 'Plutarch's 'Amatorius': A Commentary on Plato's Theories of Love?', *CQ* 51: 557–575.

Rohde, E. (1914), *Der Griechische Roman und seine Vorlaufer*, Hildesheim.

Rowe, C.J. (1986), *Plato: Phaedrus*, Oxford.

Ruiz-Montero, C. (1982), 'Una interpretación del "estilo kai" de Jenofonte de Efeso', *Emerita* 50: 305–323.

Ruiz-Montero, C. (2003), 'Xenophon of Ephesus and Orality in the Roman Empire', *AN* 3: 43–62.

Russell, D.A. (1992), *Dio Chrysostom: Orations VII, XII, XXXVI*, Cambridge.

Sanz-Morales, M. and Laguna-Mariscal, G. (2003), 'The Relationship between Achilles and Patroclus according to Chariton of Aphrodisias', *CQ* 53: 292–295.

Schmeling, G.L. (1974), *Chariton*, Boston.

Schmeling, G.L. (1980), *Xenophon of Ephesus*, Boston.

Schmeling, G.L. (2003), 'Historia Apollonii Regis Tyri', in G.L. Schmeling (ed.), *The Novel in the Ancient World*, Leiden: 517–551.

Schmeling, G.L. (2005), 'Callirhoe: God-like Beauty and the Making of a Celebrity', in Harrison *et al.* (eds), *Metaphor and the Ancient Novel, AN* suppl. 4, Groningen: 36–49.

Schwartz, S. (2001), 'Clitophon the *Moichos*: Achilles Tatius and the Trial Scene in the Greek Novel', *AN* 1: 93–113.

Schwartz, S. (2012), 'The Κρίσις Inside: Heliodorus' Variations on the Bedtrick', in M.P. Futre Pinheiro, M.B. Skinner, and F.I. Zeitlin (eds), *Narrating Desire: Eros, Sex, and Gender in the Ancient Novel*, Berlin/Boston: 161–180.

Scourfield, J.H.D. (2003), 'Anger and Gender in Chariton's *Chaereas and Callirhoe*', in S.M. Braund and G.W. Most (eds), *Ancient Anger: Perspectives from Homer to Galen*, Cambridge: 163–184.

Scourfield, J.H.D. (2010), 'Chaereas, Hippolytus, Theseus: Tragic Echoes, Tragic Potential in Chariton', *Phoenix* 64: 291–314.

Shaw, B.D. (1996), 'Body/Power/Identity: Passions of the Martyrs', *Journal of Early Christian Studies* 4.3: 269–312.

Sissa, G. (1990), *Greek Virginity*, Cambridge, Mass.

Smith, S.D. (2007), *Greek Identity and the Athenian Past in Chariton: The Romance of Empire, AN* suppl. 9, Groningen.

Sprague, R.K. (trans.) (1973), *Plato, Laches and Charmides*, Indianapolis/New York.

Swain, S. (1994), 'Dio and Lucian', in J.R. Morgan and R. Stoneman (eds) (1994), *Greek Fiction: The Greek Novel in Context*, London/New York: 166–180.

Swain, S. (1996), *Hellenism and Empire: Language, Classicism, and Power in the Greek World AD 50–250*, Oxford.

Tagliabue, A.C.F. (2010), 'The *Ephesiaca* as a *Bildungsroman*', *AN* 10: 17–46.

Tagliabue, A.C.F. (2017), *Xenophon's Ephesiaca: A Paraliterary Love-Story from the Ancient World*, Groningen.

Tatum, J. (1989), *Xenophon's Imperial Fiction: on the Education of Cyrus*, Princeton.

Tatum, J. (1994), 'The Education of Cyrus', in J.R. Morgan and R. Stoneman (eds) (1994), *Greek Fiction: The Greek Novel in Context*, London and New York: 15–28.

Taylor, C.C.W. (trans.) (1996), *Plato, Protagoras*, Oxford.

Tilg, S. (2010), *Chariton of Aphrodisias and the Invention of Romance*, Oxford.

Toohey, P. (1999), 'Dangerous Ways to Fall in Love: Chariton I 1,5–10 and VI 9,4', *Maia* 51: 259–275.

Trapp, M.B. (1990), 'Plato's *Phaedrus* in Second Century Greek Literature', in D.A. Russell (ed.), *Antonine Literature*, Oxford: 141–173.

Trapp, M.B. (ed. and trans.) (1997), *Maximus of Tyre, The Philosophical Orations*, Oxford.

Trzaskoma, S.M. (2010), 'Chariton and Tragedy: Reconsiderations and New Evidence', *AJPh* 131: 219–231.

Trzaskoma, S.M. (2011), 'Aristophanes in Chariton again (Plu. 1127)', *Philologus* 155: 367–368.

Trzaskoma, S.M. (2012), 'Why Miletus? Chariton's Choice of Setting and Xenophon's *Anabasis*', *Mnemosyne* 65: 300–307.

Turner, P. (1960), '*Daphnis and Chloe*: An Interpretation', *G&R* 7: 117–123.

Vilborg, E. (ed.) (1955), *Achilles Tatius Leucippe and Clitophon*, Stockholm.

Walsh, G.B. (1984), *The Varieties of Enchantment. Early Greek Views of the Nature and Function of Poetry*, Chapel Hill.

Watanabe, A. (2003), *Hippothoos the Lover, Bandit, and Friend: A Study on Elite Masculinity in the Novel*, Yale: Diss.

Whitmarsh, T. (trans.) (2001), *Achilles Tatius Leucippe and Clitophon*, Oxford.

Whitmarsh, T. (2002), 'Written on the Body: Perception, Deception and Desire in Heliodorus' *Aethiopica*', *Ramus* 31: 111–124.

Whitmarsh, T. (2003), 'Reading for Pleasure: Narrative, Irony, and Eroticism in Achilles Tatius', in Panayotakis, S., Zimmerman, M., Keulen, W. (2003) (eds), *The Ancient Novel and Beyond*, Leiden: 191–205.

Whitmarsh, T. (2005a), 'The Lexicon of Love: Longus and Philetas Grammatikos', *JHS* 125: 145–148.

Whitmarsh, T. (2005b), 'The Greek Novel: Titles and Genre', *AJPh* 126: 587–611.

Whitmarsh, T. (2005c), *The Second Sophistic*, Oxford.

Whitmarsh, T. (2008), 'Class', in T. Whitmarsh, (ed.) (2008), *The Cambridge Companion to the Greek and Roman Novel*, 72–87.

Whitmarsh, T. (2009), 'Divide and Rule: Segmenting *Callirhoe* and Related Works', in M. Pachalis, S. Frangoulidis, and G. Schmeling (eds), *Readers and Writers in the Ancient Novel*, AN suppl. 12, Groningen: 36–50.

Whitmarsh, T. (2010), 'Domestic Poetics: Hippias' House in Achilles Tatius', *Classical Antiquity* 29: 327–438.

Whitmarsh, T. (2011), *Narrative and Identity in the Ancient Greek Novel*, Oxford.

Whitmarsh, T. (2013), *Beyond the Second Sophistic: Adventures in Greek Postclassicism*, Berkeley.

Williams, B. (1993), *Shame and Necessity*, Berkeley.

Winkle, J.T. (2014), '"Necessary Roughness": Plato's *Phaedrus* and Apuleius' *Metamorphoses*', *AN* 11: 93–131.

Winkler, J.J. (1982), 'The Mendacity of Kalasiris and the Narrative Strategy of Heliodorus', *YCS* 27: 93–158.

Winkler, J.J. (trans.) (1989), 'Achilles Tatius: Leucippe and Clitophon', in B.P. Reardon (ed.), *Collected Ancient Greek Novels*, Berkeley: 170–284.

Winkler, J.J. (1990), *The Constraints of Desire. The Anthropology of Sex and Gender in Ancient Greece*, London/New York.

Zeitlin, F.I. (1990), 'The Poetics of *Eros*: Nature, Art and Imitation in Longus' *Daphnis and Chloe*', in D.M. Halperin, J.J. Winkler, F.I. Zeitlin (eds), (1990), *Before Sexuality: The Construction of Erotic Experience in the Ancient Greek World*, Princeton: 417–464.

Zeitlin, F.I. (2003), 'Living Portraits and Sculpted Bodies in Chariton's Theater of Romance', in Panayotokis *et al.* (eds), *The Ancient Novel and Beyond*, Leiden: 71–83.

Zeitlin, F.I. (2012), 'Gendered Ambiguities, Hybrid Formations, and the Imaginary of the Body in Achilles Tatius', in M.P. Futre Pinheiro, M.B. Skinner, and F.I. Zeitlin (eds), *Narrating Desire: Eros, Sex, and Gender in the Ancient Novel*, Berlin/Boston: 105–126.

Index Locorum

Note: this index of passages cited refers only to the extant Greek novels. For other texts, please see the General Index

General Index

Lightning Source UK Ltd.
Milton Keynes UK
UKHW020647140221
378712UK00003B/132